LE
DEAL

LE DEAL

How a Young American,

in Business, in Love,

and in Over His Head,

Kick-Started a Multibillion-Dollar

Industry in Europe

J. BYRNE MURPHY

St. Martin's Press ≋ New York

To Pamela,

with love

Note to the Reader: This is a true story, though some names
and details have been changed.

www.stmartins.com

Library of Congress Cataloging-in-Publication Data

Murphy, J. Byrne.
    Le deal : how a young American in business, in love, and in over his head, kick-started a multibillion-dollar industry in Europe / J. Byrne Murphy.—1st ed.
        p.   cm.
    ISBN-13: 978-0-312-35903-4
    ISBN-10: 0-312-35903-9
    1. Murphy, J. Byrne.   2. Clothing trade—Europe.   3. Retail trade—Europe.   4. Businessmen—Europe.   5. Americans—Europe.   I. Title.
    HD9940.E82 M87 2008
    381'.4574692092—dc22   2008017616

First Edition: August 2008

10   9   8   7   6   5   4   3   2   1

Contents

Acknowledgments

Very sincere thanks go first to Al Zuckerman, my agent, without whom this book would still remain just an idea. His immediate encouragement and subsequent faith propelled this effort all the way to publication.

My deepest gratitude is also due to Jim de Kay, distinguished author of many books, who counseled and cajoled me chapter after chapter throughout the writing process, cheerfully editing and suggesting along the way. Barbara Feinman Todd was similarly of great assistance as a sounding board and in-house editor from beginning to end.

My editor, Phil Revzin, was a gift from St. Martin's Press. Phil taught me the value of a very good editor, one who can be ruthless with the red pen, tough on deadlines, and yet sympathetic to the writer's plight. Sally Richardson, publisher of St. Martin's, has provided more support than I could have hoped to receive.

Many others assisted in this effort, including François Moss, Antoine Vignial, Claire Quill, Charlie Mathias, Brenda Bertholf, Gilles Charmey, Mimi O'Hagan, Mike Winer, Tim Cullen, and Patience O'Connor. They worked hard to ensure that I remained accurate with the facts and honest with my thoughts. Any errors remain entirely my responsibility.

McArthurGlen Europe would have never come to reality were it not for the nearly two hundred people on the McArthurGlen team who never gave up, as well as the partners of The Kaempfer Company who provided the springboard to help create the new venture. There are more people deserving credit than can be named from those ranks, but certainly those integral to the start-up success of McArthurGlen include Joey Kaempfer, John Nicolosi, George Bennett, and Peter Nash. Those who were either directly involved after the startup or supported indirectly through their contributions to The Kaempfer Company's successes include Julia Calabrese, Mitchell Schear, Steve Levin, Mark Epstein, Kevin Wade, and Larry Ricklin. There are so many advisers who guided us along the way it is dangerous to attempt such a list. Clearly, though, Simon Johnston, Lee Narrow, Joe Howe, and Steve Porter would be at the top of any such list. Others are named in the pages following.

It was our early partners in Europe who were critical to ensuring hopes became reality, most notably BAA plc in London. We were incredibly fortunate to have Sir John Egan, Barry Gibson, Gordon Edington, and Russell Walls in the positions they held at BAA when they did.

Our partners in Italy, Corrado and Marcello Fratini and Jacopo Mazzei, have been vital to the success there. The same is true of Wolfgang Kramer in Austria.

My daughters, Avery, Cara, Erin, and Kyle, were steadfast in their support, always cheering me on and permitting me to disappear as needed to "write the book." Equally steadfast over these many years have been my siblings, Sean, Drew, Chrystal, and Clarke.

A lifelong sense of deep gratitude goes to my parents, Andrew and Ann Marie Murphy. They taught all five of their children to broaden our horizons, and to never give up. I suspect that they would have never guessed that we all would take their advice so literally.

Finally, my most sincere thank-you of all to my wife, Pamela. It was she who played the pivotal role twice in this creation: first in living and counseling me through the original experience, and then having to relive it and recounsel me again as I tried to capture it in words. Pamela's sense of perspective and cheerful disposition kept me, and the entire family, persevering through the dark moments and reminded us of the joy during the lighter moments.

Prologue

I chose Paris because I didn't know any better.

I chose Paris because it was 1992, the European borders were coming down and my wife Pamela and I thought it would be an interesting time to live in Europe. I chose France because I thought it was the right place to launch a new retailing concept in Europe. And I chose Europe because my chosen field in America, urban redevelopment, had just come to a screeching halt due to a massive banking crisis. It seemed a good idea to continue earning a living somewhere. France seemed like an attractive somewhere.

Eventually, . . . finally, it turned out to be a wise choice.

By the time I left Europe, my colleagues and I had created nearly eight thousand jobs, more than a billion dollars of value, and helped to revitalize eleven towns from Scotland to Austria. If it seemed like Europe fought all this good news at every step, that's not far wrong. Along the way I encountered, among many other oddities, extortion attempts in France, threatening overtures from a would-be partner in Italy, a ruthless political ambush by the soon-to-be Chancellor of Germany, and visits by Her Majesty Queen Elizabeth II and much of her family.

I also learned a lot about what Americans know and don't know about life beyond our borders . . . enough to, well, fill a book.

ONE

"Mickey Go 'Ome!"

The first we saw of the crowd were the long shadows thrown up on the walls by flickering torches and streetlights. Then we heard the chants:

"Yan-KEE go 'ome!! Yan-KEE go 'ome!!"

"Mc-Art-TOOR Out!! Mc-Art-TOOR Out!!"

The place was Vernon, a largely agricultural town in Normandy, and the time was a crisp December evening in 1995. I had come there with my associate, François Moss, at the invitation of Vernon's mayor. He wanted my company, McArthurGlen, to present our plans for a "designer outlet," an American retailing concept we'd successfully pioneered in Europe.

By the time François had piloted our car into the town square darkness had fallen, but the floodlighting on the buildings' facades provided ample visibility. On one side of the square stood the majestic nineteenth-century town hall, the Mairie, a Beaux-Arts confection in granite and marble, housing the offices of the mayor and his cabinet. Standing exactly opposite, across an open plaza and in keeping with the historic French balance of influence between church and state, was the Gothic and very imposing Collégiale Notre-Dame. It was a near replica of the Notre Dame in Paris, except at one-third the scale. But even one-third scale was still massive in this setting. The church towered over the town hall opposite, with its soaring bell tower, enormous rose window, and rows of flying buttresses.

Suddenly, the elegant serenity of the plaza was shattered again by the sound of angry voices. Lots of them. François and I exchanged puzzled glances. François was half French, half British, and was one of the first persons I had met upon landing in Paris a few years earlier. Though only twenty-seven years old, his vital role as my cultural interpreter and real-estate adviser positioned him as someone much older. And though I was then only thirty-five, I also felt older after the few years we had just endured together.

The mayor had liked our proposal when we had first presented it to him, and had invited us back so that his six vice-mayors could have a look. The idea was to build a consensus. Once we had Vernon supporting us, the other towns in the region would then follow, to everyone's benefit. Little did we know that we had landed smack in the middle of the then-budding French antiglobalization backlash.

"Yan-*KEE* Go 'ome!! Yan-*KEE* Go 'ome!!"

"Mc-Art-TOOR Out!! Mc-Art-TOOR Out!!"

And now a new chant, the angriest of all:

"Mickey Go 'OME!! Mickey Go 'OME!!"

The mob was linking us to the disastrous Euro Disney theme park outside Paris. Disney was American, and because I and my company were also American, we were being reduced to an image as seemingly innocent and yet as potently anti-French as Mickey Mouse. It was meant as an insult and as a challenge and in time I took it as such. For the moment I was just startled.

A large crowd of men, women, and even some children filled the length of the street in front of us and around the corner onto the next, beyond where we could see. Perhaps one hundred, maybe two hundred angry locals with handheld torches were shouting the chants and waving large hand-painted signs of protest in a torchlight procession. At the front of the crowd men were carrying a black coffin with the name "McArthurGlen" crudely painted across the sides, a bold "X" slashed in red paint through it. The scene was one of a barely organized but highly emotional demonstration, made ominous and intimidating by the darkness and the echoes of the chants bouncing off the centuries-old stone walls.

François inched our car along the edge of the mob, as yet undetected. We sat in stunned silence as we crept forward. Later, François said that if we had been spotted at just that moment he felt certain that bricks would have come crashing through the windshield.

We had come that night to outline the benefits of our concept: the hundreds of jobs we would create, the tourism we would generate, the quality of the architecture and landscaping in which we would invest. I had knowingly selected Normandy not only for its demographics but also for its history of pro-American feelings. We were just miles away from the Normandy beaches of Omaha and Utah. I assumed that memories of the Americans and the British coming to liberate the French still ran deep in Normandy.

We parked the car one hundred yards from the crowds, in front of the great doors of Notre Dame. The parade had just then stopped alongside the Mairie, filling the street curb to curb. As we stepped from the car, carrying our telltale presentation boards, it was obvious that we were the ones they were seeking. We were instantly spotted. *"Ils sont là! Là-Bas!"* someone from the front of the crowd exclaimed.

François and I both turned in the direction of the voice and froze. The chanting had suddenly stopped and for a brief moment the crowd was looking past their signs, across the plaza, and over at us. A little knot of twenty or twenty-five people, clearly the leaders of the pack, were suddenly, aggressively striding out in front of the others, carrying the large black coffin and several signs, leading the crowd back into their chants.

"Mic-KEY Go 'ome!! Mic-KEY GO 'ome!!

"Mc-Art-TOOR Out!! Mc-Art-TOOR Out!!"

I whispered to François as we reached into the trunk, "No comments. No speeches. No confrontation." We each loaded up with the rest of the presentation boards and our long cylindrical cases of drawings. The boards, displaying hand-rendered perspectives of our designs, were expensive and important. They were our chief tools for the presentation.

"Let's head straight for the entrance of the Mairie," I said to François, indicating the steps some fifty yards away. "And keep moving. Let's just keep moving . . ."

As the crowd grew closer we could now read some of the signs, rendered in English for our benefit:

"Yankee Go Home!"
"No American Project!"

Just then the first tomato landed with a splat on the smooth path stones just ahead of me. A second followed a short moment later.

The coffin and its advance guard kept closing as we hurried forward toward the steps. The leaders of the crowd were angling their progress to position the coffin across the path in front of us. François and I picked up speed as we stepped off the pavers and hurried toward the steps. Suddenly there was a flash, quickly followed by several more. The press was there and started shouting questions, mostly in French, but some in heavily accented English.

"Do you think you can succeed?"

"Do you have any support here?"

"Will you kill the downtown retailers? How many jobs will you destroy? Any comments?"

A rough-looking farmer who stood near the head of the coffin was clearly the leader. He had his own sign bouncing up and down above his head. *"Mickey Go Home!"* He pushed his florid face within six inches of my own. I could smell Calvados on his breath.

"Do you see the reception you get here?" he shouted angrily. "You know what this means? Do NOT come here! Yan-KEES are not welcome!"

François and I were now surrounded by demonstrators. They were shouting their chants to us, sometimes right into our ears as we hurried onward. Now, three or four members of the press had also caught up as we started climbing the stairs to the Mairie, repeating their questions, clicking away with their flashes. Suddenly one of the chanters reached over and swatted the boards I was carrying, knocking me off stride as I swirled to catch them, the tubes in my other hand almost falling as I did. Another protester then knocked some of the large boards from François's arm and he, too, had to whirl around. Instantly, several of the men leapt in to grab the fallen boards.

"Get the *hell* out of here!" I yelled at them. "Get your goddamn hands off those!"

François had reached the top of the steps ahead of me, and had the door already open for me to shoot through. As I did I looked around and saw that inside there were ten or twelve men and women waiting for us. They were staff from the Mairie, but they made no attempt to help us. Apparently, they were content to watch, perhaps even to enjoy the spectacle, but not to help. They seemed benign and bemused, a sheepish smile on some of the faces. I was somewhere between alarmed and angry, with a mixture of defiance and confusion. I wanted to shout at the first sheepish face just inside the door. He appeared so smug and so appreciative of the action, as though François and I were the scheduled entertainment for the evening. And, in fact, maybe we were. But I wasn't here to kill any jobs, or create any turmoil. Just the opposite! *What in the hell was going on?*

The mayor's assistant, whom we knew well by now, greeted François and me meekly at the bottom of a massive marble staircase, but offered no apologies or explanations. With a silent nod, he led us up the ceremonial grand staircase into the *salon de marriage,* the large public hearing room of the Mairie. There, up on the dais, were eight name cards, and milling about were the eight people soon to be perched behind them. This was not to be an intimate little presentation to a half dozen vice-mayors as the mayor had promised. This was a setup.

Once the milling, and whispering, and furrowed foreheads had settled down, the mayor explained we were to present our project to his *conseil municipal,* his full advisory council. They would then ask us questions until they were satisfied they knew enough. At which point we would be asked to leave while they discussed the concept of McArthurGlen coming to town.

They would discuss it among themselves and without us, but not without some eighty or more members of the public, many of them from the rowdy crowd outside, who were already seated on seats behind ours. They would be allowed to ask questions of the *conseil municipal* after we had left. And above and behind us in the gallery overhead were a dozen or so members of the press who were there to hear, to record, and to report, and even to pose their own questions to the panel. But not us. We were not allowed to hear the questions of the retailers or the press, or allowed to address their concerns.

So we made our presentation. We answered the questions we were asked. And then we were dismissed, like children from the dinner table.

François and I retraced our steps back downstairs. Outside, at the bottom of those twelve steps that separated the political level from the pedestrian level, no one from the earlier crowd was still there. Our car was there and intact; leaning against the driver's door handle was the sign that the mob's leader had shaken in my face: "Mickey Go HOME!!"

In part, my anger was directed at myself. How had I allowed us to be blind-sided? I had built a career of working in close cooperation with the public sector. We were no threat to Vernon. We weren't going to steamroll local businesses or put people's jobs in jeopardy. We were there to grow the economy. Why was this so hard to understand?

Inevitably, my mind reverted to an October evening three years earlier.

TWO

Washington Goes Hollywood

Frank Sinatra strode on stage of the newly transformed Warner Theatre as if he owned the place, which, in fact, for that one evening he most certainly did.

Two thousand tuxedoed and elegantly gowned VIPs—the cream of Washington, D.C.'s see-and-be-seen set—reacted with rapturous applause as Ol' Blue Eyes, backed by a thirty-piece orchestra, launched into his signature number.

> *And now,*
> *The end is here*
> *And so I face*
> *The final curtain . . .*

Our company had hired Sinatra, along with Shirley MacLaine, to help us inaugurate our totally refurbished, state-of-the-art Warner Theatre and office tower. It was October 2, 1992, a real high point in my career. For nearly six years I had overseen the redevelopment of this grand office-and-arts complex in downtown Washington, and now, at last, the project was complete and the theater reopened.

> *And more, much more than this*
> *I did it my way . . . .*

On the closing note, the audience, which had sat transfixed and silent through the long autobiographical lyric, erupted into applause, which was instantly augmented by shouts and whistles as Frank was joined by the very leggy, very vibrant, and apparently ageless Shirley MacLaine. The two danced into the opening verses of "New York, New York," with Shirley kicking and spinning, and dapper Frank reaching his arm out to the crowd on the high notes. It was a night that Washington wouldn't forget for a long time. Nor would I.

The morning before the opening I was on stage with two of my business partners, Joey Kaempfer and John Nicolosi. We were happily watching the bustling stagehands readying the lights, props, and sound for the show. But mostly we were gazing out at the glittering theater, a classic movie palace and vaudeville house restored to its original 1920s opulence and now converted to a full-service theater. The restoration had been a complex process, overseen by the gifted architect Shalom Baranes. We were taking in the beauty of its success: the gilded domed ceiling some fifty-five feet above the reupholstered orchestra seats below; the massive hand-cut glass chandelier, an exact replica of the ornate original; the new loggias jutting out from the side walls and balcony fascia. One of the loggias was specifically designed as the Presidential Box (armor-plated, concrete floor), which President Clinton and daughter Chelsea were scheduled to use in a few days' time.

Joey Kaempfer, founder of The Kaempfer Company, a Washington, D.C., development firm, was my partner and boss. John Nicolosi was Joey's longest-standing partner, the head of construction, and the person who ensured that all our great plans were actually built, on time and on budget. I was head of overall development for our projects, and in particular had been man on point for The Warner since its inception, some 250 million dollars before. Joey and John were seasoned developers and in their forties. I was unseasoned aged twenty-seven when I began working on The Warner. In the process of bringing this extraordinarily complex project to completion, John and I had toiled side by side, covering each other's back for months and then years as one obstacle after another was thrown down in attempts to stop the project.

The theater, majestic as it was, comprised only a small part of the overall project. Fused next to and above it was a half of a city block of new construction including offices, stores, arts space, and a spectacular facade of glass and granite designed to highlight the historic theater building on the corner. Inside the office building was a soaring thirteen-story twisting-and-turning glass atrium that marked the cutting-edge design of the masterful architect Jim Freed of the I. M. Pei firm in New York. Even before The Warner opened for business, it was already recognized as a landmark development, which would help knit together the city's downtown fabric and its nascent arts district. Considered by the investment community a "trophy building," the project was already lining up for awards: architectural awards; historic preservation awards; urban development awards. The Warner, it seemed clear, was a development with more than just a profit motive driving it.

But The Warner was a paradox: We had midwifed an architectural gem and a potential cash cow, but all the profits would go to our creditors.

Like all aggressive real-estate developers who depended on the liberal bank credit of the 1980s and early 1990s to fuel their out-sized development ambitions, we had been badly wounded by the savings-and-loan banking debacle (the so-called "S&L crisis") that had exploded across the country eighteen months before. Banks had been forced to call in all sorts of loans, including the unsecured lines of credit that kept companies like ours afloat during the months and years required to take our projects from the drafting board to reality. Without such loans, we were "out of business," simple as that. As we stood there on the stage in our moment of temporary triumph, we knew that we were at the end of this particular road. The Warner would be our last project in Washington for the foreseeable future and our last project anywhere unless we could find something new to do and somewhere else to do it.

Developers dream big dreams. Then we have to pay for them. In doing so, it's possible for a single development firm to run up very large debt loads. During the boom years, the partners of our company pledged to the banks our ownership positions in our projects as collateral for the debt we borrowed, and continued to do so, time after time, as the company grew. As founder of the company, Joey had kept the largest share of its ownership to himself, but he had also kept more risk: He provided personal guarantees and thus pledged his personal assets as well as his project interests. To Joey, this was an acceptable risk and not uncommon at the time.

By the early nineties, Joey had personally guaranteed a *lot* of bank debt, just over one billion dollars' worth. At the time one billion dollars was still a lot of money, especially when it was debt attached to only one person's name. When the maelstrom of the S&L crisis hit, it was fast, furious, and left no bystanders. Loan after loan was called in for every developer in nearly every major American city. Often, the only way to pay back those loans was by selling the very real estate the loans had financed. But with everyone suddenly a seller, and almost no one a buyer, the value of commercial real estate plummeted virtually overnight, often by 40 percent or more.

When banks call in their loans and the borrower can't pay with cash proceeds from selling the buildings, the banks then invoke their right to call on the personal guarantees on which they have also been relying. In other words, Joey had to start selling his personal assets to pay back the banks. His fall from on high was swift and terrible. Suddenly, all his assets—the elegant townhouse in Georgetown; the Porsche, Maserati, and other cars; the various artwork; and the Hamptons beachfront house—they all hit the auction block and vanished in a breathtakingly short period of time. For the rest of us, the sudden and complete evaporation of our ownership positions in the projects was equally dramatic. We all ended up with our net worths a fraction of what they were, usually not too far above zero.

We were not the only development company knocked flat by the financial storm. In fact, it appeared that we were going to be one of the few survivors. In the postcrisis aftermath, most development companies had folded up and disappeared. Though we hadn't—barely—we also hadn't yet determined what we would do next. We considered the possibility of lowering our aspirations, of living off the meager management fees, which our completed projects spun off, even if we no longer owned them. We could then wait the several years—or more—needed for the development market to return to health. We considered entering the parking business, or maybe the building-cleaning business—below-the-radar enterprises that might not be glamorous but which were somehow related to the real-estate assets we knew so well. We were trying to find a concept or a niche where we could use our drive and entrepreneurial skills, even if it meant operating on a more modest scale. And then we realized our next big venture might be sitting right in our laps. It was called McArthurGlen.

McArthurGlen was a phenomenally successful operation founded by Alan Glen and Cheryl McArthur who had pioneered an updated version of "factory outlets," which they christened "designer outlets." Almost single-handedly they had been responsible for building high-quality designer outlets across America where upmarket manufacturers like Polo Ralph Lauren, Armani, and Nike could liquidate their end-of-season excess stock at 30 percent to 70 percent off retail prices. Joey had once worked for Alan before setting off on his own, and when Alan had come out of retirement (for the second time) to start McArthurGlen, The Kaempfer Company was one of his early financial backers.

Alan developed the first center just outside Williamsburg, Virginia, away from the main retail centers of Richmond to the north and Norfolk to the east. Its success was so phenomenal and so rapid that he literally couldn't build additional phases or new centers fast enough. North of Chicago, south of San Francisco, west of Denver, the people who owned the brands and the shoppers who bought them at bargain prices were demanding "More! More! More!" Early in 1992, JPMorgan led McArthurGlen to Wall Street and took them public and that, too, was a smashing success. So it was that at the time The Kaempfer Company was crawling through the real-estate equivalent of Death Valley, Alan was perched on Mount Olympus.

That was when we started considering the idea of transplanting the McArthurGlen concept overseas. Alan liked the idea.

"I'd do it myself, but I'm too busy taking care of the company here in the U.S.," he told us. "It'll be a slam dunk wherever you take it. We've proved that the concept works. All you have to do is build and reap the rewards."

The idea of practicing our trade beyond the borders of our own country should have been a little daunting, but that never occurred to Joey or to me. There was almost no investment money to be found in the USA, and McArthurGlen seemed to be the "something else, somewhere else" we needed. The only question we considered, really, was where should we take it?

"South of the border," said Alan, always a lover of the American West and our neighbor to the south. "Mexico's economy is booming and the shoppers there have always loved American brands. And it'll be easier on senior management. There are no time-zone issues."

"I don't know," said Joey. "I think Japan is even more fanatical about American brands. And as the world's second largest economy the purchasing power there is enormous. Much, much more promising than Mexico."

Maybe I was preoccupied with bringing The Warner project in on time and on budget, but I rejected both ideas out of hand. Who in the hell had the energy to start up a new company in Japan, half the world away from home, in a truly foreign culture with a nearly impenetrable language? Or roll the dice on enough purchasing power in Mexico?

"Europe," I pronounced with finality. "It should be Europe." That had been the initial idea anyway, and seemed the obvious choice to me.

"Why?" Alan asked.

An honest answer would have been, "Because I'd like to live in Europe, at least for a while. My wife Pamela and I have often talked about moving there after The Warner's finished. And I think it would be fun." That would have been my honest answer, but instead I provided analytics. I rattled off what I thought were Europe's most obvious advantages. There were 320 million Europeans, making it a larger market than America. The European Union was in the process of dropping border restrictions to foster intra-European trade. Tax regimes were being harmonized for the same reason. The European economy seemed to be gathering pace in GDP growth. Finally, and most significant, Europe was home to most of the world's great luxury brands—the most important success factor in the outlet concept.

It may have sounded as though I knew what I was talking about.

I didn't even know what I didn't know.

Joey and I had been to Europe together dozens of times on business, but even so we recognized that visiting Europe *on* business and actually *doing* business in Europe were very different matters. We started calling people and asking: What was the retail market like in Europe? In specific countries? Would the manufacturers be receptive? Would the public want to buy at discount? How would we finance it? Who should we hire?

A few months before The Warner's opening, Joey launched a transatlantic phone-calling marathon. Joey is a classic American entrepreneur, a high-energy promoter with a gift for presentation and an enthusiasm for new projects. He has an innate ability to generate and regenerate energy around him and then beyond him. At some point Joey spoke with Roger Morgan, an American real-estate investor with whom we had been working during the prior two years. Roger was then headquartered in London, where he had raised European capital to invest in U.S. properties.

Joey and Roger discussed taking Alan's concept to Europe. Was there a potential for a big hit? How difficult were the zoning approvals there? Was there an investor base that would be interested?

Roger and I had known each other at Harvard, where we had been on the sailing team together. He was always an outwardly cautious person. He listened to Joey carefully and asked insightful questions. His responses were reasoned and measured. He cautioned, "Things are a little different over here, Joey." Joey and Roger subsequently held more conversations and exchanged more information, and agreed the idea merited more study.

Which, of course, was what we were doing. But you can only learn so much from phone calls and spreadsheets, and several months later, by the time Joey, John, and I were standing on the stage at The Warner, we knew that any further study was going to have to entail real "due diligence." We had to go to Europe ourselves and conduct hands-on research.

"When are you planning to go?" John asked me.

"I'm not sure. A couple of weeks after the opening, I guess. I'm ready for a break, and Pamela and I move into our new house in a few days."

Joey gave me a look. "Well . . . I received a fax this morning. I was going to save it for tomorrow, but maybe now's the time to look at it."

He pulled a folded sheet of paper out of his pocket and handed it to me. I sensed it wasn't going to be good news. It was a faxed copy of an article from the *Drapers Record,* an influential publication for brands and retailers in the UK. Across the page was a note scrawled by Malcolm Young, one of Joey's London friends: "Is this one of your people?" I read the article by the brightness of the stage lights.

DEVELOPER ANNOUNCES
NEW CONCEPT FOR BRANDS

Roger Morgan, of R. G. Morgan Properties, yesterday announced the formation of Fashion Retail plc, to introduce into European markets the American concept of designer outlets. . . .

"WHOA!" I spat out. "What's going on? I thought you and he were talking together?"

"We were," Joey said calmly, "though we haven't spoken in a while."

"Jeee- SUS! . . ." I said, staring down at Roger's picture on the page, which was staring back up at me. "That means . . ." and my voice trailed off.

Silence, except for the stagehands shouting and clanging around us. As the news sunk in, emotions of anger, incredulity, and an intense need to react whirled through my mind.

"If he's announcing it, it means he's way ahead of us. *Months* ahead," I continued. I turned to Joey and said, "Maybe we ought to go over and see for ourselves." I shook my head incredulously. *"Jesus!"*

THREE

Landfall

J oey and I landed in Paris four days later.

"This should be fun," Joey said as we tossed our gear into the back of the rental car. "Finally, we can focus on something new, something other than creditors and lawyers."

At five-feet-six, Joey is a highly concentrated piece of work, his coal black eyes giving a hint of his intensity. Joey is fiercely bright and an incredibly fast thinker, usually faster than most of the people in the room, and his impatience can come bursting forth. He loves motion but because of that impatience, he often confuses action for progress. As he himself admits, he is often wrong but never in doubt. Despite his mercurial nature, he had made his millions—more than once. He could have retired young had it not been for his flair for pressing on with the next, even larger venture and risking those millions faster than he made them.

Joey was akin to a tight ball of kinetic energy, ready and able to rocket forward, knocking down all obstacles in the path to his objectives. But at this point in his career, financially battered after the S&L debacle, he wasn't too concerned about his manners. He was on a bigger mission—his comeback. In 1991, his net worth indicated he was a very wealthy man. By late 1992, when we landed in Paris, Joey, at age forty-five, had a net worth measured far below zero. The question was, would McArthurGlen Europe be the vehicle to replenish his balance sheet and reignite his career?

Joey and I had worked together closely for six and a half years. But we couldn't have been more different.

For ten days Joey and I sprinted wildly through France and England, meeting with leading retailers, real estate advisers, lawyers, potential investors, marketing firms—almost anyone who we thought might have anything valuable to say about our idea. We inspected whatever outlet stores already existed. We discovered a collection of dreary industrial sheds at the brands' factory sites, converted gas stations, third-rate city-center stores, and cordoned-off sections in the back of traditional retail stores.

On paper, the most promising location in France was in the textile manufacturing city of Troyes, in the Champagne region, where a group of outlet stores had sprung up haphazardly over the decades hawking their end-of-season wares. When we visited Troyes, we were charmed by the beauty of the town center. There were many narrow streets crowded with well-preserved, half-timbered medieval houses. There were also ancient churches resplendent with what the *National Geographic* has described as some of the most magnificent stained glass windows anywhere. Yet because of the town's faraway location and the outlet stores' depressing ambience so lackluster, we rejected Troyes out of hand. But we were encouraged. The Troyes outlets were well known even in Paris, nearly a two-hour drive away. Despite that long drive, and all the windy back country roads that had to be navigated to get there (no direct highway), and despite the dreary nature of the stores themselves, the shoppers were making the trek for the bargains and the brands, year after year. Clearly, French shoppers, just like their American counterparts, loved buying quality brands at discount and were willing to travel long distances to find them. We smelled potential in the air. Maybe, we thought, just maybe we could really draw out that potential by doing it better.

But not, we decided, at Troyes.

Leaving Troyes, we drove five hours south to Lyon, the second city in France and the largest in the south. We toured the city center and the outlying retail districts (slowly realizing that a couple of American office developers didn't know much about French retail—"Ever heard of the children's clothing brand Tartine et Chocolat? Me neither."). Then we were up and down the highways, getting a sense of the geography, traffic flow, and landmarks. Eventually, we split up: Joey flew to London and I drove back north to Beaune in the Burgundy wine region, and rolled eastward to the town of Nancy, and on to Metz, not far from the German border. Then back westward to Paris (stopping off to see the famous laughing angels in the Rheims Cathedral). I drove straight through Paris and out the other side, past Versailles, and into the Norman countryside. I was looking, reading, asking—trying to get a feel. Was there something to this idea, and if so where and how should we do it?

Finally, I headed up to Lille near the Belgian border, and then to Calais on the English Channel (where I wondered about combining our concept with the duty-free shops on the channel ferries). And there I was, already up on the northern tip of France. In four mad days I had crisscrossed that beautiful, mostly rural country of fifty-seven million people, trying to gauge our chances of success if we were to transplant a new-world shopping concept to the (perhaps) wiser and more sophisticated old-world consumers.

And then over to England for more of the same.

A few days later in London, I was in the spacious and classically furnished offices of Austin Reed, haberdashers, overlooking the busy traffic on Regent Street. I had read up on the company's market share, competition, opportunities, and weaknesses, and put together a presentation that I hoped would convince them that McArthurGlen would be the best way to improve their good numbers and to diminish the bad ones. The head of sales and his two chief associates had listened politely to my pitch, and now, as I stepped back from my presentation boards, I looked to my audience for questions. What I received was a polite silence.

Finally, Thomas, the head of sales, looked over to the young man on his right. "What do you think, Colin?"

Colin, still maintaining his amiable but unengaged expression, turned to me, and in the most carefully studied English public school (i.e., private school) tone of voice asked, "Surely you're joking?"

You have to admire the English. They have ways of insulting you that don't even hurt. Sometimes it isn't until much later that you even realize you have been insulted.

"Well," I said, first counting to five so I wouldn't snap back at him, "I hope I made it clear that I was not joking. I am talking about a sales concept that has been tested and proven time and time again . . ."

"In America." His voice reeked of skepticism.

"Yes, in America. It is our belief that what has worked so well in America, can be adapted to Britain."

"First of all," Colin responded, "you must realize that except for the odd sale now and then, here in Britain we don't shop at discount for the high brands." He paused for effect.

"Further," "he continued, "you are proposing that we set up shops to sell our goods to the public at prices practically below wholesale. If we did that our retailers would shout bloody murder. And they would be right to do so. I can only suppose that your American retailers are more accommodating than ours?"

"No, of course they're not. But that's where the rest of our equation comes into play. Not only do we limit our sales to end-of-season goods, which are not in direct competition with your retailers, but we severely limit the number of outlets, and deliberately place them in remote locations, far from the High Street."

At this the other sales associate took over. "It's easy enough for you to talk about remote locations. But look at the size of America. Very large. Then look at the size of Britain. Very small. You mentioned that you locate these centers a thirty-minute drive outside of town, preferably between two cities?"

"That's right," I said.

"Well, in Britain if you drive thirty minutes outside of one town, you will have already driven through and beyond the next two towns," he closed, receiving his colleagues' silent nods of support.

"There are the discount outlets at Hornsea," I countered. "I haven't been there yet, but I understand the place does a pretty fair turnover."

The mention of Hornsea elicited polite smirks.

"Ah, yes," said Thomas, head of sales. "They say that if Hornsea's not the end of the earth, you can certainly see it from there." Then, not unkindly, "You might want to see it for yourself before making any further recommendations."

Two days later, I did just that. I drove about three hours down the blustery east coast from Newcastle to find the remote coastal town of Hornsea, where the largest and most successful grouping of outlet stores in Britain was located. Thomas was right. You practically could see the end of the earth from there.

The entire complex included just thirteen stores, all midlevel brands (none of the luxury brands that MacArthurGlen counted on) clustered together around the "leisure activities" of an indoor butterfly sanctuary and a collection of nineteen antique British cars. Unexciting . . . and yet, for all its lack of glamour, this tiny, remote center, which was no match for the McArthurGlen centers in the States (which were literally ten times its size), was able to draw thousands and thousands of people who happily made the arduous journey to the back of nowhere to shop there.

Maybe the Austin Reed people were right, I thought. But then maybe they weren't. Again I smelled the potential in the air.

On the eighth day of our ten-day trip I called home to Pamela. I had left for Europe the day after we had moved into our new house, leaving her with piles of unpacked boxes and our one-year-old daughter Avery. Eventually, the conversation turned to how my trip was progressing.

"Well," I responded carefully, "I don't think you should unpack any more boxes."

"Ah, well. Between working and the baby, I haven't had time for that. Come on home and we'll get at it."

Pamela was thirteen years into her career at that point, including investment banking on Wall Street, and more recently as an executive recruiter at Russell Reynolds Associates.

"Well," I demurred again, "I think we should chat."

Silence.

"Oh, c'mon, Byrne, don't tell me . . ." Pamela knew me very well. "Oh, come on! You must be kidding."

And that was it.

Two days later we decided to move to Paris. I would move right away. Pamela and Avery would follow in a few months.

We never did unpack those boxes.

FOUR

Plunging In

No one could accuse us of thinking small. We had deliberately targeted the biggest, richest, most complicated market in the world. We weren't out to conquer so much as to charm and to entice 320 million people (USA population: 280 million), in an area of 800,000 square miles (USA: 3,000,000 square miles), divided into twenty-three countries (USA: one) speaking eighteen languages (USA: one), at the time conducting business in sixteen different currencies (USA: one).

Looking back, we may have been naively ambitious but we weren't stupid. We understood from the start that we would need help. Lots of it. And on that score we were either very smart or very lucky, because the first two allies we recruited proved invaluable from the very first meeting and continued by our side for years thereafter.

It was in London, on that first frantic reconnaissance trip, that we found the man who was to become one of our most valuable counselors throughout the hectic years ahead. His name was John Milligan, a six-foot-tall Yorkshireman, and an expert on retail properties at Jones Lang Wootten. "JLW," as it was known, was a British company that operates a global real-estate advisory agency, which helps investors purchase, sell, manage, or lease anything they want literally anywhere on earth. Whether it is an office building on the Champs-Elysées, a shopping center in Sydney, or a hotel in downtown Los Angeles, JLW has an office locally and a team of professionals available to get you what you want.

John was only thirty-four years old, but he was already a twelve-year veteran of the firm. His cherubic face expressed his most distinguishing characteristic: a demeanor of perennial good cheer, which disarmed all who knew him. John Milligan knew everybody and everything there was to know about retail in the United Kingdom. And, we discovered, everybody in retail knew John Milligan. During our first meeting it was clear that he understood the outlet concept, that he was enthusiastic about it, and that he saw great potential in it. He had already recommended it to a client who didn't know what to do with a particular property. John thus became the first and, in fact, only knowledgeable professional who gave a reassuring and unequivocal thumbs-up to our idea.

John had just been appointed chairman of a new JLW division charged with advising retailers and developers of retail centers as they expanded across borders in Europe, an emerging trend at that time. He thus had the mandate and a newly organized team under him, ready to go. All he needed was a real client who had pan-European ambitions. Just then we walked in the door.

Joey and I spent an entire afternoon with John talking through the details and identifying the types of assistance we'd need: demographic analysis, searching for appropriate sites, research on brands, etc., etc.—at the end of which John, with his infectious smile and Yorkshire accent proclaimed, "Right, then. That's a lot of talk. Shall we cool off with a gin and tonic?"

And it was while we were having drinks in his office that I related to John the story that Alan Glen had told me about acquiring a designer outlet site in Hillsboro, Texas.

McArthurGlen had already opened centers in the east, midwest, and Rocky Mountains region, and they needed one in the south. Alan found a superb location in a place called Hillsboro, Texas, located one-quarter of the way from Dallas/Fort Worth to Austin on I-35. It was a classic McArthurGlen site: a small town with no retail around for twenty miles, yet with over 50,000 cars a day driving past the town's edge on that highway. Alan had his people run all the numbers and draw up preliminary designs, and then trundled off to see the mayor of Hillsboro, to explain the concept, and to seek his support.

Alan told the mayor how the outlet would create four hundred new jobs, maybe six hundred if the center grew large enough. He estimated that there would be nearly five million dollars in property taxes flowing into his town's coffers and four million shopping visits per year. The town would no longer be a quick blur on I-35 as cars blew past. Instead, those drivers would stop, shop, visit the town's center, and come back several times per year. Alan unfurled the architectural drawings and walked the mayor through them.

"So, Mr. Glen, what do you want from me?" the mayor asked at the end of the presentation.

"Well," Alan said, "I want your support for the project. I'll need zoning approval and a building permit to get started."

The mayor thought for a moment, then asked Alan, "May I see those drawings again?"

And when Alan unrolled the drawings, the mayor took out a pen, signed his name across the top of the first drawing, dated it, and said, "Mr. Glen, you just got your zoning approval and your building permit. Let's get started."

The whole interview, from beginning to end, had lasted less than an hour.

When I finished the story, John was looking at me with an expression of amazement. "Are you kidding? Is that story true?"

"Absolutely."

John burst out laughing. "Well, brace yourselves, gents. Approvals here in the United Kingdom and on the continent—if you can get them—can take years, sometimes several."

"Well, we'll see about that," I said. "We think we have a lot to offer the townships."

"I see you have optimism, Byrne," John said with a grin. "That's good. You're going to need it."

It's significant to note that JLW wasn't the only property company we considered. Our research indicated that a rival firm, Healey & Baker, was actually the strongest in the retail field on a pan-European basis. But we discovered Healey & Baker couldn't accept our business because they had already been locked up by Roger Morgan. He had insisted on a "noncompete" clause in their contract, preventing them from working with any other development firm in the designer outlet arena. The discovery of the noncompete contract confirmed that Morgan was indeed months ahead of us.

The other alliance we made in that first foray was with the Bouygues organization, the gigantic construction company that gave us the confidence to launch ourselves into the heavy political and legal undergrowth that is the hallmark of the French property market.

Bouygues (pronounced "Bweeg") is by far the largest and most important French construction company, with 90,000 employees in France, and 112,000 worldwide at that time. There is no French town, city, or region in which the company doesn't have deep roots, both commercial and political. Company lore has it that when World War II ended, Francis Bouygues, a young sergeant in the French army, lay down his arms and began walking home, his only possessions being the clothes on his back. As he walked the roads of France and studied the devastation, he concluded that much of the country would need rebuilding. He resolved that he was going to be a major factor in that effort. Testimony to just how successful he was in achieving his goal was given by François Mitterrand, president of France at the time of Bouygues's death in 1993. Mitterrand was famous for insisting that his cabinet of ministers meet every Wednesday at the same time with all in attendance. The only time in the fourteen years of his presidency that he cancelled a cabinet meeting was for Francis Bouygues's funeral, at the Church of St. Madeleine, in Place de la Madeleine. The entire cabinet attended.

It was one of our Dutch partners on The Warner project who put us on to Bouygues. "If you want to get something built in France, you go to Bouygues," he told us. "They have enormous clout—they are not only very reliable engineers and builders, they are an important political force as well.

"But there's one caveat," he warned us. "Don't get too close to Bouygues or become too reliant on them. They will take you prisoner." He held his hands out in front of him with the wrists touching, an eloquent gesture suggesting handcuffs. "Keep your distance and you'll be safe."

Joey and I drove out to the Bouygues headquarters just outside Paris. We discovered that when you visit Bouygues, you don't just drive up, park your car, and stroll in for a meeting. First you encounter a heavily guarded gate, military gatepost style, and only after the guards have verified your right to be there are you allowed to enter.

Once through the gate we found ourselves on a long, winding stone drive, running along the side of a lake populated by white swans and other water fowl. Eventually, at the top of a slight rise, we were abruptly confronted by a breathtaking sight. Looming in front of us was a colossal building, standing like some huge, low-lying medieval fortress, and set about with columns and cantilevered overhangs, the whole structure surrounded by acres and acres of landscaped gardens and lawns. The building was not as large as King Louis XIV's palace a few miles away at Versailles, but it was clearly designed, like Versailles, to resonate power and to intimidate. The building was named "Challenger," and had been designed by Kevin Roche, the American architect who had been imported by Francis Bouygues specifically to imbue the building with its message of authority and power.

Joey was impressed. "This is the first time I've ever seen a building designed to scare the shit out of you," he said with admiration.

"I wonder," I said, thinking of our Dutch friend's warning. But then I took another look at the headquarters building. "I guess if there's anyone in France who could help us it'll be Bouygues," I concluded.

As we were in France, our first meeting with Bouygues was, naturally, over lunch. Lunch in a private cherrywood-paneled room with white-gloved waiters serving 1986 Château Margaux. Lunch consisting of our choice of poached salmon or Chateaubriand, or anything else we desired. It was there that I met the people with whom Bouygues proposed we work. Andre Pierlot, perpetually ebullient, had recently been appointed to head up a client relations department. (Heretofore, Bouygues had assumed there was no need for such a thing.) His right-hand man and my day-to-day contact was to be Olivier Jamey, a tall, lanky young Frenchman, thirty-ish in age, with a warm personality and very good English. Olivier's job was to open any Bouygues door for me that might ease my entry into France . . .

and, therefore, to hasten the day when Bouygues might be constructing multiple projects for us. Olivier and I took to each other right away. It was a positive meeting, in part because neither he nor I had any inkling of what was to come.

Back once again in Paris, I had a meeting with the head of JLW's French office that did not go nearly so well. The man, politely but firmly, simply refused to take our business.

"Whatever you heard from John Milligan in London was, frankly . . ." he groped momentarily for the *mot juste*, then gave in to his feelings, ". . . bullsheet." He waved his hand airily at the letter we had sent him describing our goals. "Your concept . . . it will not work here," he said with finality. He explained that it had been tried before and failed. And anyway even if it could be made to work it would never receive the government approvals required. It was, he concluded, politically impossible, so in all fairness he could not accept the assignment and waste his team's time.

His refusal should have set off some alarm bells, but it didn't. I chose to see it simply as a problem that needed solving, and I would solve it with a phone call to Milligan in London.

John hurried down to Paris to make peace and to work his magic. When he had done so he quickly organized a breakfast meeting to introduce me to those JLW people who would counsel me in France. The three he brought along included Elaine Anderson, a bright and well-spoken British woman fluent in French and Italian; Enrico Marazita, a strikingly handsome and soft-spoken Italian, also fluent in French, English, and Spanish; and the half-British/half-French real-estate specialist named François Moss. All were in their late twenties, all intrigued by our novel idea, and all eager to help make it work. In retrospect it was a meeting that marked a turning point in the lives of everyone present. In the subsequent years, each person at that table would play a significant role in McArthur-Glen's efforts, and each would have meaningful personal stories to tell of what evolved from that meeting. The stories included fabulous career advances, commercial successes, and life-changing decisions. The stories were also of romance, marriage, and then families. Others were of heartbreak and eventually of tragedy. All were interwoven. All started with that early McArthurGlen meeting in Paris.

On the plane trip home, I began outlining what would become the business plan for importing the McArthurGlen concept to Europe.

Business plans are almost always mind-numbingly boring, full of jargon and statistics. But a business plan is the road map defining what you will do, when you will do it, the resources you will use, and, of course, the projected "fabulous result" of your grand vision. No serious business plan projects anything other than a "fabulous result," or it wouldn't be written. "The plan" becomes your calling card for raising the money required to start the new venture, and is the guide book by which your investors keep track of what you do with their money. The prose may not be elegant, but it doesn't need to be. It is addressed to a highly select audience—the handful of people who will join you on the adventure and those who will underwrite it. If you can't persuade them that you've asked and answered the right questions, and that you're the right team to "make it happen," you'll quickly find yourself alone at the starting gate. You'll not only be lonely. You won't have a business.

Back in Washington, I holed up in an upstairs room of our little house that was still filled with unpacked boxes, and continued scribbling away for five or six days, venturing out only to join Pamela in celebrating Avery's first birthday.

Writing the business plan for a multicountry, multicultural, pan-European rollout of a new retailing concept was exciting stuff. As I sat there, alone and unfazed by whatever reality awaited me across the ocean, the possibilities were endless. Even the due diligence seemed exciting: Paris, London, Milan, maybe Berlin (why not?), and let's look at Madrid . . .

The essence of the designer-outlet concept couldn't have been simpler— selling end-of-season leftovers of famous high-fashion brands at bargain prices. Who wouldn't like Polo Ralph Lauren—or Gucci, or Prada, or Nike—at 30 percent to 70 percent off the regular prices? It's a win-win-win idea that benefits the manufacturer, the retailer, and the ultimate customer. But as usual, it is the details that matter, and our business plan covered all of them.

Where do you market such goods? How do you control the sales? How do you protect your full-price retailers? And possibly the most important question, how do you protect your most valuable asset—the reputation and goodwill of the brands you're selling?

We knew the system worked in America, and we were convinced we could make it work in Europe.

A key factor in our business plan called for identifying and securing partnerships with local business leaders in every market we entered. We needed partners who knew the country, knew the language, understood the local politics, and were familiar with the appropriate laws.

The fact that I had never worked in Europe, that I had never visited a McArthurGlen outlet center, and that our little team of merry developers had no money didn't faze me. As a matter of fact, it didn't even occur to me as problematic.

It was a grand plan, filled with passion and the smell of adventure, and we made it even grander by ordering custom-designed binders, with hand-constructed and gilded boxes in which to place them. Then we shipped them out to that tiny select audience who would control our future. The recipients must have thought the Gutenberg Bible had landed on their desks, their names written in calligraphy across the cover, announcing our vision for Europe. In retrospect, we were, naturally, short on substance so we poured on the sizzle. We were very bullish.

And very naïve.

As for the challenges of never having been to a McArthurGlen outlet center, much less developed one, and never having lived or worked in Europe, and having no money, those were simply problems and we would find solutions. We were Americans, and that's what Americans do—solve problems and move on. I assumed that was why we were in business.

To address our lack of funds, we went to our local banker, a man named Bob Pincus, the one who knew our track record so well. Six of us pooled our meager resources, and more importantly, offered up our personal guarantees to the bank, thereby pledging whatever assets remained in our names after the S&L debacle. This included Pamela's and my shiny new house and our not so shiny bank accounts. It included pledging whatever cash was in those accounts: cash saved for future tuitions and mortgage payments. In other words, if for whatever reason this concept of bringing designer outlets to Europe failed and we couldn't pay back what we'd borrowed, then the bank would take all our personal assets in lieu thereof. Just like the banks had foreclosed on all of Joey's assets the prior year. Altogether, the pledges and guarantees were enough to secure a two-million-dollar loan.

It wasn't nearly enough, but it would to have to do.

A short while later, I was sitting by myself in what had to be the loneliest hotel room in Paris—now the official headquarters of a brand-new company dubbed "McArthurGlen Europe." A company that was comprised of me, just me. I sat there with a pencil, a pad, and a phone. The only thing missing was someone to call.

Because I didn't know anyone in Europe to call.

FIVE

Children and Bureaucrats

As I would come to learn, slowly and sometimes painfully, every-thing I'd need to know about setting up the outlet business in France would be encapsulated in the complexities and, to an American, perplexities, of everyday life. Some of the most useful information I gleaned came, literally, from the playgrounds. Some came from trying to buy butter at a market. Much came from trying to accomplish anything with the government, which in France means nearly everything.

Our rental apartment was a block from the Champs de Mars park and all its open space, a key feature for daughter Avery. Green space is a rarity in Paris, a city which has dramatically less open space per inhabitant than London or even New York. What I didn't realize until we lived next to the park is that none of that Champs de Mars green space was available—not for playing on or even walking across. Those lawns are scenery only, post-card material, and the miscreants who fail to keep off the grass answer to the police.

Still, weekend strolls through the Champs de Mars provide wonder-ful compensations. They also provide testimony to the unspoken French credo that "the state shall provide." There are the sophisticated puppet shows performed two or three times daily in minitheaters seating one hundred or so; the pony-pulled cart rides along the side paths; the ever popular *creperies*; and smaller playgrounds along the side where one can be almost alone. On the park's edges are classic carousels, some that have been there a century or longer, with elaborately painted wooden horses, elephants, and sea dragons, all lovingly preserved despite their age. There are those hexagonal green refreshment stands where the large square window covers are held up at ninety degrees by wooden slats during opening hours, offering *café au lait* and warm *pain au chocolat* in the mornings, and *croque monsieur* in the afternoons. There are the live shows of renowned entertainers, performed from time to time on huge, elaborate stages set up in the public space for all to enjoy. A few weeks after our arrival, Luciano Pavarotti sang there, and we figured even with our rental apartment's third-generation Ramada Inn furniture and no dryer, it was not so bad having world-quality opera in our side garden.

All of the Champs de Mars attractions are staffed and subsidized by the state, just as they are in the Luxembourg Gardens, the Bois de Boulogne, and all other parks throughout France. All are on show for the citizens to enjoy and for the tourists to take note.

But a harsher reality emerges when you actually use the playgrounds of Paris. Two characteristics predominate: dress and decorum. The first is impeccable. The second can be deplorable, at least for the kids.

French mothers are usually perched along the edge of the playgrounds on those classic green-painted wooden benches with the black iron legs and armrests. They are dressed with that unique Parisian sense of elegance that seems so innate to them and so elusive to others, and yet when broken down into its parts, is fairly elemental. Frequently, the women don flat or low-heel shoes (though of very high quality), with a shawl nonchalantly whipped around their shoulders, a leather Hermès or Bottega Veneta bag at their side. They often also sport a hair band, elastic or tortoise shell, the hair usually positioned forward to create a crest atop their forehead. For all the elegance, makeup is only a minor factor. Far more significant is the body language declaring, in effect, that Paris is most decidedly *their* town. The ladies all seem to know each other (and, of course, Pamela and I knew no one) and would lean into their conversations on the bench while their kids were left to themselves, digging away in the sandbox and climbing on the bars twenty to fifty feet away.

While the sophistication of the mothers' wardrobe is no surprise, the outfits of their children—once you understand the brands involved—are amazing. Expensive, and always seemingly new, tops and bottoms from such well-known French brands as Catimini, Jean Bourget, and Petit Bateau are everywhere, especially during the week. These are clothes that are many notches above Gap or Abercrombie in style, quality, and price. An outfit, with shoes, can easily run $175 per child, and there it is, wrestling around in the sandboxes like everyman's Levi's.

It is on the weekends that the real fashion show starts. Then the outfits from Tartine et Chocolat, Bonpoint, and Jacadi are on display. After church the best give as good as they get in the sandboxes, as befitting the $300-or-more elegance per outfit.

But it is the juxtaposition of the children's dress with their behavior that is so remarkable. Many of the kids on the weekend Champs de Mars playgrounds could compete with any peer in American sandlot playgrounds for roughness and intimidation. Toys and the hair of the younger kids and little girls' hats are fair game for any of the high-energy boys roaming the sandboxes. The wails of protest are constant and left largely unheeded by the bench-bound mothers on the perimeter, their heads still tilted toward each other in midphrase. At first we would wait expectantly for the mothers to intervene in the macho madness, but often it would go on and on until either we or someone else (another foreigner?) would point out that limits of civility were being approached. Then, the mothers would turn their head, purse their lips a bit, and blow out an exasperated breath. They would pop their heads up just a few centimeters when attention was drawn to the fact that their marauding sons had not only taken capture of the now desperately wailing smaller ones, but had them quarantined in the playground's corner jungle gym. It was around then that Pamela and I would quietly scoop up Avery from the sands and saunter away in search of more peaceful settings.

Pamela is an athletic, vivacious woman whose energy makes her seem taller than her trim, five-foot-six frame. She has a quick and infectious laugh, made more so by her blue eyes, which add their own smile to hers. Because Pamela lost a parent suddenly when only six years old, she is a firm believer in living in the present, of knowing that relationships are paramount. Raised in her beloved Rhode Island, she was described by one colleague as being known for "her plucky New England irreverence."

Pamela's early loss and that irreverence ensure she isn't easily fussed about life's minor setbacks. Early in our courtship, we were hailing a cab near her westside New York apartment when a car zoomed past, hitting a puddle, and spraying street water all over her new suede skirt. Pamela glanced down at the mess on her clothes, arm still raised for the next cab, and laughed.

We first met while sailing off the coast of Maine in a forty-four-foot Chinese junk. She was the only person with whom I ever sailed who practiced aerobics on the foredeck, ducking whenever we tacked, happy to take the helm as soon as she finished. By the end of the ten-day voyage, I was aware a new dynamic had entered my life. Pamela has always been ready for the next day's adventure. It was a characteristic well suited for what lay ahead.

Shopping, too, would provide both a daily challenge and invaluable insights into the French character. The frustration of dealing with parking in central Paris, combined with the plethora of small specialty stores in each neighborhood, meant that much of our shopping was done on foot. We quickly fell into the Parisian routine of buying only what we could carry or haul in a small cart. We, therefore, also quickly fell into the habit of frequenting the local butcher (*boucherie*), cheese shop (*fromagerie*), baker (*boulangerie*), wine store (*Nicolas*), newspaper shop (*kiosque*), and the *pharmacie* for our toiletries. The same social ritual is performed on every visit to those small stores: the formal *"Bonjour, Monsieur,"* greets you upon entry and then offered upon exit, and you respond in kind *"Bonjour, Madame."* Unless you are well known there that is the end of discourse until you have a question or check out at the counter. Parisian shopkeepers do not smile a toothy smile and ask how they may help you or inform you of the latest special offer. That's considered too forward and insincere, even disrespectful of the shopper. It is believed that ever-present smiles must, by their nature, be insincere, so why employ them? I was often told that many French people were a little unsettled when they traveled through America, being constantly besieged by all those teeth and smiles and offers of help. Too much "friendliness," they claimed.

One of the little shops that fascinated me was the local dry cleaners. After I recovered from the shock of the prices charged (a dry-cleaned shirt in Paris was $3.25 versus $1.10 at home), I looked more closely and discovered one reason for the high cost. Over to the side of the narrow shop and set back from the counter stood an Asian man of indeterminate age and apparently infinite patience pressing the clothes there on the premises. He was dressed in nondescript trousers and a white Farmer John's undershirt, the type with thin straps over the shoulder and long hoops under the arms. It clung to his upper body by perspiration. The pressing equipment was, for me, a novelty, though in fact it was a very old design. Facing him on the wall just above his ironing board was a long thin pipe. Through dozens of tiny holes in the pipe, jets of blue and yellow flames from propane gas heated the rack directly above it, on which stood a row of fifteen or more irons absorbing the heat from the flames. These were real irons—very heavy, 100 percent iron in exactly the same shape as today's modern electric irons, but with no electricity. With an expert hand he would wield the hot iron as long as there was sufficient heat in it to press the cloth. When the iron began to cool, he placed it back on the rack for reheating and took down the next one in line. In all the times I went in to that *pressing* I never heard the man speak. He just went on about his task, shirt after shirt, iron after iron, all day long. That was, as the French call it, his *métier,* his occupation. The French system strives to ensure that wherever possible regulations should be adopted so that everyone's *métier* can be preserved, including the very labor-intensive *métiers* right in the heart of Paris.

After exploring the shops and cafés of our immediate neighborhood we expanded our horizons to include the biweekly outdoor market on Rue Cler just on the other side of the Champs de Mars. The market runs down the middle of a closed street and is a two-sided, four-block-long extravaganza of sights, sounds, and smells, of cart after cart displaying fresh fruit, meats, cheeses, flowers, pastry goods, and desserts, with colored umbrellas or canopies blocking out rain and sun. On market day the Rue Cler is a whirl of jostling shoppers and vendors. Aromas mix and swirl together, one smell riding more strongly over another every ten feet as you bumped along, from fresh baguettes to pungent cheeses, *poulet roti,* and fresh-cut flowers. It can be both exciting and daunting. In our first visits we were bewildered as to how to make a purchase amidst the throngs of the confident and fast-chattering French men and women expertly eyeing and haggling over their targeted produce. Which part of our weak vocabulary should we or could we employ? When we finally plunged in and actually purchased several items, we emerged at the other end of the market from whence we entered and flopped down triumphantly at the café there. We

felt not only buoyed but victorious that we had "done it" by actually purchasing all of the items on our list. We had met and survived the gruff
madness of a Paris outdoor market and come home with our sustenance!
Whoa! We might not only survive but perhaps even glide right into our
own version of a Parisian lifestyle—maybe even make some friends. Paris
might be accessible after all.

Accessible, that is, until we needed to sign up for a phone. Or an electricity account or bank account. Or any of the basic items needed to lead
one's life in a modern urban setting.

It's no accident that the word "bureaucracy" is of French origin. When
you are no longer a tourist in a foreign country but a resident, you suddenly realize that the entire infrastructure of your life at home needs re-
creating abroad. Not just a bank account, and telephone and gas and
electricity accounts, but credit cards, driver's license, car, doctor, lawyer,
accountant, insurance, babysitter—all the basics.

That is when the French system has you where you are most vulnerable:
up against the labyrinthine bureaucracy in that government-centric economy.
Up against the regulations and the paperwork—the endless form-filling—
and the public employees who spend all day, all career pushing that paperwork, and telling you in bored tones that you are once again missing some
key form, the one they didn't mention during your last visit there.

"Excuse me," I said on my first foray out for setting up the basics. "I'd
like to open a bank account, please. I have my passport and apartment lease
with me," I said to the man with the glasses, plaid jacket, and navy-blue
tie at the tiny Société Générale office on Avenue de Suffren. I had waited
my turn in line and was ready for him.

"Okay, *bon*. Let me read this . . . Oh, sorry—this lease is not in your
name. Impossible to open a bank account."

"Well, yes, the name there is my company. But as you can see on the
last page it is my signature as the authorized person to sign."

"Ahhh, but the lease is not in your name. Impossible to open a bank account."

"Yes, but as you can—"

"Sorry, no bank account," he says, and looks past me to the line of people, "Next . . ."

And then on to the local office of EDF, the government-owned electricity company. Our landlord's policy was to provide electricity for the first

thirty days of the lease, and then automatically close the account, to be replaced, in theory, by a new account in our own names.

"We need to see proof of identity and ability to pay," says the middle-aged, nondescript though not unpleasant lady behind the window. "Please show me your driver's license and bank statement."

"Well, I am working on that. I just arrived in Paris last week, you see, and I do not yet have a bank account; I am trying to open one now—"

"Without a bank account it is impossible to open an account here," she said quietly, the mild boredom still in her voice.

Silence while I take in a breath and prepare my story.

"How else would you pay?" she asked.

"Well, eventually with my new checks from my new bank account of course, but I'm working on that account now. In the meantime I can pay with my American credit card."

"No, no. No foreign credit cards. What's the problem with a bank account?" she asked, slightly less bored and seemingly on the verge of being helpful. My hopes rise.

"The bank wants to see the lease in my name but it is in the company's name for now—"

"Oh, *bien sûr*, that's a problem. You cannot get a bank account with that."

"Exactly, so I am working that out with the bank. But in the meantime I would like to open an account with you . . ."

"Impossible. You need a bank account . . ."

Dead end.

Later, with an inspiration in mind, I go back to the tiny office of the Société Générale and ask to apply for a credit card, bringing my spotless credit history from the existing U.S. cards with me.

"May I apply for a credit card, please?" I ask to a different man at a different desk there.

"Yes. May I see your credit report from the Banque de France, please?"

The Banque de France is similar to the Federal Reserve in the States but even more central to people's lives.

"Well, I have only just moved here and so I do not have a credit report from the Banque de France. But I do have my reports from America."

"No, no. That will not work. We need a credit history from here in France. It is, after all, a French credit card for which you are applying. You should just use your bank account and checks until you have a credit history."

"Well, that's the problem: Your bank won't open up an account for me because I do not have a lease in my name. It's in the company's name."

"Ah, yes. That's a problem. Sorry. No credit card."

And so it went with applying for a phone account, the gas account, and the driver's license. Always, there was some paperwork missing; always, another reason to come back another time; always, while time was running out on the thirty days of the landlord's grace period for electricity. All this while my time was meant to be spent setting up a new business.

Eventually, after learning a few tips from another American couple, I started all over again. With more paperwork and coordination between my lawyer back in Washington and my landlord (who wanted a credit history on me—a *French* credit history from the Banque de France—before they would change the name on the lease), I managed to get my own name on the lease, in order to make some progress. I could open a bank account, get a credit card, and secure electricity for the lights, and cooking, and hot water.

Once I had these basics in hand I could then take aim at securing the permits required to run a business in France.

"If you are serious about starting a company in France," Philippe, my young French lawyer pointed out, "the first thing you will need is the government's permission to do so." He counseled that I needed a *carte de commerçant,* which would allow me to run the business, and a *carte de séjour,* which would allow me stay in France on a long-term basis.

"How long will it take to get the licenses?" I asked.

"Each case is different. *On verra*—we shall see," Philippe responded. *On verra* is a classic French expression, one that commits the speaker to nothing other than, "I shall wait and see."

Applying for those critical work permits was the first step in what is, I was to discover, a process with no end. Legally, I was not allowed to live in France or start a company without them in place. I asked Philippe about that. "Well, I shall work on it right away," he explained. "The actual processing can take anywhere from . . . well, it is not predictable. I shall stay in touch. *On verra.*"

Meanwhile, the French government had prepared a new surprise for me, one a bit more challenging than opening a bank account.

One morning soon after we had moved into our apartment I was plodding through *Le Figaro,* the largest Parisian daily. The lead story was about the inaugural speech from the newly installed Prime Minister, Édouard Balladur. In his address to the *Assemblée nationale,* France's version of the House of Representatives, Balladur had announced an immediate moratorium on the construction of any new retail space in France . . . anywhere.

My French was still very weak, so in the hope that I had misunderstood the newspaper account, I read it again.

But no, I had read it right. The prime minister had just banned the construction of "any new retail space over the size of a convenience store at a roadside gas station."

I felt a free-floating sense of uneasiness taking shape somewhere in my gut. Here I had just uprooted my family and mortgaged our future for the express purpose of constructing a new kind of retail outlet in France, and the French prime minister was banning all such construction.

Balladur was announcing the first step in a grand plan to save the country's small retailers from the menace of the powerful "hypermarkets," the French-style megastores, which were a combination of Wal-Mart and super–grocery stores. They had rapidly spread across France over the prior fifteen years. To protect the small retailers the Prime Minister wanted to prevent any further retail stores from opening up. None. With immediate effect. That would provide time, he said, to study the fabric of the country's retailing sector and to then carefully draft new laws to strike a balance between new commerce and existing commerce. In essence, there was to be no new competition for retailers, at least until further notice.

Balladur's act is known as a *geste* in French, as in "gesture," implying a special action had been undertaken by one party for the benefit of another. Balladur had frozen all retail development on behalf of the retailers, and in making that "gesture" he would, as happens in all *gestes*, want recognition. In this case, the recognition sought was support for his party and, ergo, his party's candidate in the approaching presidential election: Jacques Chirac.

It was clear that the McArthurGlen concept was not a hypermarket, but was, in fact, a collection of small boutiques featuring one brand per store, and would actually create thousands of jobs across France. But the concept *was* retail, and thus would be subject to Balladur's decree. The granting of permits to build our outlet concept was now strictly forbidden, by none other than the prime minister.

Slowly I put the paper down and thought through what I had just read. I concluded that what I read was not a good thing. At least not for me and for my family of three.

"Pammie," I said softly to her across the table, "we have a problem."

SIX

Friends and Rivals

I had just finished lunch in London with a potential customer and was retrieving my overcoat from the Claridges's cloakroom. I turned and suddenly found myself nose to nose with Roger Morgan, college friend now turned rival. Several months had passed since Joey and I had learned via the faxed article of Roger's announcement to open outlet centers in the United Kingdom. Neither Joey nor I had spoken to him since.

"Hello, Roger," I greeted him. "How are you? From what I've read you're very busy."

My pleasant tone didn't disguise the message that his PR had found its way to my desk. No doubt my sarcasm expressed what I thought of it.

"Doing well, Byrne, thanks. You're also working pretty hard—not only here but in Paris, I understand."

Staying well informed was one of Morgan's secret weapons. Joey and I hadn't tried to hide our presence in London as we went about our various meetings. But I had been as quiet as possible with my movements in France. New retail concepts regularly migrated over from America to the British shores first, and if they are successful there, they are then rolled onward to the Continent. But our plan was a little different. We intended to go into Britain and France simultaneously, reasoning that if the concept really did work, we would be able to sprint forward both on the Continent and in the United Kingdom. Roger wanted me to know that he knew as much.

Roger was six feet tall, maybe a touch more, with straight black hair. He was lean and fit, and still looked very much as he had at college. He carried himself with a sort of casual assurance and his dark, intelligent eyes seemed to take in everything, constantly seeking, assessing, and storing information. Roger was smart. Very smart.

Just at that moment his eyes were fixed on me. He had been as surprised as I by this encounter.

"Please say hello to Laura for me," I said, deciding to wrap up this encounter.

"And a hello to Pamela for me as well," Roger responded in kind.

I had known Roger for nearly twenty years. We had met during our college days at Harvard in the late 1970s. We had lived in the same dormitory, even joined the same fraternity, or Harvard's version of one. In fact, it was Roger, one year ahead of me, who recruited me for the fraternity.

Postcollege, similarities continued to resurface. Both of us resisted the siren call of Wall Street after graduation. I embarked on a long, slow sailing voyage from Boston to New Zealand. A year after that I went on to business school at the University of Virginia. From college Roger continued straight into a four-year law school and a business-school program. Though we were never close friends, relations had always been quite pleasant.

Roger is part of the fourth generation of a highly successful New York family business focused mainly on Manhattan real estate. During his college days Roger didn't boast of his family's New York successes. That wasn't his style and wasn't appropriate. Harvard is never short on prominent families. During Roger's and my time there our fellow collegians included Caroline Kennedy, daughter of JFK; Prince Faisal of the royal Saudi family; Howard Johnson of the orange roof hotel-and-restaurant chain; Penny Pritzker of the Chicago Hyatt Hotel family. Nearly all were low-key in their demeanor. Harvard has a tradition of understatement, of letting third-party endorsements speak for themselves. No loud self-serving cheers from its quarter. My father, a Harvard man from the 1940s, described the traditional Harvardian "anti-rah-rah soft-peddle approach" as "inside out, backside to." Metaphorically, that meant that the acceptable way to wear a Harvard sweater was not with the Crimson "H" emblazoned across your chest for all to see. Better to wear it "inside out, backside to," with the "H" invisible to passersby. Other Harvardians knew and understood. Among some old-style Harvard types, there is a certain code of conduct. Roger certainly knew the code.

It was while Roger was in London that he first began working with Joey and me at The Kaempfer Company. By then, Roger had formed his company, R. G. Morgan Properties, and had raised European funds to invest in American real estate. One of those deals was a loan to our largest-ever project, larger even than The Warner. The project was called, ironically, the "Investment Building." Located just north of the White House in the heart of Washington, the project architect was the renowned Cesar Pelli. Eighty-five percent of the project was rented to one of Washington's most established law firms, Arnold & Porter, before construction had commenced. In other words, the Investment Building appeared to be a phenomenal success before it even started. But this was in 1991, just as the undercurrents of the S&L crisis were forming. Even projects as fabulous as the Investment Building were no match for the turbulence about to hit.

Roger's loan to our project was one of the many thousands of loans across America that went sour that year. Part of the security that we had posted in support of that loan, collateral that was turned over to Roger's investment group, was our ownership position in two McArthurGlen factory-outlet centers. It was during the aftermath of that loan going sour that we had discussed with Roger the idea of exporting the outlet concept to Europe.

Now, a year later, we had bumped into each other at Claridges. At that point, Joey and I estimated that Roger had a nine-month lead on us. Maybe more.

SEVEN

Two Similar Countries Separated by . . .

Even in the best of times, real-estate development requires two vital elements just to get started: ideas and money.

First, the idea—you have to know what you want to build and where you want to build it. With the McArthurGlen Europe concept, we had that.

Secondly, you need money—lots and lots of money. The Warner project in Washington gobbled up 250 million dollars. The Investment Building was budgeted for 400 million dollars. And though the outlet centers were not as costly as downtown office buildings, the first phase of an outlet center in England still required 30 million dollars, and France another 20 million dollars. After that initial 50 million dollars, if we had a success on our hands, we then wanted to roll out the concept as fast as possible, adding phases, and buying land, which would immediately require another 50 million dollars. That was a quick 100 million dollars.

The challenge was that when I landed in Paris we had a grand total of 2 million dollars. And that 2 million dollars was only a loan, and the cash was disappearing fast. Our strategy, then, was to quickly team up with a big, rich, open-minded partner in England and another one in France.

The problem was that no one wanted to be our partner. It wasn't that the English and French companies with whom we met didn't like us. They just didn't think the outlet concept would work.

As Joey and I spent months racing around trying to secure partners, meeting with the likes of British Land and Land Securities in the UK and Ségécé and SCC in France, we watched our cash balance continue to decline. Considering that the friendly banker back home who lent that money held as collateral our houses and bank accounts, not finding a partner was a serious issue. We knew that Roger Morgan had a significant advantage on us there. He had been working in London for several years, and knew his way around the financial markets much better than we did. Time and money, we had to admit by summer 1993 (nine months after our first trip to Europe), were not working in our favor. To address our cash needs, we brought in an investor, Joey's cousin, Bill Seldon, whose insight and counsel over time proved as valuable as the capital he provided.

What finally brought us together with our ultimate partner, BAA plc (formerly the British Airport Authority), were two forces at play: the shifting tides of Common Market politics, and the insight of John Milligan.

BAA had been an agency of the British government, which had been privatized during Margaret Thatcher's revolution. It was responsible for running Heathrow, Gatwick, Stansted, and several other British airports. It was big. Six billion dollars big, with one billion in cash.

In addition to running the airports, BAA owned and operated the duty-free shops inside those airports. In fact, it was BAA that pioneered the new generation of duty-free shops, offering the shopper a retail environment as convenient, as high quality, and as user-friendly as any downtown store or shopping center. And at the same time, prices on the same goods were 20 to 40 percent less than the downtown stores because there were no taxes levied. BAA's idea of upgrading the duty-free stores was an instant hit with travelers. The shops became wildly profitable, and BAA was constantly expanding their duty-free operations. Eventually, the operation became so successful that instead of referring to Heathrow and Gatwick as airports with stores inside, in some quarters they were glibly referred to as shopping centers with adjacent runways.

The fact that the source of revenue was not derived from core airport operations was very important. When BAA had been privatized the government wanted to ensure that the travelers would be well served. Therefore, the amount of profit that the airports were allowed to earn from its airport infrastructure was capped, and the annual profits were carefully monitored by government agencies to enforce this policy. But profits from "noncore" airport operations were not capped. Duty-free shops were decidely noncore. As a private company then listed on the London Stock Exchange, BAA had very strong incentives to maximize its duty-free revenue, and set out to do just that.

By 1993, only four years after the duty-free upgrade program began, its operations, according to one of BAA's Group Directors, contributed 600 million dollars per year to BAA's bottom line. It also represented 120 percent of the company's profit. In other words, the retail profits were subsidizing the airport's operations. But as BAA's management looked to the future, they could see a real threat to this golden revenue stream.

As part of Europe's desire to become more competitive with America and East Asia, the mandarins in Brussels wanted to create a "Borderless Europe," where goods and services could flow freely. Part of that concept meant that there should be tax harmonization across Europe, so that no one country created incentives more attractive than another. That in turn called for the abolishment of intra-Europe duty-free shopping. In other words, the 100 million dollars which BAA earned each year by selling duty-free goods to shoppers traveling within Europe (i.e., excluding profits from shoppers traveling outside of Europe) was to be abolished not later than 1997, four years hence. As strong an incentive as BAA management had from the London stock market to maximize its duty-free shopping in order to maximize its stock price (and, therefore, the management team's stock options), they now had an even stronger incentive to replace that soon-to-be-lost duty-free revenue in order to prevent the share price from dropping. But not just any type of new revenue stream would suffice. Management wanted "noncore" revenue, and preferably one that fit into the theme of "off-price" retailing. In that way that they could leverage the management skills they had developed in the retail sector.

It was just at that point that news of the American factory-outlet concept coming to the United Kingdom was gaining currency in the trade press. BAA read the articles and became intrigued. That's when John Milligan came into play.

BAA was one of John's many clients, as was McArthurGlen by then. John was advising us on how to enter the UK market, and advising BAA on how to replace that EU revenue stream. Naturally, he suggested the parties talk with one another about joining forces.

About this time, we discovered that in addition to our own efforts and those of Roger Morgan to begin opening outlet centers in the United Kingdom, there were suddenly three other companies also trying to launch outlet initiatives. One of them was RAM Eurocenters, a small company with roots in Freeport, Maine, home of the famous L.L.Bean outlet. Another was Prime, a fast-growing developer based in Baltimore which was the arch-rival of McArthurGlen in America. Like McArthurGlen, it had also gone public on Wall Street and was well funded. The third was a British company named Freeport Leisure, which had purchased the remote Hornsea center and renamed it. At that point none of the teams had either a first site or a local partner. It was shaping up to be a five-way sprint to see who could perform first. All five of the wannabe outlet companies had strong reason to court BAA. BAA not only had the needed capital and incentive to talk, but also, because of its successes at airport retailing, it could boast of very strong relationships with the great brands present in the United Kingdom, including British brands such as Burberry, Pringle of Scotland, and Jaeger, as well as international brands such as Gucci, Prada, and Hermès.

Our first contact with BAA was late in the summer of 1993, in Washington, D.C. The director of retail operations for Stansted Airport, Adrian Wright, was sent on a reconnaissance trip to America to learn more about the outlet concept. The meeting between Adrian and Joey went well, and was followed up by an invitation from BAA for us to visit them in London. It was the first of several meetings, held in quick succession, which made clear that their vision and ours for the outlet potential in the United Kingdom were very similar. BAA intended to expand into off-airport retailing, but knew they needed outside talent. The company was only five years out from being a government agency and had six thousand former government employees on its payroll. They needed hungry entrepreneurial talent to create the spark and to drive the process, to "make it happen." We needed a balance sheet and credibility; we were happy to do all the work. Naturally, the go–no go decision on the joint venture all came down to people. There were only three decision-makers at BAA who mattered at that time. We were lucky, very lucky, to have all three in the positions they were in when we met BAA.

Gordon Edington was head of BAA's International Group and, like ourselves, came from a real-estate background. He had recently sold the company he headed, Lynton Property Company, to BAA and had pocketed a bundle in the process. Gordon was born and raised in pre-Zimbabwe Rhodesia. To an American, he personified elegance and created a sense of presence when he walked into the room. At just over six feet with a slender frame, light brown hair, and deep blue eyes, Gordon was always dressed in elegantly tailored suits, usually double-breasted, complemented by a striking silk tie. For all his elegance, though, Gordon was known for his intensity and for driving the people around him hard. That, we figured, would be a plus.

Barry Gibson ran BAA Retail, and was the architect of the incredible duty-free cash gusher. Barry was from a modest background, carried no airs about him, and came at you with a torrent of energy and self-confidence each time you met him. In his early forties, he was athletic and affable. He was known and well respected throughout the retail industry, and was intrigued by the potential of factory outlets. His gung-ho attitude was the closest to an American outlook we had come across.

And then there was the vote that mattered more than others, that of the chief executive of BAA, Sir John Egan. Blue-eyed, silver-haired, and in his early fifties, Sir John was far from what I would have envisioned as the archetypal senior British executive. Like Barry Gibson, he was outgoing, affable, even talkative. And there was no doubt who was in charge when Sir John was in the room. He was insightful, pointed, and not afraid to make decisions on the spot and move on. And he had been quite successful in his career. A few years before we met him, he had been knighted by the Queen for his contributions to commerce and industry over the decades. And it was not long after that when Sir John pulled off his famous coup as CEO of Jaguar Motor Company. He reportedly sold the moribund firm to Ford for dramatically more than its actual value, and lore has it that the Queen had a quiet chuckle when she heard the story.

We took note that Sir John had worked with Americans before, and he, not the Americans, seemed to have done very well by the experience.

Both McArthurGlen and BAA had good reason to seek a partnership, and that autumn the dialogue progressed smoothly. Joey and I knew that during the first month or two of the dialogue BAA was still meeting with other potential partners, including Prime and Morgan, and we accepted that. Prime's advantage was that as a public company it had millions of dollars it could throw at this effort. We did not. Morgan was already well ensconced into the UK property scene, and knew many of the players and financing sources. We did not.

Late in the process an incident occurred that highlighted what was at stake in the BAA talks. We received a call from Gordon Edington to say that a fax had been anonymously sent to Sir John's office. It was an article about Joey's and The Kaempfer Company's near bankruptcy the year earlier. This didn't look so good, Gordon explained. Perhaps, he suggested, Joey could come in for a little debriefing, just so BAA knew the full story.

Hardball and dirty tricks—someone clearly felt we were getting too close to BAA, and was feeling threatened by it. Joey went along to BAA, explained everything about the S&L crisis, about The Kaempfer Company's difficulties and its ultimate survival, and put it all into the context of how many other companies did not survive. Whatever Joey said, it worked. We had a London signing for the joint venture agreement in December, only one hundred days after Joey first met Adrian Wright in Washington. Joey focused on the final negotiations while I wrestled with matters in France. Once Gordon and Barry learned more about the progress we'd already made in France, they wanted France as part of the venture as well. If the outlet concept actually panned out, they figured, they would want more geography included, not less.

With the joint negotiations focused on the topic of cash, BAA naturally wanted us to invest as much as possible so we would have lots to lose should the venture not go well. Joey sidestepped the issue of just how little cash we really had by convincing BAA that we should receive credit for the progress already made in France. In particular, Joey proposed, and BAA agreed, we should receive 1.5 million dollars of credit, in lieu of our contributing cash, for the progress we had already made in a list of towns in France. The caveat was that should we ultimately not receive the approvals needed to develop a center in any of those towns then we would have to cough up the 1.5 million dollars. That was a challenge, Joey figured, we could face another day.

"No problem," Joey-the-optimist thought to himself, "Byrne'll get those approvals in a heartbeat." Joey felt so bullish on this point that he neglected to check it with me until it was too late. It had already been agreed with BAA. It was an oversight which later was to assume a life of its own.

The management structure of the joint venture was a hotly negotiated issue. Both sides wanted as much control as possible, and eventually it was agreed that Joey was to be the Chief Executive, even though he was based in Washington. I was in charge of the venture for the Continent, and Adrian Wright was the Managing Director for the United Kingdom. In addition to Adrian, BAA also transferred Liz Bradley to the joint venture, a bright, attractive executive who, like Adrian, but unlike us knew retailing and the brands very well. The structure enabled us to pursue projects in the UK and France as two distinct theaters of activity, working along parallel lines. Situated directly over Management sat the Board of Directors, comprised of four directors from the American side, and four from the British side. The board had considerable control, and approved all major expenditures and financings.

Just before signing the final documents Barry and Gordon asked us if we would be willing to have the venture cover not just Britain and France, but all of Europe?

Joey and I looked at each other. "Why not?" we figured. It wasn't often you could sign up a joint venture along the terms we'd just agreed: We put up 2 percent of the capital, ran the operations, and received 50 percent of the benefits. If we could make this venture work it could literally be the deal of a lifetime. Not bad, we thought, given that one year earlier there was a meeting with The Kaempfer Company creditors announcing the company's state of insolvency.

At the signing, there was champagne all around. We christened the new entity BAA McArthurGlen, or BMG for short. Because of his real-estate background, Gordon was selected as BAA's point person for the venture, and he proposed a toast to our success together. International partnerships are notorious for failing, but we all felt bullish about this one. We felt we really did connect with Gordon, Barry, and Sir John.

It didn't take long before we discovered just how fragile that connection was.

With similar backgrounds in real-estate development and similarly intense personalities, Gordon and Joey were both alpha-males destined to butt heads from the outset. Joey felt strongly that, notwithstanding the fact that he was based in Washington, D.C., as CEO of the venture he should be able to run it however he wanted as long as he remained within the limits of the board approvals. Gordon's perspective was that BAA was committing the vast majority of the capital, and had its reputation and shareholders to protect. He wanted to know that matters were progressing not only according to the board approvals, but also in a style and manner with which BAA felt comfortable. This approach, Joey strongly felt, was overreaching.

The two of them clashed over the phone, in the monthly board meetings, and via backroom channels. There was frequently tension when they were in the same room. Voices were occasionally raised between them. Sir John became aware of the difficulty and expressed concern that BAA's interests needed to be adequately taken into consideration. Three months after the signing ceremony, Gordon started to wonder if, despite the energy and drive that the Americans brought to the venture, Joey might be unmanageable, and there might be more risk than return in the venture for BAA. Barry Gibson decided that a quiet little breakfast meeting with Gordon, Joey, and himself might be useful to clear the air. It was to be held at Barry's favorite venue, The Goring Hotel, located adjacent to Buckingham Palace.

The Goring is a one-hundred-year-old, family-run, five-star hotel located within an elegant Edwardian building. It has a long history of kings and queens, and, during the wars, generals and ambassadors staying there. Its atmosphere is properly British, with thick carpets, uniformed staff, and hushed tones throughout. The Goring was not Joey's type of hotel. He quietly referred to it as "The Boring."

Barry moderated at the breakfast, trying to reach common ground on how the joint venture should be managed. Joey repeatedly stated that he was the CEO, and he would manage the venture as he saw fit.

"That is totally unacceptable if it means you continue to ignore BAA's obligations as a public company," Gordon shot back, tension showing in his neck muscles.

The repartee went back and forth, and voices started to rise. Diners at adjoining tables were glancing over to observe the heated discussion. Barry tried calmly explaining to Joey that a joint venture with a large British organization required certain accommodations from a young and entrepreneurial management team, just as BAA needed also to make some accommodations to us.

"I don't want to make accommodations if it means I can't run the business the way I think it needs to be run. What kind of accommodations are you suggesting?" Joey responded with some impatience, reaching for a glass of fresh-squeezed orange juice.

"Well, for example," Gordon immediately interjected as he pulled a sheet of paper from his briefcase, "BAA is not going to subsidize your wardrobe."

Joey stopped sipping the orange juice, and turned his head slightly to look straight at Gordon, his eyes narrowing just a bit while he still held the juice glass in midair.

"Now just what in the hell is that supposed to mean?" Joey shot back in a clipped, strained tone.

"On your expense form here, which you submitted to me for approval, I note that there was a Burberry raincoat purchased in Paris for eight hundred pounds sterling. That is not the type of personal expense which BAA will condone or will reimburse. This venture is not your personal fiefdom."

"I don't give a goddamn if BAA condones it or not. I was in Paris, running to a series of meetings with Byrne, and it started raining hard. What you want me to do? Get wet, catch a cold, and stop driving the business forward while I recuperate from pneumonia?!"

"You should do what you need to do to stay healthy, Joey," Gordon retorted, his own eyes starting to slightly squint as well. "But don't expect BAA to pay for your wardrobe. You may be in charge of the day-to-day managing of the company, but the venture is half ours, and only half yours. It needs to be run according to proper corporate governance, not personal whim."

Joey's face screwed up into a tight scowl, and he brought down the juice glass from midair, slamming it down onto the breakfast table with such force that the glass immediately shattered, and fresh orange juice exploded across the table, with bits of pulp splattering all three of the men, followed a millisecond later by groans from Barry and Gordon. All others in the staid Edwardian setting of The Goring Hotel dining room stopped what they were doing in response. Forks, knives, and teacups were suspended in midair as they turned to see the cause of the commotion. Waiters started to hustle over with fresh napkins to help clean up the mess.

Gordon had had enough. He threw back his chair and stood up, wiping off the orange pulp as best he could.

"That's it, Barry. I told you—I think he's completely unmanageable.

He's out of control. Joey's not the type of person with whom we should form a joint venture. Where is the professionalism? This is absurd."

And with that, Gordon stormed out, with thirty or forty pairs of eyes around the room following him as he did.

"Joey," Barry said in the same quiet tone as before, though with a bit of a sigh to it. "It can't be like this. We can't have such strife, and such little consideration for what our side needs. Things have to change or this isn't going to work."

EIGHT

The Minuet

Prime Minister Balladur's moratorium on new retail construction, which the press quickly dubbed *le gel* ("the freeze"), turned out to be symptomatic of the times. It soon became clear that Pamela and I had arrived in Paris at precisely the wrong moment. The whole of France—indeed, the whole of Europe—was still chattering about the disastrous opening of the eagerly anticipated Euro Disney theme park the previous spring. That very public disaster, played out every day in the newspapers and on television, had been a monumental embarrassment, not only for the Disney people but for the French government as well.

With much fanfare the great Michael Eisner–led, Los Angeles–based Walt Disney corporation had exported its Disneyland concept to Europe. The move was aided and abetted by the French government, which had paid out billions from the national treasury to lure Disney from the competing site of Barcelona to the suburbs of Paris. In the process of transplanting their concept the Disney people scrupulously preserved all aspects of its squeaky-clean-family-fun package. "Made in America" worked at home very, very profitably; why change the formula? American executives were parachuted into the French subsidiary to run it from the top down, American-style. ("That's the way we do it in Anaheim. That's the way we'll do it in Paris.") Among the features of the transplanted Disneyland: there would be no facial hair on employees, and no alcoholic beverages for guests.

It wasn't just the French customers who were upset. German vacation-
ers, weaned on steins of beer from an early age, the Spanish and Italians,
who were used to their own local wines—all were at first perplexed and
then irritated. Perplexed that they couldn't get what they wanted with
their meals, and irritated that some American-based company was dictating to them what they should or should not be drinking.

But the prohibition against alcohol was only a small part of the problem. The ambience was simply not there, for a number of reasons. The
highly touted outdoor theme park did not fare well in the windy and rain-
swept plains of Marne la Vallée, the site of the theme park. Employees' relations with management, indeed French management relations with
American management, became strained and played out in public, with
ugly headlines across France and throughout the European media.

Mortified French politicians, who had put up all that tax money to lure
Disney to Paris in the first place, were just as angry as the customers and
the employees. Certainly they were in no mood for further embarrassments
from ignorant foreigners, especially Americans.

The example of Euro Disney seemed to support the gloomy predic-
tions of those luxury-brand manufacturers and retailers who had been
skeptical of our plans from the start. Maybe I should have paid more attention to their warnings. It was their market. And now the French national government was creating a whole new level of problems with
Balladur's moratorium. Barriers to my entry into the French marketplace
were being raised in real time, right in front of me. My reaction was to
move fast, before they were raised any higher. It didn't occur to me to retreat.

Property development begins with a vision. Our vision was of a new kind
of European retail center where well-known brands sold excess stock at
lowered prices without disturbing their primary retail accounts. The basic
ingredients we needed to turn our vision into a reality were talent, money,
and land. I was already in France so it was assumed, perhaps naively, that
the key talent was at hand. Our partnership with BAA provided the
money. What was missing was the land—the place where we were going
to build our vision. But it was the land that had to meet a very specific set
of requirements. It had to be within driving distance of a large catchment

of potential customers, yet away from the central cities. It had to be located in a place where those well-known luxury brands that would be our tenants would want to open an outlet. And it had to be a place where we could secure zoning approval.

The selection of that first site would be the key factor in determining whether or not the concept would work in France, and, in fact, in Europe. If I chose a site which the brands didn't like, or which the shoppers thought was too inconvenient, then the European adventure would be over before it really began. Selecting the wrong site was far worse than picking the wrong architect, or construction company, or bank. You could replace any of those elements without endangering the overall project.

It was because choosing the right site was so vital that I teamed up with both Olivier Jamey of Bouygues, and François Moss of Jones Lang Wootten. They both brought enormous energy and dedication to the process. And they brought very different perspectives.

In working with Olivier, I felt as if all of France was at my fingertips, which, it turned out, it was. All I had to do was give Olivier a one-page list of McArthurGlen site criteria and within a day it was zapped around to all the provinces of France, to all the branches of Bouygues's 90,000 French-employee network, including to all those who were charged with keeping a close watch on local mayors' wishes for new development. Knowing what they were looking for included knowing "where" and "what type" of new development would be welcomed, and most important, "when" it would be welcomed. In France, the "when" was a particularly key factor in the development equation because it addressed the reality that any new development was always a political issue, tied directly to the cycle of elections. "When" was the date of the next election, whether national, regional, or local, and that date dictated how much risk the traditionally risk-averse politicians were willing to take, which was never very much. Olivier and his Bouygues team approached each site from a political angle first. Finding a site which met the geographic selection criteria was one thing, but finding a site where we could get zoning approval, a factor that required a host of politically sensitive officials to cast a public vote, was quite another.

A few weeks after I had discussed the site criteria with Olivier, he invited me back to lunch at the company's opulent Champs-Elysées offices.

"You know, Byrne," he began with unnatural somberness, "Prime Minister Balladur still has *le gel* in place, so it is difficult to talk of shopping centers at a time when even a small roadside store is a delicate matter."

"I'm aware of that, Olivier."

"Yes, but Byrne, *really*. I am talking about true political pressure, at the highest levels. There is the presidential election in eighteen months and Monsieur Chirac's RPR party desperately needs the vote of the little retailers, *les petits commerçants*."

"But *le gel* can't last forever," I countered.

Olivier grimaced. "Perhaps," he said dryly.

And then, step by step he explained to me exactly why Monsieur Balladur had acted so quickly to invoke a moratorium on new retail development. It involved a backroom deal he had made with Chirac, who had already served twice as prime minister of France and who was determined now to be president. Chirac had handpicked Balladur to be the next prime minister, and in return he wanted an official act in support of the *petits commerçants* who were apoplectic about the growth and ubiquity of the massive "hypermarkets"—large format stores that sold everything from fruit and vegetables to clothes, gas, car parts, books, and perfume, at very low prices—which had spread to every town and city in France. In the process they were wiping out small butchers, bakers, and other independent retailers in their path. Organized into such powerful chains as Auchan and Carrefour, hypermarkets were being blamed for sucking the vitality out of the centuries-old town centers all over the country. Associations of small retailers were now organized against them, and the political arena was starting to feel their pressure. Chirac wanted his RPR party to be in the vanguard of helping them—just in time for his presidential bid.

As I listened to Olivier's description of the French political scene, I realized that I had arrived in Paris with my brand-new retailing concept—a concept organized around a shopping-center format—just at the tipping point, almost to the day, of the swing in power toward the antishopping center coalition, supported and encouraged by the new prime minister and by the president-to-be. My arrival couldn't have been timed more disastrously.

"Okay, Olivier," I said. "I get the picture. But again, *le gel* cannot last forever. While it remains in force we'll use the time to find exactly the right site for our outlet. Once we've found it, either *le gel* will be gone, or we'll convince the politicos that it shouldn't apply to us because we aren't a hypermarket. We're a collection of boutiques. We won't be putting any *petit commerçant* out of business. In fact, we'll be attracting millions of shoppers per year to a town that otherwise wouldn't have attracted them. Correctly managed, our concept will be good for the *petits commerçants* because I can direct a lot of my shoppers downtown for goods and services that I won't offer. The retail stores downtown will sell all the in-season stock that I won't. And to help lure them there I could restrict myself to not having restaurants—those who drive over an hour to reach my center, especially in France, are going to want fine cuisine for their midday meal and that'll mean going downtown. I have endless statistics from the centers in America that demonstrate this spin-off effect. Our concept is not a hypermarket— we can prove it."

Olivier sighed. "We can only hope."

For the better part of six months I spent most of my time in a car, seated beside Olivier, driving up and down the highways of France, looking at the sites identified by the local Bouygues staff. And every time Olivier climbed back into the car after viewing another empty field or run-down building, he asked me the same question. "Why are we wandering all over France, week after week, for months on end, searching for precisely the right spot to build your designer-outlet center, when you know that the perfect location is in the city of Troyes?"

Troyes, in the Champagne district, was the first French location Joey Kaempfer and I had visited on that initial reconnaissance trip. When we both agreed it did not meet our criteria, we had crossed it off our list of potential sites. Bouygues kept trying to put it back on the list.

I always gave Olivier the same answer. "*You* may know that Troyes is the perfect location, but frankly, I don't. It looks promising, but it doesn't meet the criteria."

I just wanted to find my Hillsboro, Texas, somewhere in France: a sixty-acre site fronting a busy highway midway between two cities, isolated from both. I wanted that frontage to be my advertising so I didn't need to place ads in the regional newspapers thereby stirring up the local retail trade. And Troyes didn't have those attributes. It was too far off the highway—no passing cars would see it—and too close to fashion retail stores in the center of Troyes.

"Ah, yes," he would say wryly. "The criteria—the *American* criteria!"

My other scouting companion was François Moss from Jones Lang Wootten. I was familiar with the JLW approach and comfortable with it. First, start with site criteria, move on to demographics, and then study the rules of zoning approval. Rank the possible sites from most appealing to least. Take the top twenty, visit them and the nearby Office of Economic Development. Narrow down your options. Make your choice.

Very straightforward. Very Anglo-Saxon. Not too political.

But working and traveling with François was more than just site finding. Because he was half British and half French, and had been raised in England, his perspective on France was from the outside even as he understood the culture from the inside. He was perfectly placed to be my private tutor on all matters French. He could counsel me on forms of protocol, and interpret the nuances and subtle silences that so often conveyed more of the real message than the words spoken. And with his proper British ways of approaching delicate matters, François would also gently correct me in terms of style or substance.

In the early days of presenting the outlet concept to local French public officials, I would make my presentation in halting French and in terms that I thought would resonate with the audience at hand. Because my outlet concept was new to most of my audience, I would present it using popular brand names as case studies. Polo Ralph Lauren, Nike, and Timberland were very active with the concept in America and were also well known to the majority of French. Those three brands were also keenly interested in having outlet stores opened in Europe. Of the three brands, Nike had by far the strongest brand-name recognition, and so I constantly invoked it. In doing so I made an impact, more so than I realized.

In English (as in the original Greek), "Nike" is pronounced "NI–Kee." I was fairly certain there was a different pronunciation in French. Having signed up four times for the Berlitz French course, and having cancelled four times because I was too busy to do it just then, I relied upon my high-school

French to sort out the correct pronunciation. I deduced that it must be "NEEK" because the "E" at the end on "Nike" would be silent in French, and the "I" would be pronounced like "EE."

So in those early months—when I was working alone, without François to guide me—I merrily went about my duties presenting in my broken French here and there, to mayors, to town councils, and to whomever would listen. I knew that I was making linguistic errors but because I kept postponing the Berlitz course I had no idea which errors they were. Wherever I went and presented, "NEEK" was right there with me—as prominent and obvious in my presentations as was the brand in the marketplace.

It was at a meeting with civic leaders in Lille that François accompanied me for the first time. We divided up the presentation and I took my usual part featuring that great American brand "NEEK." I was vaguely aware that every time I waxed on about the needs of "NEEK" for an outlet store, and how omnipresent the "NEEK" stores were, etc., I was met with slight smiles and glances back and forth among the town planners. I assumed they could relate to this great brand so I poured it on.

Later, in the car heading back to Paris, François warmed to the subject with his usual British reserve and politeness, but finally said, "Byrne, I think you are not aware that the brand Nike in French is pronounced "NI-k," like "night" but with a "K" at the end."

"Thanks," I said. "I'll make a note of that."

"Good," François responded. "But . . . it's important you do so, really."

"Yeah, I know. I need to improve my French. I just haven't had time for lessons."

"But this one is important, Byrne . . . really."

It was not like François to press a correction on me like this. I looked over at him.

"Why is this mistake so important, François?"

"Well, it's just that . . . well, it's a nasty word, that 'NEEK.'"

"Really? What does it mean, François?"

"Well . . . really it means *fornicate.*"

"You are kidding!" I exclaimed. But, of course, he wasn't.

Silence for a moment while I reflected on just how many times I had said "NEEK" not just that day but for all those prior meetings. Dozens of times—scores of times.

"You mean it is the 'F-word' in French?"

"Yes, well . . . but it's a bit more than that . . ." François labored on, not wanting to embarrass his client any more than necessary.

"What exactly could be more than that?"

"Well . . . it is the 'F-word' in connection with animals."

"Are you telling me that while I have been holding forth on my outlet concept featuring one of the most famous global brands, in reality I have been repeatedly speaking of *bestial fornication??* In *public meetings?*"

"Uh, well . . . yes."

I groaned.

More silence as we sped along the A1 highway back down to Paris.

"Fabulous," I concluded, "just fabulous."

Suddenly I was feeling very, very tired.

If I wasn't pitching with François, I'd be out scouting with Olivier, sometimes by car, sometimes by train. After we had managed to identify half a dozen or more attractive sites in any given region of France we would hit the road for several days—to the southeast in the Bordeaux region, or west to Nancy and Metz near the German border, or around Rheims in the Champagne region. Olivier would call ahead to the local Bouygues office, and when we stepped off the TGV we would have a full-scale scouting party made up of one or two local Bouygues people who knew the relevant politicos, perhaps one or two real-estate agents, Olivier, and me. And then the convoy would roll out, two or three Renault cars, with a half dozen knowledgeable Frenchmen, one green American, and a map with the numbered red dots corresponding to the tables and graphs.

When we thought that a particular site held real potential we would begin the round of appointments with the politicians. Over a nine-month period I had forty or fifty mayoral and town-council meetings in twenty-five or more small and midsize towns all over France, ranging in size from rural villages to small cities. After a while I began to recognize a pattern in those meetings, a pattern defined by French pride, foreign investment, and protocol. It was a slow and stately dance, very formal in its nature, a modern-day minuet in which I was one of the principal dancers though I didn't even realize it until months into the process.

A new minuet began each time I told Olivier that a certain site on our selection list was of real interest to me. He would then call the appropriate

Bouygues office, and the people there would in turn call the mayor's office to say that Bouygues had a great American company considering a significant investment in his town. Would *Monsieur le Maire,* as all French mayors were respectfully referred to, be available for a meeting with the American-in-charge to discuss this potential great investment?

Because the mayor was, *of course,* very busy with all matters concerned in running his town, his calendar couldn't possibly accommodate a meeting for at least two or three weeks, not even for the great American-in-charge. This was not, after all, Hillsboro, Texas.

So two or three weeks later I would dutifully show up with Olivier or François and one or two other advisers on the appointed day and arrive at the mayor's office at the appointed hour. Our meetings were never scheduled before 10:30 or 11:00 in the morning, doubtless because Monsieur le Maire was so busy that day. And, of course, the mayor was always too busy on that *particular* day to receive me at the appointed hour, so my colleagues and I would wait the requisite twenty to twenty-five minutes or so while the mayor hurried to make time for me in his busy schedule. Eventually, with a flourish, Monsieur le Maire would appear with two or three of his lieutenants, and we would all sit around the mayor's conference table. Monsieur le Maire was inevitably silver-haired, with glasses, in his mid-fifties to sixties, and with a respectable midsection filling up the suit he might have donned especially for this important meeting. He would welcome the distinguished American to the region, and educate me a bit about the great regional products that are produced there and enjoyed the world over—the cheeses, or *foie gras,* or wines, or oysters, depending upon which town in which region I was visiting. I would hear about the last time that Monsieur le Maire had visited America and been to Graceland in Memphis, or Trump Tower in New York, and usually Disney World in Florida. We would continue with pleasantries during the first half hour, twenty-five minutes of which it was Monsieur le Maire who did the talking.

There followed fifteen minutes during which we were allowed to obliquely discuss the purpose of my visit. Monsieur le Maire would tell me how intent he was on creating jobs and fostering new development. But, of course, he went on, creating new retail space is a delicate matter these days, *non?* He had to think about his *petits commerçants* who worked hard, and certainly didn't need any new and sometimes unfair competition. And did I know about *le gel* that had been imposed from Paris? Yes, well it was a difficult situation, Monsieur le Maire concluded.

And then, just as I thought I'd found an opening and was about to explain my concept to him, Monsieur le Maire would look at his watch and exclaim, *"Ah! C'est midi!"* even if actually it were still somewhat before noon.

And with a flourish and a gesture to the lowest lieutenant at the table he would request that refreshments be brought in to welcome this distinguished American and his distinguished Bouygues representatives. And within a minute or so, the lowest lieutenant would have corralled an even lower secretary to walk in with a tray full of aperitifs for us all to enjoy. The minuet was starting its second phase.

Monsieur le Maire would normally do the honors, offering and serving everyone a gin, or vodka, a Scotch, or a Campari. The aperitifs were a prelude to the grand lunch, which would soon start. Aperitifs were consumed straight—no mixers, no ice, no nonsense.

Monsieur le Maire would offer a brief toast in recognition of the visit from the distinguished American and his Bouygues friends. We would then be allowed to discuss the weather, the town and its history, and maybe the vagaries of Washington politics—anything but the real subject of my visit. That was for later. This was time spent ensuring that there was a *bon contact* between myself and Monsieur le Maire. This was a key component of the protocol, involving personal chemistry and ceremony.

It took me a long time to understand the concept of *bon contact*. In the first twenty or so visits I had with mayors, I didn't understand the nature of the minuet, and I was always leaning forward into the conference table, muscles taut as I tried to understand every French word and phrase that was swirling around me, trying politely but desperately to swing the topic back to all the many benefits I could bring to Monsieur le Maire and his good citizens. In essence, I was trying to do my job and conduct some business. I needn't have bothered. That wasn't the point at that stage in the minuet.

Not long after the aperitifs were poured, my host would announce that it was time for lunch, and our group of eight to ten people would follow Monsieur le Maire down the steps of the town hall, and across the street in a parade highly visible to all the voters who could witness that Monsieur le Maire was escorting important guests over to his favorite restaurant.

And inevitably as I walked alongside any one of those mayors who would be pointing out the places and people of great interest in his town, it would occur to me yet again that if you want to succeed in France, you needed to speak French. Not so Italian in Italy, or German in Germany, or Dutch in Holland. But French in France is de rigeur. Especially, as I discovered, in a start-up business that relies heavily on securing approvals from government agencies, where pride of *la langue française* is institutionalized.

Languages have never been my strong suit. My grade in French was my worst mark in all of college. I remember my father consoling me about it.

"After all," he said cheerfully, "it's not as though you'll need to speak French to earn a living."

Thanks, Dad, I thought as I strolled next to another French mayor in yet another provincial French town.

As we entered Monsieur le Maire's favorite restaurant, there would always be much bowing, and scraping, and handshakes with the owner. Then, just as we were seated at the table of honor we would be presented with glasses of sparkling champagne, a gift from the owner to the mayor and his esteemed guests. More chatter would ensue between the mayor and the solicitous owner while they engaged in a friendly debate about which of the many fine local wines should be chosen for this great event, this lunch honoring the visit of the distinguished American from the giant American company who was considering an important investment in this fine little town. This sparked a number of smiles and a few backslaps and quips, almost none of which I understood, but I smiled, and nodded, and laughed as the others did.

Inevitably, before we ordered lunch, we began the third phase of the minuet with a local red wine—perhaps a Volnay, a St-Emilion, a Châteauneuf du Pape, or a Chinon—depending upon which region of France I happened to be visiting: Burgundy, Bordeaux, the Rhone or Loire valleys. Other days it could be an Alsatian wine or more champagne. It was always from the region, and proudly so. I usually noted with rising concern that it was my third glass before lunch.

The second glass of red wine (the fourth drink overall) was usually poured as the main course was served. The main course was meant to be the *pièce de résistance* of the local cuisine and so great care was taken to comment on the freshness of the fish or duck, or the tenderness of the beef.

Sauces were also often part of the main course splendor, sauces which could leave me full on their own merits. The third glass of wine was usually poured when I wasn't looking.

It was about then that I started losing interest in conducting any serious business. It would sometimes occur to me that maybe if I could just close my eyes for a moment . . .

But no! For as the waiters cleared away the cheese, the climactic moment had arrived. Now arrived the tiny window of time—*entre la poire et le fromage* as it was known—wherein French municipal protocol finally allowed me to discuss, briefly, the object of my visit.

Entre la poire et le fromage means, literally, "between the pear and the cheese." The expression refers to a tradition of punctuating heavy and long meals with a *trou Normand* (fruit and alcohol) to assist digestion. Typically *trou Normand* is a pear served in brandy or calvados.

It was nearly 2:15 or 2:30, and I had been with the mayor and his colleagues for over three hours and consumed the equivalent of five or perhaps six glasses of wine and spirits. The minuet had reached its most important phase. Up to now all had been ceremony and prelude. Now was the serious moment when the business at hand was to be directly addressed. Unfortunately, by the time the great moment arrived I was a word-slurring, lazy-eyed, nonlistening drunk.

By that point I didn't care about the site, didn't much give a damn about Monsieur le Maire or his local cuisine, and was mostly worried that someone might place another glass of wine in front of me that I would be obliged to consume. I had given up trying to decipher what was being discussed around me. I just desperately wanted to leave. Every now and then, Olivier, seated to my right, would tap me under the table or address a question to me in simple, baby French. My problem was in answering it. By the time I stuttered out the third or fourth word Olivier gracefully took it from there and intercepted any more questions directed my way.

The climactic moment *entre la poire et le fromage* never lasted more than fifteen or perhaps twenty minutes. Time was precious. Espressos appeared around that time. Thinking that caffeine was just what I needed to regain cogency, I would eagerly knock back one or two espressos with the delicacy of a bricklayer. This was in the early months of my education in French cuisine, before I appreciated that each espresso contained enough caffeine to energize an entire can of Maxwell House. Within minutes a torrid caffeine rush shot from stomach, to heart, to limbs in a way which guaranteed that the ocean of alcohol already resident in my bloodstream went crashing into my brain in tsunami fashion, chased immediately thereafter by the raging caffeine. BAM!!

And that was it.

Game over.

My American constitution was no match for the Gallic onslaught; certainly not in my early, vulnerable days in France. Sensations combining numbness with stomach cramps and wooziness crept, and then leapt, into my physical and mental state. I found myself staring down at the empty espresso cup, down at the small grains of the killer coffee left isolated in its bottom. I was struggling to stop the spinning around me. Listening to, much less understanding, the French conversations swirling about my ears was no longer an option or even an interest. I was desperately focused on keeping down all that I had fought so hard to consume over the prior two-and-a-half hours.

It was just about then that I would hear Olivier whispering my name next to me, twice or maybe three times, pulling me back into the mayoral luncheon at hand. I looked up at all the French faces lined around the table; all rapt with attention because *entre la poire et le fromage* was already half spent. But for me it was over—the minuet was reaching its crescendo for the others at the table but I had already stumbled off the dance floor.

The irony, though, was that six or seven months into the site-selection process, by which time I had been living in France for nearly a year, I finally learned to dance the minuet. I could keep up with the pack. When the moment *entre la poire et le fromage* arrived, fortified by all those glasses of wine, I was ready for Monsieur le Maire and his team. I had been trained by forty or fifty lunches in the far corners of Burgundy, Normandy, the Alps region, and beyond. I was in French-culinary fighting shape. And after a full day's work at the luncheon tables of France I would alight from the train back in Paris, and stroll right back to my desk and keep working. And when I realized that I could easily survive the minuet, with the multiple luncheon courses, and the wines, that's when I realized just how dangerous the process was becoming.

NINE

Pregnancy and Politics

France is justly proud of its reputation as a country of romance. After living there for some time it becomes clear that not only do the French take romance seriously, but the very concept of romance is subtly and profoundly woven into the everyday life of the nation. Nowhere is this more evident than in the commercial dynamics of the French lingerie industry.

The provocative near-nudity of the French lingerie industry's advertising is a case in point. The celebration of a beautiful woman's body is taken to levels of sophistication rarely seen in America. In walking the streets of Paris one is bombarded month after month with street-side advertising campaigns for women's lingerie brands, desperately fighting to outdo each other in new and creative images to show how small patches of lacy silk or soft cotton can scarcely but romantically cover women's curves and secrets. During the height of the spring advertising season, when thousands of those sidewalk billboards and bus-stop panels are covered with the latest campaign, it can be quite inspiring just going for a neighborhood stroll.

All of this intense big-business marketing is an expression of a deeper cultural trait. For all the millions and millions of euros spent on the advertising campaigns, the French women's lingerie industry remains a very fractured one, with over sixty brands in the crowded market. For all the brand-name recognition of La Perla, Aubade, Chantelle, and other market leaders, no one brand commands more than one-and-one-half-percent market share, a fact that reflects the profound care that millions of French women take to express their intimate individuality. Contrast that statistic to Britain, where a single brand, Marks & Spencer, which for decades treated the lingerie as "a basic," commands over 25 percent of the market. In England, it seems, the presumption is that undergarments are rarely seen so "why bother?" And in France the attitude is, "You never know."

For a naïve American, the French romantic tradition can take some getting used to. One afternoon I was working in our office conference room with Yvette, an outside accountant from one of the Big Eight firms who was helping me with the relentless flood of official forms required by the French bureaucracy.

At one point Yvette apologized and told me she would have to leave earlier than scheduled, due to an urgent matter with another client. But, she suggested, we could meet the next day, perhaps between five and seven (*entre cinq et sept*)? Perhaps at her office, perhaps elsewhere? Would that be agreeable?

I usually worked until past seven anyway, so I told her sure, between five and seven would be fine. After she left, I strolled back to my office and mentioned to my assistant, Penny Coron, that I had arranged to see Yvette the next day *entre cinq et sept.* Would she please mark that in my calendar?

Standing next to Penny just then was Marie-France Marchi, the blue-eyed, attractive and regal lady who was our Director of Sales. Marie-France's nickname in the industry was "Blue Diamond," in reference to her integrity. Many people in her role would silently accept kickbacks from brands eager to be assigned a certain store location within a shopping center. It was well known that Marie-France never would; she was considered as pure as a "Blue Diamond." She was somewhat older than I, and over time adopted a role of a wiser, caring sister to me.

At first, Marie-France expressed a little surprise at what I said ("Ooh la-la," she exclaimed with a chuckle). But when I didn't laugh back, she looked at me quizzically and recognizing my innocence, burst out laughing.

"*Cinq et sept?*" she asked. "Are you serious?"

"Yes," I said, puzzled.

"Tell me, did *she* suggest the meeting?" Marie-France inquired, Penny looking on with a smirk.

"Well, in fact she did. Yvette had to leave earlier than anticipated, and suggested we meet again tomorrow."

"I'll bet she did," Marie-France replied, looking over to Penny with an even wider smile.

When again I didn't laugh, Marie-France smiled and walked me to my desk to explain a bit of French culture.

"Byrne, as you know, we French treasure our individualism. And while there is a recognition that it is important to honor our obligations in life—at work, at home, wherever—there is also our right to enjoy ourselves as individuals, to accept the opportunities that present themselves in the course of our lives." Marie-France paused, looking at me in a slightly maternal way.

"Yeeees?" I asked, playing along.

"So, in accordance with this outlook, historically some people have . . ." she paused, then continued, ". . . some have an *understanding,* so to speak. The understanding is that the hours between the end of the traditional workday and the start of the evening at home, in fact, the hours from five to seven—*entre cinq et sept*—belong to the individual, and what happens between those hours is . . . well . . . private."

"So you think that Yvette was suggesting some kind of romantic tryst?" I asked in amusement.

"Did she actually use those words—*entre cinq et sept?*"

"Yes, she did . . . but . . ."

"Ahh, no 'buts.' Those are well-known code words. She knew what she was saying," Marie-France said with a knowing smile.

"Fabulous," I groaned, "just fabulous. So how does one, here in this romantic France of yours, wriggle out of this little misunderstanding?"

"Don't worry, I'll call her in the morning," Marie-France offered, obviously enjoying the situation. "There are other code words that can come into play here."

It didn't take long before Pamela and I fell in line with the French focus on romance, and six months after arriving in Paris, Pamela was pregnant with our second child, Cara Eugenie, named in honor of her great-aunt, Mimi Eugenie O'Hagan. And as the pregnancy unfolded so, too, did an appreciation of a very different, much gentler side of Paris.

In France, pregnant women are granted an exalted status as though in public celebration of the visible end-product of all that Gallic romance. Pregnant women can and do cut in front of any line, anywhere, anytime— in the stores, at the cinema, and for museums. Men who would not otherwise cede their seat on the bus or Metro do so without reluctance for the state of pregnancy. If a woman is pregnant but not yet showing she can drop down to the local *mairie,* doctor's certificate in hand, and return with an official pregnancy badge to flash when needed, or even to wear about her neck proclaiming her special state. It is, in effect, a Scarlet Letter in reverse.

And it works. The usual curt responses, impatient side glances, and snubs often disappear. The nearby butcher, whose small store Pamela had frequented not less than thirty of forty times by her second trimester without the butcher ever acknowledging he'd seen her before, suddenly is all smiles. For the first time he actually saved a special cutlet he knows she frequently buys.

But it is while navigating the frantic *étoile* that the power of pregnancy was truly revealed. The *étoile* is where six wide Parisian boulevards, including the Champs-Elysées, flow into and then out of the massive rotary surrounding the Arc de Triomphe, disgorging and reclaiming thousands of freewheeling cars per hour into and out of a mixing bowl of metal, tires, and French aggressiveness. Over the many decades the *étoile* has become so infamous for accidents, with impatient French men and women scrambling to their next destination, that it has been declared a "no fault zone" for insurance purposes. Accidents, usually minor ones, happen so fast and with so much commotion it has been deemed not worth the struggle to unscramble the conflicting claims and counterclaims. This has, naturally, only led to more aggressiveness and chaos.

There is one official rule of the *étoile*, however, even if often ignored: cars on the right have priority. Accordingly, cars already in the roundabout slow down to permit new cars entering, and then those wanting to exit flee the *étoile* just behind the taillights of the cars they just let in.

One day Pamela was en route to a checkup at l'Hôpital Américain in Neuilly, on the other side of the *étoile* from our apartment. She launched into the mixing bowl as per usual, and not twenty yards later a car from her left came slamming into her, somewhat denting her fender but damaging more so his right front panel. The other driver was clearly in the wrong. Notwithstanding that, the screaming and waving of arms and hands from the Frenchman behind the wheel started almost before impact. He leapt from his car to press his case against Pamela, running up to her amid a howl of horn-blaring protest from the dozen other cars now blocked by the obstruction. Storming up to Pamela with epithets flying, he started shaking his fist. But then, as he looked through the car window, he noticed her advanced state of pregnancy. His tirade stopped.

There was a second's reflection.

Then he said *"Pardonnez-moi,"* with resignation before hurrying back to his car amid more horns and shouts.

In Paris, pregnancy prevails.

Though we were making excellent progress on the family front during that autumn and winter after our arrival, not so for my business. After completing desktop analysis on over two hundred sites in France, conducting visits to sixty or seventy of them, and drinking my way through lunches with twenty or more Messieurs les Maires, I still hadn't found the right site for our first project. I'd come up with a half dozen promising possibilities, but no clear front-runner. And after a full year of research the reason for my failure had become obvious: I was being stymied by French politics, and its often eccentric—not to say bizarre—local manifestations.

Several years prior to my arrival in Paris, the French Parliament had enacted a new law governing retail zoning approvals. The law was in response to what was perceived as the unbridled power of mayors to approve new projects, often with a wink-and-a-nod, which many believed had fostered the rapid growth of the powerful hypermarkets. That growth, it was felt, had been responsible for the disappearance of many downtown *petits commerçants,* the merchants who contributed so much to the unique quality of French urban life. Hence, Chirac's keen interest in courting the *petits commerçants'* vote during his election campaign.

The new law established *La Commission Départementale d'Equipement Commercial* (the Regional Commission for Retail Projects, or "CDEC" for short), which replaced the mayors' sole authority for zoning decisions with a seven-member panel. Comprised of three mayors from the area in question along with the president of the Regional Council, the president of the local Chamber of Commerce and Industry ("CCI"), the president of the Craftsmen Union, and a consumer's representative. The panel was chaired by the nonvoting *Préfet* of that specific *département* (France is divided into approximately ninety geographic departments) who was the representative of the central government in Paris.

While the new law had laudably replaced the discretion of an individual mayor with the votes of seven officials (a majority vote of the Commission prevailed), it ushered in a whole new set of issues. By the nature of the commission's composition, five of the seven votes were from elected officials (*les élus*) whose posts were by definition political. Given the nature of French politics—which usually approached any initiative with the zero-sum paradigm which assumes "if you win I lose"—the new structure often created more problems than it solved.

In the first place, it set town against town: "Why should the neighboring town get a new project and new jobs while we in this town do not?" In other words, a mayor now had a new veto power over his neighbor.

Secondly, the system provided a whole new battleground for opposing political parties. The party of the Left, for instance, would work feverishly to ensure that the party of the Right did not succeed with any new initiative, which enabled it to boast about its success in the coming elections, and vice versa. American Republicans and Democrats are generally very centrist compared to the parties of the Left and Right in much of Europe, where there are still active Communist and Far-Right Nationalist parties on the edges. The other parties work inward from there. Getting those Left and Right parties to agree on *any* initiative is extremely challenging.

Layered over the top of this volatile cocktail of sparring politicians was another wrinkle. Under French law at that time a politician was allowed to occupy up to three elected offices at the same time. If you were an ambitious French pol, which nearly all seemed to be, you very much wanted to achieve the Triple Crown of simultaneously being not only the mayor of your commune, but an elected member of the Regional Council, and a *député* or *senateur* in the national government as well. There is incredible prestige and significant personal power in wearing three political hats simultaneously. Just as importantly there are the three salaries, and three very generous sets of pensions, and other long-term benefits that trail along after all that prestige.

But the built-in problem with the Triple Crown system is that the political interests at one level may be in conflict with the interests at another level. A mayor's concern over a major initiative is likely to be different from a regional councilman's and different again from that of a senator. If you are holding all three offices, which perspective should you adopt when considering whether to vote for or against a new initiative? Which constituency do you listen to? Or do you just take turns favoring one over another?

As an outsider, a foreigner come to invest, I faced the near impossible task of discerning which crown a multititled politico was wearing when I went in to see him. Even if he assured me he was listening with his mayoral hat on, there had to be so many backroom considerations swirling in his mind that what he said was very often not what he thought. This inherent conflict of interest was the chief reason why so many mayors never declared if they were in support or in opposition of a proposed project until the very last minute. In essence, they were waiting to see from whence came the greatest pressure. As a result, I often knew who was opposing me, but I hardly ever knew who was supporting me.

In an attempt to untangle all the politics, I developed maps for each likely location, overlaying all the traditional demographic and real-estate analysis with a color-coded system, which tried to chart the political waters. For each site we would color in orange those towns with mayors from the Right, blue for those with mayors from the Left, purple for the Far Right, and, of course, red for Communists. We went on to crosshatch the appropriately colored stripes for the Chamber of Commerce president, and countercrosshatch the color for a regional councilman's political bias. And on and on, mapping out for each site the respective CDEC commission's political colors. When we were finished we stepped back to see the results—to see where unity or near unity of colors would indicate a consensus of political views and, therefore, where we should focus our energies.

What we saw was a Jackson Pollock painting: colors splashed all over a canvas with no inherent logic to it. There were no sites with a chromatic message. It was not even close. I recalled with fresh understanding General Charles de Gaulle's famous observation, "How does one govern a country with two hundred forty-six different cheeses?"

In addition to the labyrinth of political intrigues stirred up by the CDEC law, I had to keep in mind the even more daunting obstacle on the horizon: Balladur's *gel,* ready to stamp out any attempt to construct a retail outlet.

So there I sat in my office, staring at a polychromatic color-coded political map of all our final site possibilities. As I understood the situation, before I could even start addressing the normal business challenges of buying land, negotiating construction contracts, setting budgets and time lines, managing the risks of leasing, and coordinating the marketing, all in a foreign language I didn't speak for a product type I had never before developed (i.e., outlet centers)—before even contemplating any of those "normal" challenges, I would first have to master the full spectrum of French politics. Local politics, which pitted one mayor against another, or against the Chamber of Commerce, or against the Regional Council, or maybe against all of them. And national politics, where I was already in direct conflict with the presumptive next president of the Republic and his prime minister.

In other words, instead of following the three cardinal rules of Anglo-Saxon real estate, i.e., "Location, Location, Location," I found myself faced with the three cardinal rules of French development: "Politics, Politics, Politics."

"*Okay, bon!* Now you understand!" said Olivier with a wide smile when I dejectedly recited my analysis to him. "*Now* you begin to understand France. It is not only about statistics, and demographics, and purchasing power. It is about votes, and elections, and political parties. So, *now* will you listen to me? Will you meet the man I have been telling you that you have to meet?"

"Fine . . . sure, why not?" I said in resignation. "Let's meet him. And let me guess—I'll bet he comes from Troyes."

"Yes, he does," Olivier said with a grin. For months he had still been urging me to settle on Troyes, but I had steadfastly resisted him. It wasn't as though I was totally negative about the site. There were lots of reasons to like Troyes. It was an historical jewel, for one thing, a little city of seventy-five thousand souls nestled into the Champagne district, with narrow little streets lined with charming half-timbered houses dating back to the Middle Ages, all still in active use. And it had been a center of the textile trade ever since the thirteenth century. Troyes still boasts the headquarters and manufacturing presence of the LACOSTE company, and others. And with that manufacturing heritage came a legacy of outlet stores. Importantly, the town was also situated right along on the main north-south highway (the A26) of France, connecting Calais (on the English Channel) to Marseille (on the Mediterranean). In addition a new highway (the A5) was under construction, which would run the 100 miles southeast from Paris, and connect with the north-south highway right there at Troyes. Proximity to highways was critical to our concept: they ensured an easy, pleasant trip to the stores, prompting a shopper to conclude it would be worth returning in the future.

The negative aspect of Troyes was what Joey and I had discovered on our first visit there: The existing outlet stores were downmarket, in grotty industrial zones, and well off those important highways. The route from the highways to the stores was not straightforward, and the first-time shopper could easily get lost—an experience which would strongly discourage repeat visits in the future.

"Don't worry, Byrne," Olivier assured me, "the man I want you to meet is a key political operative in Troyes. He is an important member of the UDF, one of the political parties of the Right, and the Right is now in power in Troyes as well as here in Paris. His name is Antoine Rochefort," Olivier said, still smiling as he rose from the conference table. "I'll arrange it immediately."

And out the door he went, in search of just the right Bouygues person to place just the right call to Monsieur Rochefort of Troyes, someone who, apparently, was just the right person for me to meet.

Soon afterward, Pamela and I were walking through the Tuileries Gardens on a wintry Saturday, weaving a path amongst all those sycamore trees laid out in the straight-lined geometry, which define so many French gardens. We were well into the third trimester and the walks were both doctor's orders and a pleasure for us. I had just updated Pamela on the results of all the research, the site visits, and mayors' lunches. We walked on in silence as she absorbed the information. A minute or two later she stopped and looked at me.

"Byrne, are you telling me that in order to continue with our one- or two-year adventure in France you have to go head-to-head against the interests of both Prime Minister Balladur *and* Jacques Chirac? *And* a host of local mayors and xenophobic retailers?"

"Apparently," I said.

"Well, as a former investment banker, can I ask you one question?" Pamela continued.

"Shoot," I replied.

"Are you sure you've picked the right country for this startup?"

TEN

Focus on Troyes

Y ou are a businessman, Monsieur Murphy, looking to make money," Antoine Rochefort said dryly. "I am a politician, looking to win votes. Perhaps we can help each other."

Once again I was in one of the private dining rooms of Bouygues's Champs-Elysées office, surrounded by the cherrywood paneling, polished silver, and white-jacketed waiters ghosting about, replenishing glasses with Premier Cru wines. The windows offered a fabulous view of Paris. Off to the right, just up the boulevard, was the Arc de Triomphe. Straight ahead was the Eiffel Tower. To the left was the Rond-Point des Champs-Elysées.

Olivier Jamey had invited me there to meet two people. The first was an elegant colleague of his named Jean Dumont, whose specialty was knowing the who's-who in the Right-wing parties in towns and cities all over France. The second person was the man Dumont brought to the table, Antoine Rochefort, who would tell me more about Troyes.

Rochefort was a mayor of one of the small towns ringing the city of Troyes. All the townships around Troyes were in one economic development initiative together. Importantly, Rochefort was active in the UDF (Union for French Democracy) party, the party which was in a loose coalition with Chirac's and Balladur's "Rally for the Republic" (RPR) party. He was a man of medium height and high forehead, sporting rimless glasses, and dressed with a crisp sense of fashion, though never overstated. Olivier had already told me that Rochefort was ambitious . . . intensely ambitious. For years it was rumored he had planned on adding another crown of political office to his mayoral position, that of *député*—i.e., congressman—for the Troyes district. Receiving credit for attracting my designer outlet to Troyes, along with the jobs it would create, might help him accomplish that goal.

"This project of yours might be very good for me," Rochefort continued. "If I decide it would be good for Troyes, we go forward. If we do go forward, I will be your *interlocuteur.*"

I wasn't sure what an *interlocuteur* was but I gleaned it was important to Rochefort so it was important to me. Later I learned it was a cross between a presenter and a guide.

Olivier ran the meeting in a businesslike manner. He explained why he believed Troyes was an appropriate location for McArthurGlen, citing the highways and the fact that the existing outlets were already well known to the buying public as far away as Paris. He pointed out the value to Troyes that such a project would generate in terms of employment and revenue, and pronounced it a win-win proposition for all concerned.

When he was through I then explained my reasons for not completely sharing Bouygues's strong enthusiasm for Troyes, citing the unglamorous nature of the present outlet stores, the distance to the highway, and the modest purchasing power in the catchment area immediately around Troyes.

Rochefort was busy making notes. There was a nervous intensity to the man, as if he constantly needed some release for his pent-up energy. You could see it in his eyes. Despite their light-blue tone, they were fiery, and when they bore down on you there was no doubt on whom he was focused. And just that minute he was very focused on me.

"Come to Troyes in two weeks, Monsieur Murphy. Come see what we have to offer you," he stated in accented but fluent English. "You will like it. I will do some research; I can address your concerns. As we say in French: *Il faut préparer le terrain*—the groundwork must be done. If I think the political conditions are good for you I will say so. If I think your project will only be killed later, I will also say so. You know, of course, that we still have *le gel*?"

"Yes, I do. Unfortunately, I know it only too well. Do you think a project such as mine can survive with *le gel* in place?"

"*On verra:* we shall see. First, I look around."

Rochefort was nothing if not frank. After all the opaque feedback from so many mayors and elected officials all over France, his candor was refreshing. I had to admire his bluntness.

Despite my doubts, a fortnight later François and Olivier and I were back in Troyes. There was no denying the great charm of the little city. The centuries-old architecture of the town center served as a tourist magnet, and we discussed the degree to which that might be an asset for us. Despite Troyes's heritage as a textile center, its days as a manufacturing capital were now being challenged by the lure of cheap labor in North Africa and, more recently, in China and Eastern Europe. Troyes's plants were shutting down, though the outlet aspect of its textile heritage seemed to be growing. A recently completed outlet center at one end of town, named Marques Avenue, had been built in a former factory. It joined those grim stand-alone outlet stores I had seen before. It was a poor imitation of the McArthurGlen concept, but nevertheless it had fifty stores, and the indications were that they were selling well.

As we toured Troyes, with memories of so many rejections from so many other towns all over France, I thought, "Well, maybe Troyes could work. Just maybe . . ."

"I have good news for you, Monsieur Murphy," Rochefort said when we arrived at his office in the town of St. Royale on the edge of Troyes. "I can get an approval for your project here in Troyes. It can be done, yes, even with *le gel,*" he said, reverting to speaking in French here in his hometown. Rochefort was very much at ease. He was in shirtsleeves, his jacket hung on a peg on the back of the door. He was leaning back in his chair and swiveled sideways to his desk. He clearly was feeling comfortable with his surroundings and with himself, clicking a long unsharpened pencil on his desk throughout our conversation, sometimes with force to make his point.

"You need a CDEC approval, Monsieur Murphy, and I can get it for you," he promised. Suddenly, he whipped his chair around toward me and leaned forward across the desk. "No matter where you decide to locate,

Monsieur Murphy, whether here in Troyes or elsewhere, you will find you have enemies. You need a CDEC in a time when they are very hard to secure. And you are American—that helps and hurts your case. We all know about Disney, don't we? But if you select Troyes for your first project, I will know who all your enemies are even before you are aware of them . . . and I can bend them to my will." Dramatically, he cupped his hand and slowly closed it into a fist. Then, in a whisper, he said, "No matter where you decide to build, Monsieur Murphy, you will need a fighter at your side. At Troyes, I will be your fighter! And . . ." he paused for just a moment while he tap-tapped the pencil on his desk, ". . . and, I will be your *interlocuteur.*"

I was surprised by his intensity, but it was effective. And I had to admit, it could be very comforting to have someone like that on my side. "There is still the question of *le gel,*" I said.

Rochefort smiled.

"Ahhh," he said with confidence, "that is why I will be your *interlocuteur.* It will not be easy, but we can do it. But be clear on one thing, Monsieur Murphy: You will have to do as I say. French politics are difficult. French politicians can be vicious. But everyone has a skeleton; you just need to know what it is, and how to use it. I know all the skeletons around Troyes, Monsieur Murphy. And I am not afraid to shake them until the bones start breaking. But . . ." another pause for effect as his beady eyes squinted slightly across at me, "but if you decide to come here you *must* do as I say, eh? Okay?"

It was a compelling performance. Clearly, he was positioning himself as the visionary politician who brought the foreign investor to town, and the slight unease I felt over his hunger for power was more than offset by my keen interest in having a fighter by my side. I hadn't met anyone willing to play that role in the scores of other French towns I had investigated. Lots of wine, lots of *geste.* But no one offering to stand up and fight.

"If I decide to choose Troyes, I will be delighted to work with you," I said, wondering if he had noted I didn't promise to always do exactly as he proposed.

The fact was that despite the drawbacks of Troyes, it had real advantages. Its heritage as a textile town could help with the political process. I had a fighter in Rochefort—and Bouygues had recommended him, so they had to be committed to the fight. The town did have a reputation for outlets as far away as Paris; that would help in the marketing. And, of course, I didn't have any other town or mayor promising to fight against *le gel.*

Lastly, there was the million-and-a-half-dollar credit we Americans would receive in the deal with BAA if a French site received a zoning approval to proceed. A million and a half dollars that we would otherwise have to fund in cash if it were not approved. And we didn't have any more cash.

The next morning, in one of the most crucial decisions I was to make in Europe, I called Olivier and told him I was ready to bet the farm on Troyes.

ELEVEN

Taking Aim

Cheryl McArthur, cofounder of McArthurGlen, is a very attractive woman. Slender, blonde, and five-foot-seven with high cheekbones and wide brown eyes, she had been a model earlier in her career. At the time I was in Paris, she was in her mid-forties, very fit, and svelte almost to the point of too much so—but not. She and Alan Glen had made a fortune by taking McArthurGlen public on Wall Street the year before I moved to Paris. Alan was in charge of land acquisition, development, and finance. Cheryl was in charge of marketing, PR, and client relations. She was the front person with the brands, the VIPs, at the marketing events, and especially with the press. She performed her role well.

When I heard that she would be visiting Paris with her husband about the same time that I was scheduled to make the key presentation to the town fathers of Troyes, I hopped all over it. Having Cheryl there, as the name founder of a successful New York Stock Exchange company whose affiliate wanted to open in Troyes just might help cement the support I was seeking. The fact that her involvement in our European effort was essentially limited to lending her name, and that the USA McArthurGlen held only a small fraction of ownership in Europe and provided no financial support, wasn't important. I had counted on the impact of her presence and her track record.

But I hadn't counted on the jet. As I stood there on the tarmac of the tiny Troyes airstrip, watching as Cheryl stepped out of her husband's company's sleek white Gulf Stream, I was relieved by my decision to not publicize that she would be flying into Troyes. Her husband's firm was active in international financings, which necessitated his being in France that week, and Cheryl was being dropped off as the jet was en route to points south. I always wanted to present McArthurGlen as a solid American company, financially strong enough to undertake a European expansion. I had not wanted to present it as an over-the-top splashy American company coming in for a quick profit and only to fly away again. Just that moment, as Cheryl was waving to me from the jet doorway, I was wondering how do I hide a dual-engine white jet on a small airstrip in the middle of alfalfa fields?

I had counted on Cheryl's smarts, good looks, and *haute couture* sense of fashion to help position McArthurGlen as a company Troyes would want to welcome. But like the jet, I hadn't counted on the outfit. In bright morning sunshine on a crisp autumn's day, Cheryl was delicately stepping down the jetway stairs in white Chanel three-inch heels with a snug white Lycra dress that came down from shoulders to just below midthigh. It was a striking scene in a striking dress in little Troyes. I noticed several of the airstrip's maintenance workers strolling out of the tiny terminal building for a better view. The fact that Cheryl brought way more to the table than met the eye, the fact that she had steely resolve, was incredibly streetsmart, and kept an unflinching eye on the goal at hand didn't enter into the initial impression. It didn't need to.

Moments later, when I escorted Cheryl into Rochefort's mayoral office, where he was waiting with Olivier and François before we all moved on to the main event, I presented a smiling, charming, tanned Cheryl McArthur. In retrospect, it was the first *grand geste* that I myself had made since arriving in France. I introduced her to the three men, and then unconsciously moved back a half step in the way the French do when they have made a *geste,* as though saying, "*Voilà!* See what I have brought you."

It worked.

Rochefort must have immediately concluded that he was going to be inducted into the *Interlocuteur* Hall of Fame. Not only was he going to earn credit for bringing a great foreign investor to town, and credit for creating new jobs, advancing economic development and diversifying Troyes's employment base, but he was surely going to earn serious credit among his political brethren (all of whom were men) for bringing . . . well, for bringing Cheryl McArthur to town.

"Welcome," Rochefort said in English, the first English I had heard from him since our initial meeting on the Champs-Elysées. "Welcome to Troyes."

Rochefort stood there for a second, with no fidgeting, no hands and arms waving about, no pencil tapping.

"Would you like a *coupe de champagne?*" he offered upon recovery.

"Champagne?" Cheryl repeated in surprise with her big smile and large brown eyes. "Well, no, thank you. I don't drink during the day," she said as she then turned to shake hands with François and Olivier.

"Pardon?" Rochefort said, confused by her accent and rapid English.

"*Bien sûr,*" I responded for her in French, "she would love a glass."

Cheryl looked over at me in puzzlement when Rochefort held out the glass to her.

"Welcome to France," I whispered to her. "When a mayor offers you champagne, especially when you're in the Champagne region, you accept."

"But I can't drink during the day," she protested in a whispered return. "It makes me sleepy."

"The good news is that I'm your *interlocuteur* today, Cheryl. Just do as I do and it'll all be fine."

"You're my *what?*" she whispered in a rush, leaning back my way to hear better.

"Voilà!" said Rochefort as he walked back with flutes filled with champagne made from the centuries-old vines we could see on the hillsides straight out his windows.

"Voilà!" I responded. Another minuet was starting; a very important one.

Thirty minutes later we arrived at the Hotel de Ville, the magnificent town hall of Troyes. Rochefort almost skipped up the broad marble staircase as he led us up to the second-floor Grande Salon. He was the *interlocuteur* here, and he was obviously eager to demonstrate his interlocution skills to the visiting Cheryl McArthur. With a beaming smile, he introduced us to the dozen or so assembled public officials from the town of Troyes and its environs. There were officials from the mayor's office, from the vice mayor's office, from CAT. All eyes came over our way, but mostly they stayed on Cheryl.

Among all the officials there were four of significant note. Firstly, the seventy-year-old Robert Galley, Monsieur le Maire of Troyes. Politically, Galley was the most powerful person in the room. Not surprisingly, he was a Triple Crown politician. He was not only mayor of Troyes, but also a member of the Regional Council, and a *député* in the National Assembly in Paris. Monsieur Galley might have looked like the distracted-professor type in his rumpled suit and unkempt hair, but Rochefort assured me he was a very cunning pol who knew all the tricks from the back halls of Paris to the side streets of Troyes.

Secondly, there was *Monsieur le President* of CAT, a calm, wise gentleman named Jacques Pallencher, whom I had met a few weeks before. In his mid-sixties, he carried a full head of almost white hair, and a trimmed, narrow white beard along a strong jawline and pronounced chin, but with no mustache, Abe Lincoln style. If the meeting went well, I knew I would be seeing Monsieur Pallencher again, privately. It was Pallencher with whom I would negotiate the price of entry for coming to town. His office had spent many hundreds of millions of French francs over the years putting in infrastructure for the roads, signage, sewer, and water lines. It was not unusual for CAT to expect a contribution for these past expenses for supporting a new arrival. Pallencher would handle that process.

The third significant figure in the room was the president of the Chamber of Commerce (CCI), Monsieur Tockenburger, a man I knew I had to handle with kid gloves. He was president of his family's distinguished textile manufacturing company, Dore Dore, which specialized in men's hosiery. He was tall, refined, well spoken, and had made it quite clear that he was maintaining some distance from our plans for Troyes. The CCI represented all of the Troyenne commerce, and everyone knew the power of the downtown retailers in the Chamber and their visceral dislike for any new retail competition in town.

The fourth and final important figure was Monsieur Bischoff, the mayor of a small township adjoining Troyes, Pont-Sainte-Marie, which hosted many of the outlet stores already operating in its industrial zone. Monsieur Bischoff was open, honest, and simple. He was unequivocal in stating his desire to attract McArthurGlen to Pont-Sainte-Marie.

As the senior official present, Monsieur le Maire Galley offered the welcoming remarks, but kept them short, and quickly turned the floor over to me.

With a slide projector and large screen (no PowerPoint in those days), Cheryl and I alternated in presenting our outlet concept, providing vivid color images of the McArthurGlen centers in the States, very American in their crisp, clean design and heavily landscaped format. Cheryl, of course, spoke only English, but no one complained. She was impressive in her presentation of what it meant to be a public company on Wall Street, and how seriously the company, therefore, took its commitments. Expressing a desire to open in Troyes was just such a commitment.

After we finished with our presentation I left on the screen a slide of a regional map of France with Troyes in the middle. I spoke of Troyes's unique heritage in the textile industry. I pointed out Troyes's strategic location along the Route du Soleil, the A26 highway that bisected France north to south, and how the soon-to-be opened A5 highway from Paris would come eastward to meet the A26 right there at Troyes. I spoke of the success of this new generation of outlets in America, how I would like to work in partnership with Troyes to create a win-win-win situation for the town, for the retailers, and for McArthurGlen. I explained further how I had studied the existing outlets in Troyes and that I had walked all the streets of *centre-ville,* examining the downtown retail, the strength of *les petits commerçants,* and how I had no interest in upsetting the delicate balance of the retail downtown and the outlets on the edge of town.

I ended with the conclusions that what was good for the town of Troyes was good for McArthurGlen, and vice versa.

After a moment's silence one of the city officials raised his hand and asked in very precise French, "Why, if Troyes's location along those highways is so important to you, why then does your map not even show the A26 highway? It is very important to the town," he pointed out, "and it has been opened now for several years."

All heads turned toward the regional map still on the screen. With a sinking feeling in my stomach I saw that the questioner was right. There was no indication of the A26 whatsoever. And, I thought, if one of the most important visuals in this key presentation was inaccurate, well then . . .

I felt my neck muscles tense up. This could end in a serious embarrassment. I didn't know if my French was subtle enough to delicately brush off the error.

Cheryl knew something was amiss but, not speaking French, didn't know what. In the silence that hung in the air for a few seconds she whispered, "What's wrong?" I didn't have time to answer her.

I glanced over and saw Rochefort looking intently back at me, his expression and body language clearly saying, "What the hell is this?" Any embarrassment for me would certainly be an embarrassment for him.

"You're right," I responded in French, looking back to the man who asked the question, hoping to retain credibility as I spoke. "The A26 highway isn't on this map and worse still, the A5 isn't there, either. And you know why?" (*Dear God,* I thought, *I hope this works* . . .) "It's a map from America, and you know Americans," I said with a smile. "They know much less about life beyond their borders than they think they do . . ."

A few chuckles; many nodding of heads. A reference to the debacle of Euro Disney's opening, another example of America's "know-it-all-approach." A dig at myself in the process.

It wasn't elegant, but it was an escape route. And it worked.

Monsieur le Maire Galley stepped in and thanked us for the presentation, suggesting we move on to lunch and to save questions for afterward. He was orchestrating his own minuet, and I was grateful for it.

Monsieur Galley's minuet included an appropriately regional menu for lunch. As we sat at one long table under the two-hundred-year-old hand-carved wooden ceiling thirty feet above us, waiters began pouring bottles of Chambolle Musigny wine from Burgundy, and later brought in *Boeuf Bourguignon.* Cheryl was seated to my left, and Rochefort to my right. The four key politicians were directly across from us. Cheryl and I happily offered them anecdotes of how well outlet centers worked in various American locations, and the benefits they generated for the townships around them. But they were more interested in asking Cheryl questions about being the head of a Wall Street company, and regaling her with their favorite stories of past trips to America.

At the usual climactic moment *entre la poire et le fromage,* came the surprise.

Monsieur le Maire Galley announced that Monsieur le President Pallencher had a few words to offer. Whereupon Pallencher stood up, and an assistant brought him an easel and several presentation boards.

Pallencher told us how impressed he was with the McArthurGlen concept and what he had seen that day. He went on to say how indeed the town leaders had decided they really would like to work with us. To help move the project forward, he said in very calm, low tones, the town fathers had two different sites to propose to us.

I stared at him in amazement.

I had expected the minuet to wind its way through lunch and to end with the usual platitudes. It would not be for another week, I thought, that we would learn whether we had made any real progress. But Pallencher was moving much faster than that. I looked to Rochefort and he smiled proudly back at me, offering a slight nod of his head in acknowledgement. Obviously, my *interlocuteur* had been hard at work.

Pallencher described one potential site out near where the exit from the new A5 highway was being built. He explained the advantages of its location, commented on the timing of its availability and how CAT would work with us to analyze it. He then presented the second location. It was in Mayor Bischoff's commune of Pont-Sainte-Marie, and comprised sixty acres of open land next to the grotty industrial zone where those dozens of downmarket outlet stores were already operating.

He then closed with the classic French phrase articulated as usual in the passive voice, the one I had heard so often: "*Il faut faire une étude. On verra.*"—"It is necessary to study it. One shall see."

I certainly didn't need any time to make a study; I could already see. Despite the surprise, I was ready to make my decision that very moment. It was a no-brainer: I wanted that site near the highway exit.

As I was starting to get up to respond I said to Rochefort next to me, "This is easy. I can choose right now." Rochefort immediately grabbed my arm and pulled me back down to my seat. He leaned over until we were almost head-to-head, and whispered quietly but very intensely.

"Pallencher has just made an important *geste.* You cannot make a choice, just like that. You have to acknowledge his *geste.* You have to make a study. You have to make consultation. We then need to get together again. Then, at the right time and in the right way, *then* you make your choice."

"But I know what I want," I said pointing over to the boards. "It's clear." And after all those thousands of miles driving up and down France, and all the minuets, and the waiting to speak during those precious minutes *entre la poire et le fromage,* it *was* an easy decision. I wanted that highway exit site.

But I could see Olivier signaling to me from two seats away that Rochefort was right. I couldn't just jump in and make a decision. That was too American. There needed to be a process, a time for reflection, and I had to respect the process. In effect, there needed to be the next phase of the minuet, and for once it was up to me to orchestrate it.

Later, during the car ride back to Paris with Cheryl and François, we reviewed the day's events over and over. François and I were beyond excited. We had never had such a positive session with the full slate of a town's leaders like that, and certainly not one which included the anti—new retail CCI vote.

I asked Cheryl how this all compared to site selection in America. After all, no one in the presentation had discussed the needs of the brands or the shoppers. No one had looked at the whole process from the customer's standpoint. What did she think about that, I asked?

Silence.

I looked back. Cheryl had been right. Wine during the day didn't work for her. She was passed out across the backseat, white Lycra dress hidden by the overcoat pulled over her.

TWELVE

Shuttle Diplomacy

Thirty-two landowners? What do you mean *thirty-two* landowners?"
I couldn't believe what I was hearing from François. And he
couldn't have liked reporting it, either.

"Pallencher and Rochefort both said the site was ready to go!" I carried
on. "That should mean there is one site owner, ready to sell, and I assumed
that owner would be CAT! How could there be *thirty-two* different
landowners on a site that's 'ready-to-go'?"

François had recently paid me the ultimate compliment by making the
transition from outside adviser to in-house director of acquisitions. His top
and only priority was securing the site in Troyes, which didn't seem very
secure just then.

"Well," François responded in a steady, methodical voice, evidence of
his theatrical training, "actually, there are thirty-two different pieces of
land. But some of them are held by multiple owners. There are thirty-six
owners in all."

"*Thirty-six!!*" I exclaimed. "How am I supposed to deal with that?"

Combining contiguous pieces of land from different owners into one in-
tegrated ownership is a standard part of real-estate development. It's known
as creating an assemblage. I had never heard of an assemblage involving
more than ten or twelve owners. Thirty-six was beyond comprehension.

"Who *are* these thirty-six owners? Are they all investors in a partnership, speculating on the land?"

"No," said François, staying calm as a way of calming me. "They are not speculators. They are farmers mostly, or brothers and sisters, sons and daughters of farmers. There are so many owners because under French law when an agricultural landowner dies the heirs inherit the land in equal strips unless there are other provisions made, which in the traditional farming family there are not. As a result, much of this land is broken up into long skinny strips, most with a separate owner, some with coowners. And there are thirty-six owners in all. That's why the city is proposing a project on this land—there are too many owners for coherent agriculture, and it's located next to an industrial zone."

I sat there shaking my head for a moment.

"Are we never going to get a break on this project?" I took in a deep breath, and let it out slowly . . . audibly. I realized I needed to do it again, this time emitting even more slowly.

"And we need to submit our application for the CDEC in three months. What does that mean for these thirty-six owners?"

"At the time of the application we need to demonstrate control of the land on which we are applying."

"And what does 'control of the land' mean in this case?" I pressed further. "Does it mean we actually have to own it?"

"Well, no. You have to control the land, so we should have it under a signed *promesse de vente*—a 'Promise to Sell' contract. And you submit evidence at the time of the application that that is the case."

"A signed contract? From all thirty-six owners?"

"Yes."

"Fabulous. How do we do corral thirty-six French farmers and friends in three months' time?"

"Well," François said, his voice still calm, "you go to the local *notaire,* the government-licensed person who must attest that all transactions of land or buildings are in good order. With his seal on a purchase and sale agreement, title to the site is guaranteed to have been exchanged. He or his father have usually been working with the same families in a given area for generations. They have the trust of those families, so it's best to go through the *notaire.*"

"Right . . ." I said. I kept trying to deal with the fact that we now had thirty-six owners with whom we had to haggle.

Troyes was now my new Warner—a single point of focus, which would encompass all my energies and all my hopes. Everything was riding on Troyes, personally and professionally. If I couldn't secure an approval there, then two years' investment in money, effort, and angst would be a complete loss. Pamela's earlier question about whether I had chosen the right country would have received a resounding answer: No! The strategy to open on the continent as well as in the United Kingdom would have backfired. And it would have done so just after we had sold BAA on the pan-European concept as a key reason for forming the joint venture with us.

The first hint of how much I still had to learn came when I discovered that Pallencher and Rochefort had been right about the two sites they had proposed: I needed to study them both before making a decision. In my let's-decide-now style, I had wanted to choose the site by the highway and to forget the site next to the industrial zone. But I had dutifully kept my mouth shut when Pallencher proclaimed that "*Il faut faire une étude. On verra.*"

Once we'd had a chance to examine the properties and to run the numbers, I came to realize that my first choice was wrong. The property near the highway was a mess of access, utilities, and even title-clearance problems. Suddenly, the land next to the crumby industrial zone looked much more promising.

In order to have a chance at winning the CDEC in Troyes I had to make some seventy-five round-trips in the three months leading up to the presentation. That's seventy-five round-trips over a period of ninety days, of which twenty-six were Saturdays and Sundays. I went back and forth, back and forth, with meeting after meeting with all the players in Troyes, rounds and rounds of meetings with those with whom I already met, to ensure we clarified and secured their support.

I could have accomplished much of the business—probably most of it—with well-chosen conference calls from my office in Paris, but that was not to be. I was repeatedly told by the Bouygues people that meetings had to be in person, commuting to Troyes. I was a newcomer and a foreigner, they explained, and because the CDEC approval was so sensitive it was of paramount importance to cultivate and to maintain a *bon contact* between myself and each politician, and each of their key advisers. The only way to do that was to meet . . . again . . . and again . . . in person . . . in Troyes. On this, Olivier and his political advisers were adamant.

So there were meetings with Pallencher and Rochefort; sometimes meetings with just Pallencher, sometimes meetings with just Rochefort. There was so much positioning for political considerations that there were meetings just to discuss which meetings to have and with whom.

There were meetings with Mayor Galley and his advisers; others with advisers to Tockenburger of the Chamber of Commerce; repeated meetings with Pallencher to determine the exact nature of the relationship between McArthurGlen and the municipal authorities; meetings with Mayor Bischoff of Pont-Sainte-Marie, to review exactly what his support could do for us and what our center could do for his voters. And there were meetings with the powerful Préfet, who had no vote but, as Olivier constantly reminded me, wielded immense influence. As part of my strategy to keep my team as French and as local as possible, I hired the Troyenne architectural firm of Téqui-Pointeau to design the center. The firm was headed by the incredibly warm and affable Jacques Téqui, who was an important asset for us. But still, hiring him only meant more train rides to Troyes.

As part of my early-morning commuting routine I always tried to make time for a quick double-espresso from the café concession near Track 7 at the Gare de l'Est. It was from Track 7 that I began the one-and-a-half hour train ride to Troyes. Eventually the concessionaire came to recognize me, and when he spotted me coming his way he would, with an elaborate flourish, start to prepare my usual serving. He performed the same ritual each time.

It began with the swift and expert measuring and firm packing into place of fresh grounds, the two-step motion of popping the silver cup back into place on the espresso machine (up into the slot and then a quick jerk to the right for a tight connection), followed by the precise flip of the steam lever. There immediately followed a short cough as the valve holding back the highly pressurized water opened up, followed by the hissing of the steam as it went whistling through the fresh grounds to create the espresso. The man behind the counter busied himself during this interlude with a few wipes of clean cloth over freshly washed cups, and an arm-outstretched wipe-down of the counter in the spot just vacated by a departing customer. As the hissing behind him died quickly down to silence, he spun around and back again in one fluid motion with a triumphant *geste* to me of the steaming espresso in its tiny china cup and saucer, two cubes of sugar, and a demitasse spoon on the side just in case. The sharp smell of fresh coffee arrived before the cup even hit the counter.

Drinking the espresso involved my own ritual. It took both hands— one for the cup, one for the saucer—which meant I parked my briefcase on the ground between my feet and the concession's wall. The act of actually consuming the coffee often only took a minute-and-a-half. But it was a fabulous minute-and-a-half. The explosion in my mouth of double-roast espresso hurriedly imbibed in open air on a wintry Paris morning clears the mind and tunes the nervous system for the coming day like few other sensations can. The stationmaster's echoing announcements on the loud-speakers continued on overhead, and the swirl of rushing travelers continued just behind me, but both seemed muted during my espresso moment. It was more than a ritual: It was an event, a quiet Paris moment when everything went as I wanted it to go. It was an event which I couldn't replicate in ambience and ritual at home, and so made it more memorable.

Sometimes, if I was running late, I would have to skip the ritual and ride to Troyes without benefit of espresso, slowly emerging from that vague, ill-defined state of half wakefulness.

Once, when I arrived at the station slightly earlier than usual, I asked the coffee man had he ever considered also offering the coffee in Styrofoam cups, thus allowing his customers to enjoy his coffee on the run.

He stopped his whirl of motion for just a moment and looked straight at me. Deciding that I was neither joking nor meaning to insult his *métier,* he made a short, quick sound of shooting breath through pursed lips that let me know I had said something inane, but he wouldn't hold it against me.

I instantly understood the nature of my gaffe. I realized I was taking into account only one small aspect of his work. In my mind's eye, I pictured those other parts of his work life I never actually witnessed—the daily bargaining with his vendor for his freshly roasted beans, the meticulous cleaning of his coffee machine after each day's rush hour, the careful examination of his china for chips and pitting—all the dozens of tiny but vital steps that would eventually culminate in the presentation of a glorious espresso or café creme to a grateful customer, delivered with the *geste* that would, over time, establish a bond of trust between coffee maker and coffee drinker, which would validate his place in the overall flow of Parisian life.

I never again mentioned Styrofoam, and the coffee man, whose name I never learned, had the grace to overlook my naiveté.

I was learning.

At 5:15 each evening François and I would climb back on the train in Troyes and reverse our movements. Arriving back at Gare de l'Est at 6:35, it was then off to the office in a desperate attempt to catch up on the French paperwork, the calls with London, and then the calls with Washington, which as often as not came through much later, after I'd left the office and returned to our apartment.

"You understand, Byrne, we do not have any more cash," Joey would say on yet another late-night call. The six hours that Paris was ahead of Washington never seemed an obstacle to Joey. As he was in midstride in afternoon workflow he thought it natural to call at nine o'clock or later my time.

"In fact, we have no more cash to put into the venture. And I am out of places to go find it. You have to get that approval—I mean you *have* to. I really mean it."

Silence on the line while Joey waited for me to respond.

"Byrne, did you hear me?"

"Joey—I've heard you on this score many times. Question is, have you heard me? We're talking about complicated French politics here, politics emanating from the national level. I am focused on getting an approval because it's what we need and what I have been working toward for over a year and a half now. If I can pull it off, then great. If not, we'll face the problems that arise then. I can't do any more than that."

Another silence; this one a bit icy.

"I hear you, Byrne," Joey came back in a slightly conciliatory tone. "But you know what happens if you don't get the vote and then we cannot come up with that cash . . ."

"Yeah, yeah, I know. Inability to put up our share of the cash, dilution to our ownership interests, and all that. Joey, it's late, and I'm tired, and need some sleep. I think we should call it a day."

We did call it a day. But nearly the same call with the same themes would happen a few days later. The cycle continued as the vote inched closer and closer. Eventually, I started unplugging my phone after nine each night. That sometimes left Joey even more frustrated, but I slept better.

It was in struggling to get the land under control that I had some of the more memorable visits in Troyes. François had been right. All efforts to assemble the thirty-two different pieces of land and coordinate the thirty-six owners were directed straight through the offices of Maître Thomas, the *notaire* who knew all the families of Pont-Sainte-Marie area so well.

His office was in one of the old homes on the edge of Troyes, an elegant house converted to office use, with the reception area placed in what must have previously been the dining room. The former kitchen in the back of the house was now a room lined with rows of oak cabinets where the smoked hams had once been stored.

Maître Thomas's office was upstairs, in the former master bedroom. As we entered he greeted us formally from behind a massive oak desk. He was a man in his sixties, with a straight posture, and a presence that radiated an aura of profound gravitas. He was wearing a three-piece navy-blue wool suit with the vest all buttoned up (including the bottom button), a crease-less white shirt setting off his muted red tie. The room was as somber and crisply organized as the man himself. Dark-stained wood cabinets and bookshelves lined the walls, supporting leather-bound and gold-embossed folders and legal reference books.

François and I introduced ourselves, and I mentioned that I was seeing him in connection with a project that I was hoping to bring to Troyes.

"Yes, yes," acknowledged *Maître,* "the McArthurGlen dossier," indicating that Rochefort had already been in touch with him.

As it turned out, *Maître* knew all the people involved, and could assist with the land acquisition. It was likely to be a bit complicated, he intoned, as in some cases there were three or four siblings who had inherited land from the father, which was now broken into narrow and parallel ownership strips.

"Yes," I replied, "I have been told this is a complicated situation."

But that wasn't the complicating part, *Maître* responded. No, no. That was normal. The slight complexity was that sometimes there was the siblings' uncle or aunt who had owned part of the land with the father, and though he (the uncle) or she (the aunt) had not yet died, he or she had turned over the farming of all of the land—the siblings' and the uncle's—to the uncle's son-in-law, now married to the uncle's daughter, who was cousin to the siblings. And that son-in-law farmer didn't have a lot of land to farm, and so would want to keep as much as he could in production. Of course, it wasn't his land, it was his father-in-law's.

"The problem," *Maître* continued, "was that the son-in-law had been farming the land for more than seven years."

I must have looked bemused.

"Well, in France once a farmer has been farming land for a certain period of time he had earned rights to the land—it was part of his *métier,* so to speak—such that he could not just be thrown off of it whenever the owner so declared."

"Even if the owner is his father-in-law?" I asked.

"*Bien sûr,* even if the owner is his father-in-law. The law is there to protect farming. But I will have to check the documents to see what arrangements are possible. I drew up the papers for this some time ago."

"How long ago?" François inquired.

"Oh, well, the first papers would have been worked on by my father or grandfather either eighty years ago, or perhaps sixty years when some local families first bought land there. I am sure I updated them as recently as fifteen or twenty years ago," the *notaire* replied, giving us our first lesson in generational agronomy.

"But, *Maître,*" I asked in starting to sum up, "is that family situation the only complication in the assemblage? Are all the rest fairly straightforward in nature?"

Maître looked at me blankly for a few seconds. I thought perhaps my still creaky French had failed me in communicating, and he hadn't understood me. Just as I was about to restate my question, he answered me.

"Monsieur Murphy, I am sorry if I was not clear enough. The example I cite is not the only one with such a tangle of siblings, cousins, heirs, and owners. There are thirty-two parcels of land on the site in which you are interested. There are thirty-six owners. The parcels are *all* like that. That is why I said it was a little complicated, and why I cited an example. Some are more complicated."

"Dear God," I said to myself, thinking of the dwindling number of days left before the CDEC filing deadline, "tell me this is not happening . . ."

"But I will study the file," said *Maître* in closing. "*On verra.*"

One day, as I was walking down the corridor to Rochefort's office, I could see even from a distance that he was really steaming. He came striding down the hall to meet me, and ushered me into the first empty office he could find.

"You are *so* lucky that Pallencher is so weak," he said angrily, finger pointing, without offering a greeting. "You would *never* have gotten away with that from me!" he seethed, before the office door was even closed behind us.

"What do you mean?" I asked, bewildered.

"You know exactly what I am talking about," Rochefort continued. "Your last meeting with him. Pallencher, that weak old man, he has given you a deal that is too good for you! It is a steal!"

"A steal?" I replied, feeling uncomfortably close to the reddening face before me.

"Yes; a steal. Pallencher has in effect granted you full support, has opened all these other doors to you, and what do we get in return? Nothing!"

Aha, I said to myself. Rochefort's talking about the payback—the contributions he wanted Pallencher to squeeze out of us for all of CAT's prior work—the contributions that would have added great luster to Rochefort's reputation for his having brought McArthurGlen to Troyes.

"One moment," I said firmly, "the town of Troyes is getting a lot in return for supporting us. Troyes will have a fabulous project that is going to propel your outlet industry here to a whole new level. I am putting in my own roads and a public rotary for the entrance, as well as sewage and electrical infrastructure that will serve the local community as well. The number of jobs we'll create . . ."

"*Bairn* (that was as close as his French accent could get to my name): Do not bother me with your speeches. Remember: I have heard them all before.

"Just know this, *Bairn*. If I had been in charge I would have you contributing millions of francs in addition to all that. I would have held the CDEC in one hand out here," holding one hand outstretched to the side, "and I would have held your balls in my hand down here," indicating just about crotch level. "And I would have squeezed them until your eyes were blue and I had millions from you. I would never have stopped squeezing them until I had what I wanted," he said, pausing for a moment, "and then squeezed them some more."

All this from my *interlocuteur,* my in-town coach—the man I had thought was on my side.

It was a clear and unambiguous warning to me. In a foreign culture, in a foreign land, it is hard, very hard, to know who really is on your side. And if it seems as though someone really is, then ask yourself, "Okay, but for how long?" From then on, I made it a point to keep my relationship with Rochefort in perspective. I was merely the means for him to be popular, from which, as he candidly told me, he would derive power.

There was the day I put down the phone and glanced up at François. I must have looked a little funny. "The mayor of Troyes just asked me if I'd mind putting off our application for a year. A year, for God's sake! Who are these people? I told him that would be impossible."

"Byrne, you have to understand. The only time frame a French politician understands is the time left until the next election. And the only steps they're really concerned with are the immediate steps at hand, the ones involved in making the next *geste,* and getting credit for it. Or, conversely, not taking a step because they think doing so may make some voters unhappy."

I looked up ruefully. "After that meeting with Cheryl and the town fathers I thought the key CDEC members were with me. I was convinced I could count on their support, you know? They never really said they were with me, did they?"

François was sympathetic. "Everything in France is political, Byrne, and all politics is governed by the calendar."

We had ten months until France's presidential elections, and six months until Troyes's Chamber of Commerce elections. Those two dates clearly affected our chances of securing a majority of the seven votes cast. Schedule the vote too close to either of the elections and we'd lose support right off the bat. It was well known that Tockenburger was running for another term as president of the CCI, and the CCI retailers would be sure to punish him if he voted to support us. The closer to his election day the more he'd feel the heat. On the national level, the Chirac/Balladur machine would certainly not permit a favorable CDEC vote for a large project in the middle of a national moratorium just a few months or weeks before the presidential election. If we missed the window for a CDEC vote before these key dates it would be another year before another window would appear. That would be a year of sitting still, waiting for the political stars to align.

"Oh, Jesus. . . . How long is it supposed to take before I am able to think like a French politician, or to at least understand what they're really saying?" I wondered aloud.

"I am not sure you want to," said François, the half-Frenchman in consolation.

I was sitting in an elegant conference room overlooking the Rue Royale, just down from the Place de la Madeleine, in the offices of the prestigious law firm Fried, Frank, Harris, Shriver & Jacobson, one of the well-respected American firms active in Paris. Across the conference table from me was Eric Cafritz, head of the Paris office. I didn't know Eric but had been advised to come to him for counsel on how to work with the *notaire* in Troyes. It was nearly a month since my first meeting with Maître Thomas and there was, as far as I could see, no progress. Should I worry?

Eric nodded sympathetically. "If you're here to ask if it can be tricky working with *notaires* in the countryside, I am here to tell you to watch out—they can completely screw up your project.

"I mean I have seen it before on deals I have worked on," he continued. "Don't be fooled by the quaintness of the little country-office setting and stories of father and grandfather *notaire*. All *notaires* have those stories. It's a family monopoly on living the good life handed down from Napoleon's day, generation after generation. And there certainly are good *notaires* out there, even in the provinces. But believe me, there are bad ones, too, and, as I say, they really can screw up your project. And yours sounds like a complicated one already. I mean, *le gel* is still on and you're trying to secure a CDEC in the middle of it."

I had gone to meet Eric Cafritz, in hopes of hearing reassuring words. I walked away with a pit in my stomach.

Time was running out. François and I were back in the *notaire*'s office, and he was briefing us on the glacial progress of his negotiations with the thirty-six owners. He explained how he had to be careful which owners he saw first as the interrelationships of owners involved some of the usual sibling issues of lifelong rivalries and mistrust. He wanted to start the process with an owner who would be reasonable but also one whose decision would be respected by the others. And working through all the interpersonal issues he concluded by saying, therefore, the first meeting would be in two-and-a-half-weeks' time.

Voilà!—there it was: the *Maître's geste*. He'd derived a plan and had delivered it, even if prematurely by his calculations.

François and I took a moment to appear respectfully appreciative of his *geste* (I had been learning . . .) but at the same time, his plan meant waiting another two and a half weeks before even starting the round-robin of meetings. It barely seemed possible. It meant that almost seven weeks after our first meeting no real action would have been taken.

"*Merci, Maître,*" said François, "but one question. Why wait another two-and-a-half weeks?"

"Because he is harvesting his winter crop right now."

"Yes, and so . . . ?" I asked.

Maître broke a small little smile for the first time that day, one which said clearly we didn't know much about something he seemed to know a lot about.

"Well, one cannot interrupt a harvest. It starts early, goes late, and continues seven days a week until it is finished. It would do no good and earn no time to intervene until he is finished."

Knowing that I had a McArthurGlen board meeting in London the following week where I was to update my fellow board members on the progress in Troyes, I was turning over in my mind just how was I going to explain to my erudite, urbanite, and hard-nosed colleagues that all was on track provided that this year's winter alfalfa harvest was plentiful and on time?

We debated the point a little longer but *Maître* was not budging, and, in fact, became irritated that we didn't understand the psychology of harvesttime.

Trying to salvage the situation I finally asked about price. What did *Maître* think would be the all-in costs?

Maître patiently explained that the reasonable price was known to all. It was the market price for agricultural land, approximately fifty francs per square meter, which equated to sixty thousand dollars per acre.

Knowing that I had budgeted much more than that amount, I murmured something about, "Well, should we need to offer a higher price to one or two owners to speed up the process then I might be willing to consider it."

"Not possible," *Maître* responded.

"What's not possible?"

"Offering to pay more. Not to even one of the owners."

"But why not? If it helps to speed up the process?" I asked.

"Because the price has to be reasonable, and going above a certain number is not reasonable."

"But, *Maître,* if I am a willing buyer and they are a willing seller at a somewhat higher price, surely we can proceed on that basis?"

"No, you cannot."

"*Maître,* if the buyer and seller do not set the price, who does?"

"The market does."

"Yes, exactly. And, therefore, who decides what is the market?" I asked, thinking I had backed him right into my definition of willing buyer and willing seller.

"*I* decide what is the market," *Maître* said with finality.

Amid all the frantic activity relating to the upcoming CDEC hearing, there was a personal issue weighing on my mind as well, contributing to the numbing fatigue of those months. I had learned the prior week that my father had been diagnosed with throat cancer, and had started radiation and chemotherapy immediately. Though there was not yet any long-term prognosis, it was the realization of the ultimate risk Pamela and I took when we moved abroad: What about our parents? They were getting to the age where any week could bring news of some grave illness, and we'd be three thousand miles away. And here it was—just such news. I knew Dad had not been feeling well, but the news of his cancer stopped me short. Despite Dad's gruff protestations to the contrary, I had arranged to return for a visit the following week. I hadn't been home much since I landed in Paris eighteen months before.

Maître Thomas took some time to kick into gear. But once he did, his process was a joy to witness. He did indeed meet with the key farmer after the winter's harvest was complete. He started by going to the farmer's house and breaking the news to him, telling him why a sale to me was in his interest. *Maître* then called me in and explained why my underwriting the costs of switching fields for the farmer to cultivate was in my interest. It only took a week, and three meetings, to finalize terms, to finalize the need for a new tractor, the underwriting of the next three-year crop yields for the farmer, while he "became accustomed" to the new land barely a mile away. I dared to ask, once, did I have a choice? *Maître* ignored the question, and moved on with the list of items for which I was to pay.

"The other landowners all trust this man," *Maître* explained. "He has . . . integrity . . . *probité*. When he agrees to the terms, they all will."

And so they did.

At our final meeting at Maître Thomas's office, the farmer arrived with his wife and their son. The farmer had scrubbed up and wore a jacket and tie for the occasion. When all the paperwork was completed, I shook hands with him. It was a true farmer's hand—rough, and chapped, and calloused with cracked fingernails permanently stained the color of the soil of France. It was one of those moments when I was face to face with the real France of the provinces. Over time the farmer and I became quite friendly, and he and his fellow farmers were nothing but supporters throughout.

During one of our many train trips, François and I were seated together one evening on the way back to Paris, quietly reviewing the day's meetings. Our carriage was two-thirds full. There were probably thirty minutes left to the ride and most of the passengers were silent. Two young businessmen were seated directly in front of us. The staccato clicking of steel wheels rolling over the end-to-end connection of steel rails was a repetitive background sound, made more mesmerizing by the occasional lurching as the train pulled around another bend. A slight smell of cigarette smoke permeated the air, even in our *Défense de Fumer* car.

At one point I leaned my head back onto the high leather seat and closed my eyes for a moment's rest. Just as I did so I heard the unmistakable French pronunciation of my tiny little company: "Mc-Art-TOOR," coming from the seat directly in front of me.

"Did you hear that?" I whispered to François.

"Hear what?" whispered François in return, looking up from his *Figaro*.

Silently I pointed to the seat in front of us. We could hear the two men talking but could only discern every fourth or fifth word. After a minute of murmuring and pauses, the word came again: "Mc-Art-TOOR." We instantly looked at each other and François nodded his head in acknowledgment, his eyes lit up in surprise.

We continued listening intently, but could never quite understand the flow of the conversation. At one point François walked forward to the car ahead of us, turned around, and strode back to our seat with a full frontal view of the two men. What he saw confirmed his suspicion—one of the men was Gilles Bureau, the number-two person from the company which developed Marques Avenue, the recently opened outlet center in Troyes. In the few remaining minutes before we arrived at Gare de l'Est, we could hear enough to confirm that they were discussing outlet shopping in general, and referring to McArthurGlen in particular. Just prior to arriving in the station we could also hear Bureau crumple up some paper and toss it to the side.

At the station François and I busied ourselves in our seats while all the passengers streamed out of the car and onto the platform. When we had the car to ourselves, François spied the crumpled paper on the floor, scooped it up, and jammed it in his suitcase.

Minutes later, in the taxi, we uncrumpled the paper to reveal a short but sharp memo written from Alain Precaire, Bureau's boss, dated the day before, and entitled "McArthur in Troyes."

It has become clear that McArthur is being taken seriously in Troyes and the situation has now become dangerous for us. Now is the time to stop them. You occupy yourself with the retailers and others in Troyes and I will handle the officials in Paris.

I hadn't known what to expect when we opened the paper, but I definitely hadn't expected this. In my years of developing projects in very competitive environments in America, never had I witnessed one company actively working to sabotage another company's project. We competed on price, on product, and through marketing and salesmanship. But never out and out sabotage. It was a stark reminder that despite the eighteen months I had spent in France, and despite whatever progress I had made in establishing McArthurGlen, I was still learning about context. And until I really understood the context, surprises were inevitable.

There was no question that the memo's directive to stir up retailers and "work with others" in Troyes and Paris was a call to arms. Clearly, securing a CDEC in Troyes had just become dramatically more difficult.

THIRTEEN

The Defining Moment

Entrepreneurs are like explorers, constantly operating in uncharted territory, dealing with new experiences, stumbling across surprises.

Sometimes those surprises can be highly unwelcome. Such unexpected moments can result in resounding victories or devastating defeats, and often it's a thin line that separates the two.

The fate of my business in France now lay in the hands of the Troyes zoning board. Those seven people would decide our future. I had already anticipated that, win or lose, their vote would be a defining moment for me and for my company. As it turned out, the defining moment came long before the vote, and from an entirely unexpected quarter.

The year and a half I had spent in France had reminded me just how "foreign" I was. It wasn't the French who were "different"; I was different. For someone with a Type A, always press-on personality, it took quite a while for me to absorb that. I had been raised in a classic, solid, middle-class, Irish-American family of five kids, two parents, and a dog. It was a kitchen-centric upbringing where the family operated like a team. Everyone had to pull his or her weight: take out the trash, wash the dishes, cut the lawn, clean up after the pup. Nobody was exempt. If, for whatever reason, you tried to rise above the fray—if you began to feel special due to some recent social or athletic success—there were always four siblings to bring you back down to where you belonged: in the kitchen, scraping away the left-over beans and greased-up broiling pan. Family came first, and family duties foremost. Playing your part on the team was the top priority.

This team approach was reinforced at school. Athletics played an important part in the curriculum, and preparation, team spirit, and winning were emphasized. In soccer, football, and basketball winning was important, but team play was how you arrived there. In college, the same philosophy prevailed. On the sailing team you sailed your boat according to the overall team points. Team winning was the best winning.

When I began property development, I learned that teamwork was crucial there as well, sometimes life-or-death crucial. Before acquiring a site for development, the acquisition team had to be in sync with the sales team to know the market ("location, location, location"). Likewise, the design team needed to know costs from the construction boys who were in turn given budgets by the project management team, and so on. Throughout the two to six years it took to deliver a complicated 100-to-200-million-dollar urban, mixed-use redevelopment project, the team was guided by monthly meetings that kept everyone focused on the overall goal.

When I landed in France I knew that one of my first priorities was to put together a team, but whatever my original plans might have been, macroevents intervened. Because I had arrived just after the Euro Disney disaster, I was a ready-made target for the antiglobalization, anti-American meat grinder known as the French political process, the same political process I was depending on for the key public vote to approve my project.

I had the advantage of witnessing the Disney disaster firsthand, and was determined not to make the same mistakes. My first and easiest decision was not to hire Americans to introduce my American concept to skeptical French politicians and to the public at large. Instead, I hired French. All French. The head of marketing, the head of sales, the finance team, the construction team, everyone was French. It would be their mission to help me promote my concept, which I was certain held great potential for the shoppers, the workers, and the brand names of La Republique.

Smart?

Maybe.

Maybe not.

Philippe Bourguignon, the very savvy Frenchman who became chairman of Euro Disney after the initial debacle, was sympathetic but unimpressed with my decision. I had been introduced to Philippe by Steve Burke, an American friend in Paris who was Philippe's number two at Euro Disney. Philippe's reaction was that by hiring exclusively French employees I had made an even greater mistake than Disney. Greater, he explained, because after his many years of living and working in America, he knew that the French do not think like Americans, and, therefore, I, as head of the company, would not have anyone with whom to talk, really talk, when the problems arose. I was, he said prophetically, destined to be lonely.

The French way of thinking is systemic, he explained, and the indoctrination begins early. French schooling is a highly structured, highly centralized effort. Overstating it a bit (but only a bit), on a Tuesday morning at ten o'clock, all nine-year-olds throughout France are studying precisely the same lessons at precisely the same time, and in the same rote fashion. And so it goes with all other classes at all other ages in the system. A key element of this highly focused, highly controlled educational program is the study of philosophy, and in particular, Cartesian philosophy. As in René Descartes, the legendary seventeenth-century scholar whose works, both mathematical and philosophical, remain today influential throughout French life, law, arts, and education.

As a mathematician, Descartes is famous for creating the system of "Cartesian coordinates," which remain the bedrock of modern geometry. Carried into the more abstract fields of thought, Descartes's thinking was less formulaic, and intentionally so. His philosophic credo, *"Cogito, ergo sum"* ("I think, therefore I am") rejected the authoritarian scholastics of his time, most of whom were clerics espousing strict church doctrine. Descartes believed those doctrines were insufficient to explain the world around him, and instead began his search for truth with "universal doubt," which meant not accepting anything as stated. (I often wondered if this was the genesis for the skepticism that I encountered time and again in France.) From his position of doubt, Descartes extolled the virtues of intense examination and reason. The problem at hand, he argued, must be studied and reflected upon, and restudied. Through such examination all would eventually be revealed.

The practical effect of this Cartesian logic, I discovered, was that problems were often studied and not solved. It seemed that when faced with a problem my French colleagues, or the French politicians and administrators with whom I dealt, would discuss and observe it from many angles. They would walk around it, examine it, stroll to the other side, and look at it from there. In time, they had been taught, all would be revealed. But for impatient Americans such as myself, under duress and watching time gallop by, such waiting for revelation was not an option. I was not on a monastic retreat. I wanted action. I wanted to assess, to analyze, to derive, and to solve. I wanted to personalize the problem, and then attack it and move on. "I will do this," and "We will do that." Job done. Next?

But that's not Cartesian. That's not French.

The French approach is to remain impersonal, even passive to the problem as it is being studied, as though time will somehow take care of it. This sense of distancing oneself is buried deep into the very language of daily French life: *Il faut réfléchir* ("Reflection is needed"), *On verra* ("One will see"), *Il faut discuter* ("It is necessary to discuss"). Always third person, always distant. Not personalized.

This difference in approach can be seen in French movies (amorphous plot, heavy on questioning, lots of reflection, and without a conclusive ending), versus those from Hollywood (boy meets girl, conflict arises, and then happy, conclusive ending). You can even see the difference in the way each country conducts its diplomacy and foreign affairs. Americans, in the French view, veer toward black-and-white analysis, oversimplified solutions, and a rush toward action without taking into account the subtleties of history and relationships. The French, in the American view, become so obsessed with reflecting upon nuances and shades of gray that history will be made and moved on before they take action.

The fact that I operated on a different wavelength from the rest of my team meant that when a defining moment arrived, I wouldn't be able to connect intellectually or philosophically with them, and would be on my own.

Philippe Bourguignon had another insight for me. The French not only think differently, he cautioned, they have a particularly high regard for the individual as opposed to the team. Solo efforts and solo triumphs are prized, solo accomplishments lauded. If I was aiming to mold a team out of a group who had been taught to think as individuals, act as individuals, and to particularly admire the accomplishments of individuals, I was going to have to deal with that reality.

It didn't take me long to see his point. As I observed life around me more carefully, I saw that in France, as in America, significant athletic, professional, and social achievements were highly admired. But in France there always seemed to be more glory for those who pursued solo endeavors. More identification. Tennis players, skiers, ocean sailors, mountaineers, arctic explorers—the Charles Lindberghs of the modern era in a French setting. America, of course, has its own modern-day Lindberghs. And conversely, France certainly has its own teams that perform brilliantly and are greatly admired, notably the 1998 World Cup soccer champions and the 2006 runners-up. But as I looked closely at France, individualism seemed always to be loudly proclaimed, while the praise for team effort seemed to me to be distinctly muted.

I saw this national trait play itself out regularly in our weekly managers meetings. There were only seven of us in attendance (out of only fifteen in the Paris office), one from each discipline of marketing, leasing, construction, etc. At every meeting, I would review our overall corporate objectives, each department's objectives, and ensure everyone agreed and understood how those goals fit into our day-to-day operations. Very Anglo-Saxon. Very MBA. We'd discuss problems, and progress, and agree on actions. I'd always end each meeting with my exhortation to coordinate all efforts between departments, so that each was aware of the others' activities, to ensure there would be no time lost, no surprises.

But there were always surprises.

Each week I'd leave the team meeting full of optimism that this time we were all in the same boat, all coordinated, all members of one disciplined crew team, all pulling our oars together, all moving rapidly forward in a straight line. And the next week I'd realize I was not only full of optimism but also of naiveté. Because I'd discover we weren't in the same boat. We weren't in any boat. A more accurate analogy was that they were running in a footrace, each in separate lanes. Marketing in Lane 1, Sales in Lane 2, Finance in Lane 3, and so on. And as each runner sprinted through the week, they didn't look left or right, or even acknowledge there were other runners. And it took me several days to realize I was still seated in the boat, shouting out "Stroke! Stroke!" to a row of empty seats.

Usually (though not always), the runners would stay in their own lanes. But coordinate? Marketing would never inform Sales what he was doing until he aired his achievements, making his *geste,* at the next "Team Meeting." ("But I'm not in charge of sales," he'd say, in response to my plea for more coordination.) Construction didn't think of informing Finance that he had changed the facade design, which significantly drove up the costs and, therefore, the cash needs. ("It is a better design," he concluded.)

"Why," I continued to ask myself, "do they all think so differently? Why can't they coordinate their actions before problems arise?"

Eventually, belatedly, I came to realize that the issue was not how they thought and acted. It was how *I* thought and acted. After all, designer outlets may have been my concept, but it was their country. It finally occurred to me that even if I was, at age thirty-three, pretty set in my ways, it was simpler to change my behavior patterns than it was the behavior patterns of fifty-seven million French citizens.

I made a mental note to try at next week's managers meeting to explain my concept of teamwork within their context.

Then there were the consultants, the professional specialists I hired to help navigate me through the labyrinth of Gallic regulations, cultural traps, and political minefields into which I was continually stumbling. I had lawyers, contractors, architects, engineers, fix-it men—anyone to help me understand that puzzling part of the globe called France. But, of course, advisers could only be what they were intended to be: hired guns, providing advice by the hour. They were advisers as long as they were paid, ready to help as long as the invoices were answered, and not a moment longer. I couldn't blame them. They were used to advising big corporate clients on big international matters, clients who had the resources to invest millions and millions of French francs to penetrate a new market in a foreign land with foreign rules and a different culture—clients like Goldman Sachs, Gillette, Coca-Cola. My advisers perceived me and my struggle precisely the way I was trying to portray it—a smart, well-funded American effort that was merely a small advance guard of a mighty corporation behind it. They didn't know that the small band of Americans spearheaded by my halting French had bet everything that we had, mortgaged ourselves through tomorrow and beyond to make this work. My advisers did not realize that for me everything had come down to the impending vote in Troyes. I was praying that vote would be in our favor, because that would in turn unlock the financing for future projects. But I couldn't tell my advisers that. In other words, their advice was extremely useful, up to a point. The most worrisome aspects of the project—balancing risks, return—was strictly up to me.

So there I was, an explorer in an unmapped wilderness, working with my team of individualists, all of whom had been trained to observe and to reflect, but not necessarily to solve. Sometimes I felt very alone.

Not surprisingly, I turned to the one group that understood my perspective, my background, and my style of thinking. I called Joey and my other colleagues in America. I called to keep them informed of my progress, or, sometimes, lack of it. At first, it was reassuring to hear someone view the obstacles in the same way that I did. Someone who shared the same sense of urgency, the same awareness of the scarcity of resources that I felt. Someone who could help me formulate arguments as to why the Chamber of Commerce should vote for our project even though powerful retailers vociferously opposed it. Or, how to convince key politicians that a high-end outlet center would create hundreds of jobs and generate millions in tourist revenue. But as the months clicked by, I found I had to spend more and more time explaining to my American colleagues—my three-thousand-miles-away partners—that given the French context, the issues that I was describing couldn't be addressed in a traditional American way. The solutions were not as straightforward as the American analysis indicated. The thinking, the point of reference, wasn't the same. The storm-the-beaches assault tactics didn't work in this culture of nuance and shades of gray. Not in a Cartesian context. After a while I realized I was spending a disproportionate amount of my time explaining to my American partners why their reactions and recommendations were appreciated, but were wrong and would not work.

Eventually, I sought their advice less and less. My partners didn't understand. They couldn't understand. And my efforts to get them to understand only frustrated me more.

In July 1994, with one month to go before the crucial vote in Troyes, I assessed my situation. I realized that one of the real challenges before me was "whose judgment could I trust?" I was surrounded by a well-meaning French team that I had handpicked but which was on a different psychological wavelength from me. I was surrounded by advisers who were equally well-meaning, but didn't understand what was at risk. I was being observed by the French press, which was hungry for more errors by aggressive American capitalists who, like Disney, wanted to import new concepts into France. And my American colleagues were too far away and too disconnected to offer me any meaningful advice. I realized that the only counsel I could depend on was my own. And that was just the business side of it.

The fact is, I was not working in a vacuum. My family was very much part of the equation. Pamela had abandoned her thirteen-year career in support of this effort. She was refused a work visa, didn't know anyone, and didn't speak French upon her arrival in Paris. She was my constant, my confidante, but so, too, was I hers, and that needed attending to. With us was our two-year-old daughter Avery, and now our two-month-old Cara. Homes with multiple babies have their own ebbs and flows of stress, of sick infants in the morning's wee hours, and no fresh diapers in the dark. And now, I had just learned, my father's cancer had just been diagnosed as terminal. His timeline was months, not years, and I was on a monthly commute home to be with him. Personal issues have a habit, I have discovered, of piling up on you just when professional challenges are reaching their peak.

And it was at that crucial moment that my defining moment arrived.

Phone calls began coming into my office from a man I didn't know. He wanted to talk to me about some property in the village of Lavau, immediately adjacent to my project. I sat up and took notice. Lavau is a charming little cluster of rustic stone houses surrounding a village church, the whole surrounded by a quintessential French countryside of green, gently rolling farm fields. Though my project did not lie in Lavau, the entrance to it did. And I needed that entrance.

I sensed that the person on the telephone knew I needed it, and seeing that massive, great American-financed project on his doorstep, had decided that fortune had indeed smiled upon him and the picturesque little village of Lavau.

The phone calls kept coming. I left messages that I was "not in for a few days," and suggested "please call back next week." Other times, I was "in a meeting." But finally, when the calls became more and more insistent, I grudgingly agreed to meet with him. I asked François Moss to join me and to help interpret what was really going on.

At the appointed hour, not one but three Frenchmen showed up. The leader, the man who had been doing the telephoning, Mr. Jean-Claude Estephe, introduced himself and his two companions. All three were in their thirties to mid-forties, all with well-coifed hair. No gray. Each was impeccably dressed in crisply tailored suits, Hermès-style ties (pushed up tight to their necks), polished cuff links, and Italian-cut loafers. They arrived with an air of knowing what they were doing.

Mr. Estephe began talking in long, slow, elliptical French, congratulating me on my success to date, and making references to how he really wanted to cooperate with me. He and his colleagues had been appointed by the mayor of Lavau as the outside Development Manager for the land adjacent to ours, including the land which we needed for our entrance. Estephe stated that he recognized that we "must all work together," and that he felt certain that I would come to appreciate their cooperation. He repeated the theme of cooperation over and again. I wanted to point out that I didn't realize we were "working together," or that I needed their "cooperation." But instead I responded by playing the dumb American, struggling with my basic French, and thanking him for his "cooperation." I adopted the French custom of ending every sentence with a rising inflection to imply the end of the conversation and, hence, the meeting. "Okay, *bon. Merci bien pour votre visite.*"

Not to be.

Estephe became impatient and more direct. He pointed out that the entrance to my project, *"le grand project Américain,"* went right through Lavau, and that the main entrance to my "giant project" needed the road widened and a rotary built to handle the traffic flow. In fact, he went on, these improvements had been demanded by the highway authority as a condition for its consent. The highway authority in Paris, he added. The reference was unmistakable, and my suspicions were confirmed. To secure my vital zoning approval, which required road improvements, Mr. Estephe pointed out, I needed local official approval, and to ensure that approval (and here Mr. Estephe's voice took on a deliberately casual tone) would require a payment of 20 million French francs.

"Vingt million Francs."

Almost four million dollars.

He said it almost in a whisper at the end of a long lead-in, with the slightest shrug of his shoulders, the dropping of his head, and the raising of his open hands on the mahogany conference table. Almost as if one has to do what one has to do as, of course, we all understood.

But in fact I didn't understand. I didn't want to understand.

Twenty million francs—four million dollars. Payable to him. This seemed to me to be nothing less than pure extortion. One month before the vote.

Suddenly, all the effort and all the risk and all the strain and stress over the last year and a half—the flying back and forth to America with politicians and brands and advisers, the relocating of my family, my wife giving up her career, my father's illness, the stress of being a foreign person in a foreign land, introducing a foreign concept and being the only Anglo-Saxon on an otherwise French team—all of this came crashing down on me. Flashes of that Cartesian-based education of reflecting on problems, casually and over time and through the third person, not making it personal to them, and not solving the problems.

Well, this was *my* problem, very personally *my* problem, and there was no time to reflect on it. And the bearer of this problem, in fact, very probably the creator of this problem, was sitting across from me. This was not a problem where I could say, "Oh, let me think about that and consult with my American colleagues three thousand miles away, and my multitude of hired French consultants scattered around Paris. Let me reflect and we'll see. *On verra.*" It was too late for that. I was on my own.

In that moment of moments, as I struggled to control the fury that was threatening to consume me, I felt myself rising to my feet, not knowing what I was going to do, not even knowing what I was going to say. I deliberately forced myself to pause while I stared at the shoulder-shrugging, "one-has-to-do-what-one-has-to-do" man in front of me. Then I counterattacked.

"I will never, *ever* pay one French franc to you, or to anyone that you send to me," I started. My voice was firm but not harsh. My French was clear, simple, restrained.

"This is my project, this is my company, and I will do it *my* way." The tone was tough as the voice began rising. "And you will *NOT* chase me down by phone, harass me with your messages, demand meetings, come to *MY OFFICE,* and threaten me with extortion." I was now leaning forward and pointing my finger at his chest, glaring into his eyes, my voice louder but still clear.

"You think that you can threaten me? Is that what you think?" Now I was shouting—red-faced, eyes-bulging shouting. I had launched and was going off into space, into free-form ascendancy. There was some intellect in my delivery but mostly emotion. I spat out my broken French in my American accent, but it was forceful French, meaningful French.

At this point I could vaguely sense François at my side. He was offering soothing words of counsel, telling me in whispers to calm down, to sit down, to tone down, to back down, anything. Apparently this was too much drama, even for François. I could feel my left hand waving him away. I was not to be stopped.

"Do you *understand* me? Do you *hear* me?"

Estephe started sliding to my right, slithering along the wall and toward the door. I continued shouting.

"I will *NOT* be intimidated, do you *hear* me?" He had the door open and was stumbling out. I was ready to follow him, but François held me back, beseeching me to calm down. I don't think anyone in the room had ever seen a spectacle quite like this and not anyone in the room knew quite what to do. Except me. I was on counterattack and I was ready for more.

"*OUT!* There is no *goddamn* way I am I paying you one goddamn French franc!"

I ended up shouting in English with yet more conviction and more emotion. I slammed the door behind the rapidly retreating Estephe.

I had confronted a threat and faced it down. I was still full of anger, and rage, and energy, and wanted to fight more. I felt flush and victorious as I turned to François.

"I was not going to be held-up by him or anyone after all of my work," I told him. "Not after all the risk and trips and bullshit I've put up with!"

But then I glanced past François and remembered that the threat had arrived in the form of three men and not just one. The two remained there in the conference room, somewhat taken aback, but steadfast in their chairs. One looked straight at me and said calmly, "*Monsieur Murphy, s'il vous plaît, asseyez-vous. Il faut discuter.*"

More Descartes, even now.

I realized that our vote was only one month away, and I had scared off the lead spokesman, but the threat was still there. They controlled the land. They controlled the access. I didn't yet know if, therefore, they controlled the approval I so desperately needed.

Suddenly, I wasn't sure that I handled the situation at all well. I had prepared myself tactically and intellectually for this moment, but not psychologically. Not emotionally. The result was not exactly grace under pressure.

I had not solved the problem. I had only put it off. It dawned on me that my defining moment had only just begun.

FOURTEEN

The Vote

Who really was behind the extortion attempt? Was it the mayor of the adjoining commune smelling an opportunity? Could it have been Marques Avenue or another competitor using it as a way to stop me? Perhaps it was someone directly involved in the CDEC process who had seen the vulnerability of my application and pounced on it? I couldn't be sure and nor could anyone else.

The only certainty was that the timing of the extortion was nearly perfect. It created maximum leverage for the blackmailers. There were now only three weeks left before the CDEC hearing. Though I had chased Estephe out of my office, the problem hadn't disappeared.

I couldn't put off my hearing date without losing several months in time and all the momentum in the political process. The hearing was scheduled for late June, just before the summer break in France. If I missed that date I couldn't be back on the schedule until late autumn at the earliest, just weeks before the presidential election. By then whatever political support I may have secured would wilt away under pressure from the national political parties. In addition, the delicate balancing act I had achieved on the purchase contracts with the farmers would certainly be at risk if I went back to them asking for more time.

I could, perhaps, find a compromise solution. I wouldn't pay anything myself but could hand the problem over to Bouygues. They would have been no stranger to these tactics. But if I pursued that route I knew two things. Firstly, I would bear the costs of any payoff anyway as it would just show up hidden somewhere in the Bouygues construction contract. Secondly, if I were willing to go that route, the word would inevitably get out and everywhere I went in France I would be marked as a soft touch. One could play this game only on a slippery slope, and I had no desire to end up on one. Paying off the blackmailers, whoever they might be, was not an option.

I could also call Estephe's bluff—just show up at the hearing as though nothing had happened. But something had happened, unmistakably. And to ignore it could only put everything at risk.

When I concluded that none of the solutions involving time, politics, or money would work, I looked to physical solutions. Could I avoid the land on which my proposed entrance was sited and still have a viable project? In other words, if I couldn't have a front door for my project, could I find a back door? Or rather, a back door which could serve as the front door? And the answer was—maybe. But to achieve that would require a complete redesign of the project, from where the buildings were sited to how the road system would work, to the signage, the store's visibility— everything would need rethinking.

Because of the time limitations we had to do everything at once. The day after Estephe's visit, I called a meeting of everyone involved in the project, in-house staff and outside consultants. I wanted to examine new entrance concepts from every perspective: design, construction, sales, marketing, legal, financial. In essence, I wanted to spend one week redesigning the project we'd just spent several months designing. We started pulling out the land records, identifying possible locations, resurveying the properties, laying out a new master plan, checking rights of way, checking titles, checking with the *notaire* on likely negotiating terms on potential additional land.

We plunged into simultaneous meetings and conference calls, and new plans and then newer plans, and faxes and FedEx packages arriving and going, and late-night sessions, and early mornings with croissants, cappuccinos, and baggy eyes. It was a full-scale project development marathon that went through the first weekend, the following week, and was headed for the next weekend.

And somewhere in the middle of it, a call came in from Estephe's colleague, asking for me. I passed the message back that I wasn't available. It was the last time they called. Though thankful for the respite, I recognized that Estephe and I were engaged in a waiting game.

I concluded a back-door plan was possible, and we were able to design it and gain control of the land in time for the CDEC. It was a solution, but it certainly also was a compromise. Instead of shoppers exiting the highway and entering into a new luxury designer-outlet center passing by fertile farmland and a well-engineered and landscaped entrance, they were going to reach our center via a circuitous route around the site and enter it from the back side. The cars would first pass by what would have originally been the entrance point, drive across railroad tracks, take a left into that dreary industrial area, proceed along a tight road past some blighted factory buildings, take another left to double back across the railroad tracks. They would then travel along a new road (which just then was a tractor path), and enter into the center's parking lot, having driven nearly three quarters of the way around the site. God knows what would happen when a wave of cars arrived all at once. That was tomorrow's problem.

It was not a pretty solution. But it was a solution. And there was no blackmail.

My most worrisome concern was technical. The application we had submitted months before to the CDEC Commission showed an entrance scheme that was no longer there. Anyone who wanted to oppose our application—and there were now several competitors and retailer groups working hard to do just that—could use the disparity between our original application and our amended site plan to force a new application. We could lose months in the process. Months which would drag us so close to the presidential elections that, again, for political reasons, a year's delay was very possible. It was the weak link in our solution.

The person on my team with whom I worked most closely on the CDEC process was Eric Marron, a bright, twenty-seven-year-old from Burgundy and a Harvard Business School graduate, a combination that sometimes proved a challenge in itself. But when focused on the CDEC, Eric was determined, insightful, and of great assistance.

On the morning of the vote, Eric pulled the car up before the massive Prefecture, and we began unloading our presentation boards. The building in front of us was large. Impersonal. Deliberately intimidating. Built of limestone, the Prefecture was fenced off from the streets by a fifteen-foot-tall black iron-rod fence with guardhouses at the entrances. It stood back from the fencing with a forecourt of stone pebbles and granite walkways, inducing a processional approach from guardhouse to guarded doorways.

Inside the Prefecture, the great stone staircase that led from the ceremonial ground floor to the offices and conference rooms above had been deliberately built with shallow risers and broad treads to ensure that anyone going up or down would be forced to do so at a measured, dignified pace. The tall, leaded windows in the spacious foyers created a cathedral-like atmosphere. The high stone walls echoed every sound and induced visitors to speak in whispers.

When we arrived in the anteroom to the Grand Salon minutes before our scheduled hearing time, we found we were not alone. There were two other applicants for a collection of outlet stores, both modest in size. One was located just outside the new entrance to my center, the other near Marques Avenue across town. They stopped talking when we entered. Rochefort had been right. While the downtown retailers had clamored against our application on grounds of unfair competition, these two applicants had decided to wrap themselves in the French flag in protest against the overly fair treatment for *les Américains*. Should *les Américains* win a CDEC by the vote from *les élus*, they reasoned, then they, too, should each receive approvals if only to show that the town still cared for French interests. I studied them for an instant as I walked into the anteroom. I certainly had enough battles raging just then and didn't need to play into their hands by opposing their applications.

It would have been useless to point out that for McArthurGlen I was actually the only American involved, that the capital deployed was 99 percent non-American, and the jobs created would be 100 percent French—none of that would register. So I remained discreetly silent as these interlopers played their hand on the back of my struggles and, therefore, strengthened their positions as my future competitors.

We settled down to await our turn, all of us choosing silence to discourse. After several minutes, a bespectacled clerk emerged from the counsel chamber and summoned us inside.

It was a large, long, and tall room built in keeping with the grand dimensions of the Prefecture building. Yet, it was unexpectedly sunny and almost cheerful from the effect of a half dozen of those massive windows along one side. The seven members of the Commission who would judge my application sat on either side of a massive walnut conference table with the Préfet at the head. The whole room was quiet. I was directed to the empty chair at the other end, where I sat with Eric and our boards at my side. My position as the supplicant was clear.

The preliminaries were quickly dispensed with, at which point all eyes turned my way. I stood up to address the board. By that time I knew each member well, and had spent the last three months trying to ensure that they all knew me equally well (*le bon contact*). Yet, for all the time I had spent with each member, for all the meals and aperitifs we had shared, for all the movements in the minuet we had engaged in, for all that I could be sure of only one vote. I had hopes and reasons why we should win more, but I could be sure of only one.

Once again, I presented my project—the concept, the design, the team—using renderings and architectural plans. I described how we would be positioning our center as the high-end alternative to all the other outlet offers in Troyes, and in fact to all others in France. The architecture, the landscaping, the amenities, and most of all the high-end brands, each in its own store offering prices on end-of-season goods at 30 percent to 50 percent off retail prices—this was the McArthurGlen concept. After the months of our minuet about town the Commission members knew well what I was about to say, and I knew to be succinct. After fifteen minutes I sat down and Eric rose to present our marketing program—the plan to attract three million shopping visits per year, the majority from an hour's drive or more from Troyes. These were high-income shoppers, Parisians mostly, who would otherwise not be visiting Troyes. Eric outlined our plan to welcome them to McArthurGlen but then direct them to visit downtown Troyes as part of their day out. As Eric spoke I studied one Commissioner after another, remembering what each had last said to me, and what their body language indicated today. I was hoping I could count on at least four favorable votes around the table.

At the far end of the table, next to the Préfet, Mayor Bischoff of little Pont-Sainte-Marie, sat with his broad smile and rumpled suit. He had been clear in his allegiance from the start, the most clear and consistent of all the Commissioners—absolutely in favor of McArthurGlen coming to his commune. I felt confident he was "Yes" vote Number One.

Next to Mayor Bischoff was Mayor Lancoin, mayor of La Chappelle

St. Luc, the second largest commune in the Troyes agglomeration. Cool and calculating, he had always made encouraging comments but had never come out with a clear statement of support. I thought he was playing a political game, waiting and leveraging his vote to receive something in return from CAT and the town of Troyes. I didn't know if a deal had been made or not. His was a hedge position, and so his vote was "Uncertain."

Seated next was the Consumer's Representative, a woman who lived well outside Troyes. She was elected to the position because a certain group of local activists took turns in the role. As Rochefort had warned at the outset months ago, she was inconsistent and unreliable from application to application. At least she hadn't told us she was out and out opposed to the project, and so represented "Uncertain" vote Number Two.

To my immediate right was the president of the Craftsmen's Union, the *Chambre des Métiers*. As the members were small craftsmen, they were allied with the *petits comerçants* in the town center. To my knowledge their association had never supported a CDEC application for a commercial center anywhere in France. We had met with the president and his council several times and proposed programs to ensure ongoing jobs were directed their way. I thought I had a *bon contact* with him, but politics were politics, especially in France. His was "No" vote Number One.

So far, one "Yes," one "No," and two "Uncertains," with three votes to go.

Mayor Galley was to my left, and throughout the hearing he never looked me in the eye. The elder statesman of those present, he was the only person with two votes to cast, as befitted his double crowns in this setting: first as the Mayor of Troyes, and second as president of the Regional Council. He had the power to swing the project one way or the other. Cagey as always, he had espoused support for our coming to Troyes but had always sucked air in between his teeth as he said, "difficult with *les petits comerçants. On verra.*" Officially, he had backed Pallencher's and CAT's vision of focusing on the outlet sector as a key economic development program for Troyes, and had gone public in saying so. The only way he could say that and then not back my application would be to cave into the nationalistic argument that *les Américains* were not the answer. His waffling was the most frustrating and, I thought, the most dishonest and spineless. I never felt I had a *bon contact* with him. Realistically, his was "Uncertain" votes Numbers Three and Four.

The final voter was Monsieur Tockenburger, president of the CCI. As always he appeared distinguished sitting there in his crisp deep-blue suit and two-blocked silk tie. I had the most sympathy for his political position, as he had always been straight with me while he worked to see if there was a way the CCI could possibly support us. He understood well the outlet concept as his own company's outlet store downtown continued to prosper. But as the elected representative of all the Troyenne businesses, in particular the *petits comerçants,* and with his re-election vote only three months away, he was feeling the heat from all sides. Again, politics were politics. His was, reluctantly I thought, "No" vote Number Two.

Final tally: "Yes" votes: one; "No" votes: two; "Uncertain": four.

In other words, after nearly two years of working on this new venture, and with the vote to decide whether it was go, or no go, only minutes away, I still had no idea, really, whether or not the politics of the town was with me or against me. And if I did win an approval, a four-to-three vote, or maybe four-to-two with one abstention, was about as favorable a vote as possible.

Eric concluded his presentation, sat down, and we waited for questions. I expected many, and had hoped that they might provide a clearer indication of how the "Uncertain" votes were likely to be cast. But there were no questions. One by one the Commission members, in what I suspect was a prearranged agreement, deferred to the Préfet at the far end of the table. He, it turned out, would ask the only questions. There was a brief pause as he consulted some papers in front of him, then looking over the top of his spectacles he addressed me directly.

"Monsieur Murphy, will there be any restaurants at your proposed project?"

"No, Monsieur le Préfet. There will not be any restaurants. There will only be fast-food outlets. In addition, we will have a program, organized in cooperation with the Chamber of Commerce, to advertise all the area restaurants, accompanied by hand-out maps and signage directing our customers to the *centre-ville* to find them."

That was Accommodation Number One, made on behalf of the downtown restaurateurs and hoteliers, permitting them to benefit from the influx of shoppers driving in from so far away. The French, after all, take their midday meals seriously, and offering only fast food at our center was akin to offering nothing at all. Hence we would direct them downtown for "real cuisine."

"Monsieur Murphy, will the shops at your center offer any products other than textiles?"

"No, Monsieur le Préfet, there will be only textiles. We will not have china, pottery, housewares, perfumes, or other nontextile products."

That was Accommodation Number Two, made on behalf of the downtown retailers. It represented a major sacrifice on our part, a serious blow to providing a fully merchandised offer to the shoppers who spent a full day driving out to Troyes, shopping, dining, and driving back again. It was also a restriction that was not being applied to any other outlet offer, notably Marques Avenue. But I was dealing with politics here, not perfection.

"Will there be any resellers involved with this project?" the Préfet continued.

"No, Monsieur, only the brand manufacturers themselves. That is why we have branded our center: *Boutiques de Fabricantes*—'Manufacturers' Boutiques.' "

That was Accommodation Number Three, again to protect the downtown retailers. Resellers are freelance merchants who sell products they have purchased on the "gray market," usually at distressed prices. They have no long-term relationship to the brands' normal sales distribution and, therefore, no loyalty to the brands' regular retailers. Brand manufacturers, on the other hand, are highly protective of the retailers who carry their brands, and will go to great efforts to ensure they do not compete directly with them. It was an important distinction that the general buying public was not likely to understand, but which local retailers would recognize and appreciate. It also differentiated us from other outlet stores.

The Préfet followed up on this point: "And will you have a method of working with these manufacturers in their boutiques to help protect the downtown *petits comerçants?*"

"Yes, Monsieur le Préfet, we will. Whenever there is a manufacturer whose brands will be present in both the McArthurGlen center and with a *petit comerçant* downtown, we will ensure that the store in our center does not offer the same goods as the downtown store. We will ensure there is no direct competition."

That was Accommodation Number Four, a program I had worked out with Tockenburger and the CCI to further assist the downtown retailers in deriving benefit from our arrival on the scene. It was not a restriction the manufacturers would like, and could certainly hinder our leasing efforts as the CCI had also insisted on a policing program to be undertaken by an independent government agency.

"Okay, *bien,*" the Préfet said matter-of-factly, indicating he had known the answers to all these questions before he'd posed them. My responses were for the record. After consulting his papers again, he leaned over to his right and conferred briefly with the Secretary to the Commission. Accommodation Number Five was not discussed. It involved the center's design. Two times I had presented our proposed design to the political leaders of Troyes, and two times they had said it was "too nice," and requested that I make it "less fancy." They wanted to ensure that the center not compete with the charm of downtown Troyes. Thus, the final design was based on the materials and architecture reflecting the industrial heritage of Troyes: glass, brick, and steel. It was also a much simpler, more basic design than we would have preferred. The Préfet's next question was in the most solemn of tones, as if by a prosecutor at a trial.

"Monsieur Murphy, have you direct control over all the land you need to develop this project?"

"Yes, Monsieur le Préfet, I do," I responded, hoping this line of question wouldn't go any farther.

"Monsieur Murphy, have you secured the entrance to your project?"

This was what I had feared. At first I thought all the commission members seemed to lean forward just a bit, as though eager to hear my response. It may have been, though, that it was I who leaned just slightly forward. It was obvious that everyone there knew about the extortion attempt and understood precisely what the Préfet was really referring to.

"Yes, I have secured my entrance," I said, hoping that it wouldn't be necessary to show them my new site plan, which might alert someone to the discrepancy in the master plan.

The Préfet, after listening to a comment from a Commission member to his left, looked at me sternly over his spectacles and said, "Are you sure you have secured a suitable entrance to your project, Monsieur Murphy? And that you have control of the required land for that entrance?"

"Yes," I affirmed. "I am sure."

The Préfet paused for a moment, digesting my answer. It seemed as though he was pondering the same issue I was—wondering whether he should delve any deeper into this. After a long thoughtful pause—long enough to permit me to add more commentary, which I didn't—the Préfet nodded his head.

"Okay, *bien,*" he said. Scanning the faces of the commission members he secured their silent agreement, then turning back to me, he nodded.

"Thank you, Monsieur Murphy, for your presentation. That will be all."

I expressed my thanks to the Préfet and to the commissioners, and Eric and I picked up our boards and turned to leave. As I did I wondered if, after all those months of meetings, after all the politics and intrigue, might there be anything I should add, anything that could strengthen my case. But I remembered the French expression that Olivier had taught me: *Il faut préparer le terrain*—"One must prepare in advance." All the hard work, all the positioning, had been done before this hearing. I decided best to leave the situation as it lay.

As we walked out of the Grand Salon and into the waiting room, all eyes of the other applicants were on us. The two young guys from Marques Avenue, as well as the other applicant, all studied our faces, searching for clues as we walked past, scanning us as we had just scanned the faces of the commissioners inside. The outcome on our application was very likely to dictate the outcome of theirs as well. I was sure that none of the restrictions that had just been formally applied to my project through the Préfet's questions would be slapped onto theirs. But I said nothing, and offered no assessments, nor could I. I couldn't guess where we stood at that moment.

The rest of the team was waiting for us at a little café opposite the Prefecture. Eric and I were peppered with a half dozen or more questions from our colleagues before we could even sit down. I understood their curiosity. The fate of our project, and very likely the fate of all of their jobs, was being decided at that moment by those seven commissioners. But there was very little to say. We ordered our coffees and Oranginas, and sat at two small round tables facing the Prefecture. We waited, chatted a bit, and watched for any commissioners to exit. But no one appeared.

Ninety minutes later still no one had appeared. We began to speculate. Were the members locked in an impasse? Had some new issue arisen that we were unaware of and not prepared for? Could the French projects receive approvals, and ours not?

Instead of letting the anxiety continue to build I suggested we lunch at our favorite bistro a few blocks away. As we left the café, I detoured to the office of Jacques Téqui, our architect, to invite him along as well.

When I arrived there the receptionist recognized me and waved me on. "He's on the phone, but go on in," she said cheerfully.

Jacques was standing by his desk, jacket off, nodding eagerly as he listened, a broad grin on his face. The smile grew broader when he saw me, and he said into the phone, "He's just walked in. I'll get back to you later. Thank you so much!"

"*Bairn!* I've just heard!" he said, running over and vigorously pumping my hand. "Congratulations!"

"Congratulations?" I said vaguely, not daring to take in what he was obviously saying.

"You don't know? You've won! What a triumph, *Bairn!*"

I hadn't expected the news just then, not from Jacques, and I couldn't quite process what he was saying. I'm not sure I remember well the next few seconds.

"I won? We got it?"

My thoughts raced beyond the good news. Did I dare trust it? How had the vote gone? Was it the four-to-three I had counted on, or had I been able to pick up another vote? A five-to-two decision would make it easier to defend against an appeal.

"What was the vote?" I asked.

"You really haven't heard, have you?" the architect said, leaning back and forth from one leg to the other in his excitement. "It was unanimous, *Bairn!* Seven-to-zero!"

Unanimous?!

Seven-to-zero?

Never, ever had I ever dared hope I could win all of the votes. How was that possible?

"And, *Bairn*—unanimous means there cannot be an appeal against the approval. There is no one to appeal it. They all voted for it!"

Jacques was ahead of me there. Because I never contemplated a unanimous vote in our favor, I hadn't thought through its implications.

Maybe he was right. When there were split CDEC votes in favor—say four-to-three, or five-to-two, as there nearly always was—then those who voted against the majority could appeal the vote up to the national Commission to try to overturn the result. But if there was a unanimous vote at the regional level, seven-to-zero, who had standing to force an appeal? There had never been a unanimous vote before. This was almost more good news than I could manage.

I asked Jacques if he was kidding—surely he wouldn't joke about this would he? "No!" he practically shouted. "Of course not!"

"Then come to lunch," I practically shouted back. "Come along—come celebrate!" The news was sinking in and magnums of champagne seemed particularly appealing just then. Jacques promised he'd be along in just a moment; he wanted to tell his staff.

I turned and strode out of his office, out of the building, and turned left onto Rue Girardon, a tiny street that led over to the bistro. It was one short block that was bordered on both sides by tall stone walls providing privacy to the gardens behind. But at that moment, with no cars or people along that block, the walls also provided privacy to me.

And it was there, in that very private moment, that the news really struck me. Suddenly, a great inchoate surge of relief and amazement, of triumph and pride welled up inside, and nearly took physical control of me. I walked alone down the center of the lane, between those centuries-old walls and clutched my fists and uncharacteristically punched both my arms up into the air, skipped along a step or two, and then pumped them a few more times.

That rare feeling of absolute, pure elation began taking over and I felt as if I was moving in slow motion, weightless. I sensed stillness: I could see cars passing just a block away but couldn't focus enough to hear their engines. I could smell the light fragrance of jasmine growing behind one of those stone walls, and could feel the gritty roughness of the road beneath my shoes, but couldn't take notice of any of it. There was no one specific image in my mind as it raced along, clicking though endless imagery, one scene after another. I thought of what it had taken to get to that point, of the sacrifices, the surprises, and the obstacles. I thought of the two years of taking risks I hadn't even realized I was taking, of the naïveté involved, and of desperately trying to get my bearings. I thought of putting our house and bank accounts on the line, and having nothing left if we lost them, of Pamela and Avery moving over to join in the adventure but also in the risk—of Pamela giving up her job and putting her career on hold. I thought of Balladur's moratorium, of Cara's birth there in France, and my family's support from America. I thought of my father's illness. I thought of so much as I simultaneously soaked in the thrill of having really, finally, planted a stake in this foreign land to launch this new venture, my venture.

I have no idea how long the pure elation held. Probably not more than the fifty or sixty seconds it took to reach the end of that little lane and reenter the world of shoppers, sounds, and traffic lights. But it was a full sensory stand-alone moment in time.

I had created a team in a foreign land from scratch, and against all odds we had won. An idea borne out of desperation two years before and a world away was really, actually, going to become reality.

Events, it seemed, had finally turned my way.

FIFTEEN

Land and Church

Much has been written about the ramifications of Henry VIII's rupture from the Catholic Church in 1533. Among other things, King Henry effectuated one of the greatest land grabs in history. Dotted all across England, north and south, east and west, in cities, towns and villages, were the great cathedrals, the chapels, churches, rectories, artwork, and vast landholdings of the Catholic Church. Overnight and without compensation these assets all became holdings of King Henry. The King promptly turned all the property over to the bishops of his new Church of England, forever cementing their undying gratitude and loyalty. In some ways this hijacking of property was as cataclysmic as the break with Rome itself. This was so because, besides the clergy and parishioners, there is nothing about which a church feels so strongly as its property holdings.

Just over 460 years later, Joey and I belatedly discovered that for the Church of England that axiom was absolutely still the case.

Having established the joint venture with BAA just before Christmas 1993, our European venture suddenly had money, credibility, vision, and drive. By virtue of BAA's wildly successful duty-free operations, we also inherited superb relationships with dozens of the most important fashion brands in Europe, brands such as Burberry, Versace, Armani, and Pringle. The only ingredient missing to launch the new venture was the first site on which to build the first outlet center. The pressure for finding it couldn't have been more intense.

We estimated that the United Kingdom could support up to ten or twelve outlet centers for a total capital value of 1.5 billion dollars or so, averaging 100 million dollars to 150 million dollars per center. Being the first to open a center not only meant becoming market-leader in the United Kingdom, but also meant that we could develop two or three more centers than if we were an also-ran. So, being market-leader equated to 200 million dollars to 400 million dollars of capital value we might otherwise lose. For a couple of Americans fresh off our company's near-bankruptcy, fighting to win 200 million to 400 million dollars of capital value seemed like a smart thing to do.

There were several reasons why being the first to open translated into market leadership. The first company to announce an outlet site in the United Kingdom would garner enormous PR benefits for bringing a new, appealing form of shopping to 57 million Britons. At the very least the fashion-trade press would give the story wide coverage, which in turn would raise our profile to the fashion brands. The first company to open would also likely secure some of the most important British brands to test the new concept. These brands would then be hesitant to open stores in the second and third outlet centers (i.e., our competitor's centers) until it was certain that their first store actually worked well. Such PR and brand-relation advantages would be extremely beneficial in opening future outlet centers.

Notwithstanding that Joey was based in Washington, he remained active in the day-to-day activities in the United Kingdom, with Adrian Wright (UK Managing Director) reporting to him. I stayed focused on France. Every three or four weeks, Joey and I would both fly to England, and join in the semimonthly site acquisition meetings where we reviewed all efforts to scour the British Isles for our first site.

Joey has always had enormous energy, but even for him commuting back and forth across the Atlantic once or twice per month was at best a tiring exercise. Add in the stress of any start-up venture, plus the pressure we put on ourselves to catch and then pass Morgan, and it was no wonder that Joey's demeanor could be pretty itchy by the time he arrived at those site-acquisition meetings. The McArthurGlen venture remained his vehicle to redemption after the S&L debacle. At that point the only obstacle to starting that climb back was securing our first site. Joey literally couldn't sit still until he had it.

We attacked the process of finding that first UK site with palpable intensity. We placed full-page, four-color ads in the real-estate trade magazines, introducing ourselves, and asking for site submissions. Our lawyers combed through databases to find every site in the United Kingdom, which had any form of shopping-center approval already in place.

We also attacked the United Kingdom just as we attacked France, with similar site criteria: forty-five to sixty minutes' driving time from two major cities (so we didn't disturb any downtown retailers), fifty acres right along a highway (for perfect visibility), adjacent to an existing junction (for ease of access to the center), with at least thirty thousand cars passing by per day (to ensure there would be enough shoppers), and with zoning approval for a shopping center in place (to gain time). As in France, we wanted our own Hillsboro, Texas, site somewhere in England.

John Milligan, on behalf of his Jones Lang Wootten site-finding brokers, gently reminded us that, alas, England was not Texas.

For one thing, our requirement that the site be forty-five to sixty minutes outside of any major town meant it would be located somewhere in the North Sea. Such a site, John humbly noted, probably did not meet our "ease of access" criteria.

This was Britain, John repeated, and we would need to be more flexible in our approach.

And yet for all our intensity to find the first site, we needed to be extremely careful in choosing it; a mistake on the first one would be extremely costly. The land costs alone were stratospheric compared to France and America, and for good reason: There is not a lot of land in the British Isles, though there are a lot of people.

Milligan's reports indicated the population of the United Kingdom in the mid-nineties was approximately 57 million people. That was about the same as in France, but France had nearly five times the amount of land. Supply and demand alone dictated that UK land be more expensive. Prices in the United Kingdom versus France were sometimes twenty times higher, costing approximately one million dollars per acre in the UK. Our analysis indicated that sites in England could cost 20 million dollars. Add on top of that another 10 million dollars or so for construction, marketing, leasing, and other costs. Choose the wrong site—a site which does not generate enough shoppers to drive up sales high enough to justify the development costs—and not only do you disappoint the brands with low sales, spoiling those key relationships before you even really get started, but you quickly lose your 10 to 20 million dollars of nonrecoverable costs.

The risks were enough to keep one's mind very focused, even if already fatigued with the pressure to be the first to open.

By early summer 1994, it had been nearly six months since we had signed the joint venture with BAA, and despite the intensity of our search effort, we had nothing. Sites were either not on the highway (Milligan had been right: Britain's land-use laws were usually too protective to permit that), or would never grant zoning permission where we wanted it (ditto), or the landowner wouldn't sell—endless reasons.

And then, finally, we had a break.

Milligan strolled into one of the acquisition meetings with a wry smile.

"I have found the site for McArthurGlen's first center in the United Kingdom," he announced before even reaching the conference table.

As everyone there sat back in our chairs to hear more, he continued: "But I can't tell you where . . . yet." A shower of pens, notepads, and half-eaten apples came raining down on John until he was forced from the room, instructed not to come back until he could tell us everything.

Eventually, we learned that the site was located west of Manchester, in the county of Cheshire. It was situated immediately alongside a busy highway, just north of the intersection with another one. The UK pharmacy chain Boots had applied for and received zoning approval to develop a shopping center there. Because Boots was a client of Milligan's, he had heard about their recent decision to sell rather than develop the site. We immediately swooped in before it went onto the open market. Boots had actually leased the property on a long-term basis, and the underlying owner of the land was the Church of England. It was the Church with whom we would have to negotiate a ninety-nine-year ground lease, structured with a massive upfront rental payment. Nearly five hundred years after its founding, the Church of England still had its strongly held ethos never to lose control of its property. Long-term leases enabled then to retain ownership while also capitalizing on land values.

The group of individuals who ultimately looked after the affairs of the Church of England is known as the Church Commissioners. For all matters regarding church property the commissioners in turn engaged real-estate agents to represent them, though all decisions remained with the commissioners.

From Washington, Joey quarterbacked the negotiations. The terms were agreed fairly quickly, and final documentation pushed along rapidly as well. But then, during the week before the scheduled closing, a fateful phone call came in to our lawyer at the firm Winthrop Eliot. The call was from the agent representing the Church Commissioners.

"Sorry to bother you," the gracious agent started out. "But . . . sadly . . . I must advise you that we've received a higher offer on the Cheshire site. As you can imagine, really, the Church Commissioners have their fiduciary responsibilities to consider, and yes, well . . ."

We had been "gazumped."

The earliest known appearance in print of the word "gazump" was in London's *Daily Express* newspaper on December 19, 1928. While its origins are disputed, the word's meaning is not. It is a verb which connotes "to swindle."

There is a major difference in how a transaction is structured when buying and selling property in England or Wales, versus how it is structured in America.

In the States, once both buyer and seller have signed a valid sales contract, both parties are then legally obligated to complete the transaction as contemplated in the documents. The signatures are usually secured sixty to ninety days prior to the "closing," i.e., the process of actually transferring a property's title from seller to buyer in exchange for money.

In England and Wales, when a buyer and seller have agreed terms for a sale, it is in effect "an agreement to agree," but not legally binding until the moment when the transfer of title and money actually takes place. In reality once the seller has "accepted" an offer for a given price from the buyer, the seller can then accept another, higher offer right up to the moment the closing occurs, notwithstanding the fact that Buyer Number 1 continues to spend very significant sums of time and money on lawyers, title searches, inspections, and the like. When a seller does accept the higher price from Buyer Number 2 and sells the property to Buyer Number 2, Buyer Number 1 has been "gazumped."

To an American used to a different legal structure, gazumping is an odious method of conducting business. In England and Wales, it is legal, it is accepted, and has been practiced with regularity for many decades— clearly at least since 1928. The practice is especially widespread in times of rising real-estate values, where an offer today may be less than another one tomorrow. In all the years and transactions in which Joey and I had been involved in real estate, neither of us had ever seen or experienced gazumping.

"What do you *mean* we've been *gazumped* and *lost* the site?!" Joey screamed through the phone from Washington to London. Our lawyer at Winthrop Eliot could almost hear the words rocketing across the Atlantic without the benefit of copper wires. "Just what does '*gazump*' mean and why the hell didn't *you* protect us against it?!"

It was not an especially good day to be a Winthrop Eliot lawyer representing McArthurGlen.

Joey was practically strangled with fury.

He had called Milligan, asking for an update on the site status. Hearing the news Joey then ricocheted over to our lawyer who, poor guy, was blown backward in his chair so strongly from the rage blowing down the lines that he apparently went for a walk around the block, and didn't come back until the next day.

"How could we be gazumped?! How could the Church Commissioners *of all people* conduct business like this?! Isn't there any sense of probity—at least from them?!" Joey bellowed.

The problem was that it wasn't the lawyers' fault, or Milligan's fault, that we were being gazumped. Gazumping is a fact of life in the English real-estate world, and we were learning our trade while on a feverish tear to be first across the finish line with an outlet site. In fact, it was very likely that our obvious eagerness to buy the site had led to a gazumping. Zealous buyers have a way of radiating their need to buy. Prices have a funny habit of escalating under those circumstances.

The fact remained that the Cheshire site was still a fabulous one for us, with a shopping-center approval in place, situated next to a major highway, with thirty-five thousand cars passing per day, and not located in the middle of the North Sea. It met all of our criteria.

The question was what would it take to close the deal with the Church Commissioners? How much to *re*-gazump?

After a feverish round of negotiations, of expressions of outrage and double-dealing, the facts were laid bare. If we really wanted this perfect site, the site by which we felt we could leap ahead in the race to be market leader, we would need to increase our offer by five million dollars for the first half of the land (the contract allowed us to buy half the site initially and the second half later), and by a similar amount for the second half of land. So with one call from sellers to buyers, ten million dollars can disappear before the phone is even back in its cradle. And that was a call from an agent representing the esteemed and venerable Church of England. It could, I guess, have been worse.

We agreed to pay the increased price. And we hoped we hadn't overpaid to the point of negating the ultimate profitability of our investment.

And yet our baptism into gazumping wasn't over. Soon afterward, we received an even more intriguing call on the matter.

We learned that Roger Morgan had selected a town named Bicester, located in the well-to-do county of Oxfordshire, north of London, for his first outlet site. A week before he was scheduled to close on the site, we received a phone call from the seller, who called to describe an "opportunity." The opportunity, of course, was to gazump Morgan. But to gazump him would require a price increase to the seller, which made it worth the seller's while.

Now this, Joey and I discussed on the phone, was an interesting situation.

Because this was Morgan's first site in England, if we could steal it his start-up efforts would receive a serious body blow. We would surely then have a clear run to be the first to open in England, and from there to be the market leader in the United Kingdom. Market leaders on new retail concepts in the United Kingdom have a wonderful history of having very successful rollouts across Europe. That was a compelling argument for a gazump.

But as compelling as that was, we had just been through a gazumping ourselves, and knew well just how slimy the whole process was. Perhaps because of our American backgrounds, where gazumping wasn't practiced, this "opportunity" was a step too far and too slimy.

We couldn't do it.

So instead of calling the seller back, we called Morgan, our number-one competitor in the United Kingdom and, therefore, in Europe.

We told Morgan of the type of seller he had, and the risk he faced. He thanked us. He hung up. He fixed his problem.

It was, we were to discover many times over the ensuing years, an insight into our own naïveté. No development company to whom we told the story in Europe would have done the same thing under the same circumstances. Oftentimes a listener to the story would shake their heads in reaction.

"That's not how it's played out here," they would usually say. "You have to take your chances when you get them. And you had a chance to nearly put a competitor out of business before he'd even started."

We don't regret what we did. But we did learn the property world in Europe is a different kind of jungle. The incident put us on guard for how else our naïveté might make us vulnerable.

SIXTEEN

Boomerang

With the Troyes approval finally secured, Pamela and I felt there finally was a reason for staying in France and making our home in Paris. I checked in with the lawyer handling my *carte de séjour* application: Was our residency legal yet, I asked? Well, no, not yet, he responded. But the officials were working on it. Keep a low profile, he advised, and he would call the Palais de Justice and check on the file.

During the slow summer months after the June decision, we found an apartment we liked in the Seventh Arrondissement, and finally had our furnishings from Washington shipped over.

The new apartment was located on Rue de Bourgogne, halfway between Rue de l'Université and the Musée Rodin. Like all such apartments in Paris, it gave a new meaning to the word "unfurnished." The kitchen had no sink, counters, cupboards, stove, refrigerator, or any other appliances. It was void of everything save a plumbing pipe sticking up through the floor indicating where the sink should go. In Paris, when you want to make an apartment your home, you work at it. By late August, our kitchen was in, the furniture had arrived, and we were hanging art on the walls.

While we were busy setting up house, the project in Troyes was generating its own momentum. Not only had the local and regional press broadcast the news of the project's approval immediately after the vote ("Green Light for the American Mega-Project"), but the story had also caught the attention of the national press as well. It turned out that the combination of Balladur's moratorium, the project's unanimously favorable vote, and the unusual nature of our outlet concept had created a story with legs. *Le Figaro,* the largest daily newspaper in France, was the first to break it in mid-August, and the national business periodical *La Tribune* followed a week later: "Troyes Euphoric in Advance of McArthurGlen's Arrival." Almost all the news items featured "the giant American McArthurGlen." What never made the headlines, and usually not the story either, was that we were not exactly alone. The two other, smaller projects, both sponsored by French companies we had seen in the anteroom on the day of the vote, had also been approved.

On a Saturday morning shortly after those stories ran, Pamela and I were hanging prints in the tiny half-bathroom in the front hall of our new apartment. I was standing on a little stepladder, hammer in one hand and picture hook in the other, when the phone rang. Pamela and I looked at each other with a mixture of puzzlement and a little foreboding. Who could that be? The phone had just been hooked up and almost no one knew our number. It was too early in the morning for anyone in the States to be calling. I gingerly placed the hammer on the toilet's white porcelain top and walked to the living room.

It was Rochefort, calling from Troyes, and he sounded serious.

"*C'est tombé,*" he said. "It's happened. The Préfet was forced to lodge an appeal."

"Oh my God," I responded, not at all able to absorb the news.

Technically, there had always been the possibility of an appeal, but as the lazy summer months passed with no hint of one, I had hoped the project could silently sneak past the deadline unnoticed. There had been rumors for over a week that something was stirring in the halls of the ministries around Paris, but on that Saturday we were literally only one day away from the end of the appeal period. I had reason to hope we would get through unscathed.

"It was *Matignon,*" Rochefort said, using political shorthand. "Matignon" was the Paris mansion that housed the prime minister and his staff. His meaning was clear. It was people at the very top of the French government who took action.

"But why?" I asked, a hint of anger in my voice. "On what grounds can the Préfet appeal?"

"Politics," Rochefort replied. "He doesn't need any more grounds other than that the minister told him to do it."

There was a pause on the line. I felt rooted in place. I stood in the middle of my new living room, the movers' boxes still piled up all around its edges. In the center were two familiar couches from our home in Washington, our favorite coffee table between them. The apartment was one floor above street level. I remember staring down onto the streetscape below and marveling at the sculpture of flowers in the window of the florist shop opposite our building. Everything seemed a bit too normal, too orderly, to be receiving a call such as this, in the middle of a day such as that.

"The Préfet will undoubtedly write something about regional commerce and your new concept of designer outlets," Rochefort continued. "But the reality is that Balladur declared *le gel,* and for you to get a zoning approval of this size, with its unanimous vote, just months before the presidential election, could make him look weak. I would imagine his boss Chirac is not at all that pleased, either, and Balladur will be feeling the heat."

I didn't have any meaningful response.

"So that's it," I said finally. "It's an official appeal."

"Yes, it's official," Rochefort said. "I'm sorry, *Bairn.*"

I thanked him for calling and hung up. I stood there for a few seconds before turning back to Pamela.

She had heard my end of the conversation and had guessed the news. I found her seated on the floor, leaning wearily against the wall and looking up at me when I walked in.

"It's an appeal, isn't it?" she asked quietly.

"Yes, it is. From the prime minister's office."

"From the prime minister's office," she repeated slowly, meaningfully.

We both remained silent for several moments. I leaned against the opposite wall and slid down until I was also seated on the floor opposite her. The bathroom was so narrow both of us had to bend our legs at the knees. We suddenly had no energy or interest in hanging art. We sat in stillness, the type of stillness where you notice the gentle humming of the refrigerator's motor two rooms away. The street noise outside seemed significantly louder than usual. We sat there, absorbing one of the lowest moments we had experienced together since we'd met. Two years of exhausting work, of facing up to the obstacles one after another as they appeared, of trading all of our support systems at home for a foreign environment abroad, of putting everything on the line for that moment sixty days earlier when a fabulous victory had finally been achieved. And in one call, in one quick moment that interfered with what was just starting to once again be the smooth progression of our lives, all was undone. Suddenly, it was not at all clear we had a reason to make a home in Paris.

"I am sorry, honey," Pamela said to me. "I'm sorry that what was to be our great Paris adventure has ended up becoming such an ordeal."

During my early high-school years, I attended a three-week winter program similar to Outward Bound, a program that taught students how to deal with adversity. The program consisted of hiking and camping trips, some solo, some in teams, in the Green Mountains of Vermont during a bitterly cold February. One of the final exercises was to climb up the north side of the area's tallest mountain and to descend down the other side in time to make camp before sunset. The north side was known as "The Ledges" because of the numerous protruding rock formations there. As we began our hike up the mountain we could not, because of those protrusions, see past the first ledge to view the next. When we reached the first ledge we were able to see the next one, but again could see nothing beyond it, and so on. We never knew how many ledges there were before we would reach the summit, and the counselors would never tell us. The end was never in sight. The only thing the counselors told us was that we needed to hurry in order to make it back to camp before sunset. Hiking in darkness was not an option.

Six hours after sunrise we were still hiking upward, having only reached the fourth ledge. As we continued to climb the wind grew increasingly bitter, and temperatures remained far below freezing. Time was growing short, we were told. Stopping for lunch wasn't possible. We ate as we hiked, and still we couldn't see the summit. By the sixth ledge, several of the students dropped out, turning back drained and discouraged. By the seventh, in midafternoon, tempers flared as the counselors pressed us on with increasing urgency. A few more students turned back. We all had perspiration around our necks and down our backs from the exertion of the hike and the weight of the packs. The frigid wind would sometimes mix with that perspiration and create a chill, which shot to our bones. By then the sunlight was beginning to fade. Hike on, the counselors told us. There was no time to waste.

At the eighth ledge, the sun was about to sink behind the mountain to the west. The hikers banded together and demanded to know, on safety grounds, how many more ledges? Just climb one more, the counselors said, and we would assess the situation from there. The ninth ledge, the last one, involved the shortest hike. We finished it as twilight was ghosting in. As we stumbled over to the highest outcropping of rock, the actual summit of the mountain, we could see a spectacular sunset taking place. We could also see some two hundred yards in the distance the shadowy outline of the vans, which were there to drive us back down the bumpy winding lumber road on the other side of the mountain. We learned it was never in the plans for us to hike down. Those hikers who had persevered to the summit would arrive back at base camp long before some of those who had dropped out.

The lesson, of course, was simple. When adversity hits, sometimes there's no end in sight.

I had other experiences, many other experiences, which taught similar lessons. During college, I became ill with osteomyelitis, an insidious bacterial bone disease that is extremely difficult to vanquish. Three times in college it flared up, punctuating my final two years with long and dispiriting hospital stays.

After college, unexcited by the lure of Wall Street, I embarked on a sailing voyage that would eventually take me from Boston to New Zealand. We were sailing from the Cook Islands to New Zealand when two small cyclone systems collided together to create a much larger one, and bore down on us just where the edge of the Tasman Sea meets the Southern Pacific. We were one thousand miles from any land. We prepared as best we could. We shortened sail down to a storm trysail, and lashed the helm all the way to windward. We precooked meals, secured and stored all movable items, and prepared for the forty-foot ocean swells headed our way. We attached leather belts to our bunks to keep us strapped in when the oceans began its really violent toss-and-turn movements. When the storm hit, it came lashing in with a fury. We were blown backward over sixty miles in two and a half days. On the second day, two massive albatross appeared, circling silently around and around us with their massive twenty-foot wings spans, circling in their grim waiting game made famous to all sailors in Samuel Coleridge's famous ballad, "Rime of the Ancient Mariner." In the end, the boat suffered damage but there were no injuries. We survived the storm because we had prepared.

Sometimes, there isn't time to prepare. When leaving the Marquesas Islands on the same voyage I was swept overboard by a freak wave just after a storm had passed. It was just before sunset with not much time left for real visibility. I only survived by luck and masterful boat-handling by the skipper.

Later, when I finally landed in Auckland, New Zealand, thirteen months after departing Boston, I was greeted once again by a bout of osteomyelitis, cutting short my circumnavigation for good.

Three years later, in graduate school, the disease once more came roaring back, reminding me that, like The Ledges, it was not clear where was the end of the struggle.

After graduate school, there were the usual challenges of starting a career, made all the more acute by working at The Kaempfer Company, which was short on capital and long on ambition. The five-and-a-half year duration of The Warner project was nothing but surmounting one obstacle after another. That in turn was capped by the ferocity of the S&L crisis, which quickly decimated our company's financial foundation, a platform that we had spent so many years building up. I wouldn't exchange any of those events for more tranquil moments. Facing adversity is underappreciated, especially when experienced at a young age. It provides valuable rehearsal time for challenges later in life.

Now, in Paris, faced with the grim reality of the French government's determination to quash my project, all those experiences seemed like background training. The prime minister had declared that there should be no more retail projects developed in France, and when mine popped up on the political landscape as the sole exception to his ban, he slapped it back down again. This, I thought, was some serious adversity, and I could see no obvious route around it.

SEVENTEEN

Never, Never, *Ever* Give Up

It is often said there are two distinctly different worlds in France: Paris, and everywhere else. Paris is the world of high culture, renowned cuisine, and liberal sophistication. It is the part of France that the tourist most often sees.

Then there's the France the tourist usually does not see: the France of the provinces, the relatively unsophisticated France—closer to the earth, slightly suspicious of strangers, often stubbornly conservative. The two worlds are radically different, and both sides often admit there is a gulf between them.

For nearly two years I had been conducting business in the second France, the provincial France, where negotiations might be difficult but are usually straightforward. It was a world where you tended to know who your friends were and could safely assume who were your enemies.

But now I was catapulted into Paris and an entirely new challenge. Suddenly I found myself in the world of *Matignon* and its ministries, a world of the highest and subtlest political nuance, where all those Triple Crown politicians were trying to determine to which agenda they were playing on any given issue. It was a world in which those in power danced a thousand intricate minuets all across the city, in a world of suggestion and managed perceptions.

To begin an assessment of whether and how to respond to the government's appeal I called a meeting of both my legal team and my

Bouygues team, along with François and Eric, for the following Tuesday at 9 AM. This was the first of what became a series of such meetings every Tuesday for the ninety days we had until the national commission hearing in mid-December. It was an impressive group. From our law firm, Gide, Loyrette Nouel, was Maître Gerard Tavernier, known throughout the French legal community as a leading expert on all matters dealing with real estate, and renowned for his acumen and subtlety. Along with him were two young, very smart lawyers, Antoine Vignial and Eric Martin-Impératori, who had advised me on my every legal move since I had arrived in France. From Bouygues came Olivier Jamey, of course, and Jean Dumont, the political specialist who had originally introduced me to Rochefort. Accompanying them was Rene Albert, who headed up Bouygues's construction activities for all of central France, and who was, in consequence, a man with considerable clout. Bouygues had put itself on the line for this project and was not about to lose it without a ferocious fight.

In those first weeks we were usually joined by Rochefort as well, who commuted in from Troyes. He was consistent in advising that "this is the year of presidential elections and this situation is *all* about politics. . . ." Eventually, Rochefort became convinced that the political opposition to my project was too strong to allow for any positive outcome, and he stopped attending the meetings.

As had been the case at Troyes, my fate would once again be in the hands of a seven-member commission, this one comprised of a panel of highly distinguished national figures. It would be presided over by a member of the Conseil d'État, the French Supreme Court. The members of the commission included another representative of the Conseil d'État, as well as a member of the Cours des comptes (the highest court dealing with public funds), a member of the Inspection Générale des Finances (an independent panel charged with auditing the government in power), and three eminent private sector individuals, one appointed by the president of the Sénat, another by the president of the Assemblée nationale, and a third by the Ministre du Commerce. In other words, the commission was a collection of the best and brightest in France, a who's-who of the Powerful and Influential in Paris. It was the type of governmental commission which, if you were working with them for the right reason, you would brag about it to your mother, who would then naturally spread the news far and wide. I, however, wasn't seeing them for the right reason. I didn't call my mother.

I knew I was going to need all the help possible to persuade this august group. So, in addition to my regular Tuesday morning crew, I called an acquaintance whom I had met just after my first visit to France. He was Maurice Herzog, one of the most renowned French public figures of the twentieth century. As a young man in 1950, Herzog became the first person ever to climb Mount Annapurna in the Himalayas. In doing so he became the first to climb any peek over 26,000 feet. Herzog arrived home a national hero, but he had paid a heavy price for his success. He lost his gloves on the mountain's summit and, in the process of descending, incurred severe frostbite on his fingers and toes. Gangrene appeared soon after and there was no choice but for the expedition's doctor to perform amputations out in the field. It was amputation without the benefit of any anesthetics or proper operating-room safeguards.

The book Herzog wrote of his adventure, *Annapurna,* sold more than 11 million copies around the world, and became one of the all-time international bestsellers. Known for his good looks, charm, and elegance (the ladies were frequently smitten), Herzog went on to become Minister of Sport and Culture under President de Gaulle, and served on the Olympic Operating Committee for twenty-five years. He was a legend in France, and a widely respected man. Maurice Herzog wouldn't boast about being associated with the members of the national commission hearing my case. But they might boast about being associated with him.

Maurice was from Chamonix, in the French Alps, and had been mayor there for nine years. Coincidentally, Prime Minister Balladur was also from Chamonix, and had also been mayor there, after Herzog. In fact, Herzog had sold his Chamonix house to Balladur, and knew him well.

I visited Herzog in his office and explained my situation. I asked if he would consider assisting me in my fight against the appeal.

"Let me study this," he said, gracious as always. "*On verra.*"

To a certain extent, those Tuesday-morning sessions were nearly dysfunctional. Each party brought to the table a completely different perspective.

Bouygues's outlook was purely political and didn't consider what the official rules dictated. Maître Tavernier and his colleagues read only the laws and procedures, and were adamant that I adhere to them closely. Herzog was focused on personal relationships, especially with the prime minister, and was all for knocking on his door for a convivial dinner and backroom chat. I was there to listen to all of them, to keep them analyzing with me at the same table, and to develop a strategy for moving forward. I needed all their expertise.

One of our first tasks was to gauge the depth of our opposition. We needed to analyze the myriad rumors circulating as to which interested parties had lobbied for, and which against, an appeal of our original approval at Troyes.

We heard rumors about several of the larger French development firms—the very ones who had two years before refused to consider being my joint-venture partner. They had told me that I "would never get an approval in France," and even if I did, "the McArthurGlen concept would never work" there. The word on the street was that these firms, the likes of Segece, and SCC, and other large development companies, wanted to prevent me from getting a foothold in France. The retail development world, they determined, was a shrinking pie in France, and they did not want to give up even the smallest slice of it to any newcomers, much less an American newcomer.

On the other hand, we heard that the very large and powerful chains of hypermarkets had at first lobbied in favor of an appeal against us, reasoning that if it was impossible for them to secure zoning approvals, why should I get one? But then we heard that they'd changed their minds, and started lobbying aggressively in support of our approval. Apparently, they concluded that if even a unanimous zoning decision could be appealed to Paris, what hope was there for the much more controversial hypermarkets to ever secure an approval?

In the end, there were so many rumors, counterrumors, and conspiracy theories, we finally tossed them all out. Who knew what was true and what was the point of shadowboxing? Better, we thought, to focus our energies where we might have an impact. And so we focused on three areas: the Ministry of Commerce, the advisers within Matignon, and the staff of the panel that would judge our case, especially the executive director, a man named Philip Caton.

In the midst of all this, Herzog, a man of action, decided that the most effective way he could help was to contact the prime minister directly—to go right to the source. He drafted a letter by hand, and, of course, his penmanship—written by a man having no fingers beyond the first knuckle—was highly distinctive, and would be recognized immediately by his old friend, the prime minister. In the letter he explained that I was a family friend (which I was, but not exactly a *long-time* family friend), that I had a novel concept for France, a concept that would create jobs and help the textile manufacturing industry, which needed help (this was all accurate). Herzog went on to say that he was certain that the appeal against my project was merely due to lack of accurate information and not made on the merits. Could the prime minister take a look into this for the sake of the French manufacturing industry? Having popped the letter into an envelope—addressed with the same distinctive writing—Herzog then called on the personal secretary to the prime minister, a woman from Chamonix he'd known for many years. Naturally, she was flattered to hear personally from *Ancien Ministre* Herzog, and gave Herzog her word that she would hand-deliver a letter to the prime minister herself. The next day. Without fail.

Herzog had completed all this within a week of my seeing him. When we met over lunch at his favorite table in his favorite restaurant along the Champs-Elysées, he recounted what he had done. He ended the tale with a *"Voilà!"* his arms open wide, hands turned up, a gesture clearly saying, "See what I have just done for you!" It was one of the grandest *gestes* I had witnessed in France, and I was properly impressed. And, indeed, he had pierced through to the political heart of the Republic, to the man who very likely had been personally involved in the decision to appeal my approval.

I could just imagine the prime minister sitting behind his desk in Matignon, reviewing correspondence with his personal secretary, coming across Herzog's letter and looking up to her dolefully, thinking, "Is this that American project back to annoy me *again?*"

From our Tuesday strategy sessions we fanned out for meetings around Paris. Suddenly I found myself, two years after witnessing my company's meltdown in the S&L debacle, sitting in the Louis XIV salons of

Matignon, one of the great mansions of Paris, former home to Tallyrand himself, waiting to see the prime minister's adviser on the national economy. As I waited, mentally reviewing again my arguments as to why my zoning-board approval should not be overturned, it didn't seem to me at all odd that I was there, seated in the heart of the French government. The long arm of the Parisian political machine had reached all the way down to Troyes, 100 miles away, to quash my project. So, I was reaching right back into the heart of that machine to try and take back what I earnestly believed was rightfully mine. I kept wondering, would an American president interfere with a zoning approval for a midsized shopping center outside of Omaha, Nebraska? If the prime minister of France, head of one of the world's top five GDPs, wanted to be such a microman-ager of the national economy, then that prime minister shouldn't be too terribly surprised to find an American sitting stubbornly on his doorstep, surrounded by the best legal and political advisers Paris had to offer, ready to annoy him *again*. Rochefort may have been right. All the political odds may have been stacked against us, but I wasn't going down without my own ferocious fight.

One Thursday morning, as our presentation date approached, Pamela and I were standing in the foyer of our apartment just as I was about to leave for another day of meetings.

"By the way," Pamela said, "I am arranging a Sunday afternoon family outing with Isabelle and Ricky Ernst." The Ernsts were good friends and fellow ex-pats from Washington D.C. who lived upstairs, and had children our girls' age.

"Fine, fine, fine," I said absentmindedly as I packed a few more files into my briefcase. "Whatever you and the girls want to do is okay with me. I'm not over here for fun."

There was a moment's silence.

"Well, *that's* a ridiculous statement," Pamela said. There was a distinct change in her tone of voice. "And in fact, that's a pretty stupid outlook," she added with conviction.

"What?" I responded distractedly, looking up at her. Now she had caught my attention. "What was that?"

"Well, for you to say 'I'm not over here for fun,' just shows that the whole situation is out of control. If you can't keep the situation in perspective then maybe we shouldn't be doing this. The fun factor was always a major element in our decision to come to Paris in the first place, remember?"

"Yeah, I guess," I said ruefully. I was having trouble disengaging my thoughts from my upcoming meetings, but Pamela was insistent.

"If you can't sit back even for a minute from your laser-focused efforts to turn this project around, then I've got bad news for you. You're putting all your energies, *all of them,* into a fight that is completely stacked against you. This is *their* country, not yours. These are *their* politics, not yours. We've been here nearly two years and we've been living on the edge the *whole* time. Everyone needs to have a break, to have some fun, especially under these circumstances. That's why that was not only a stupid statement but a dangerous one. You have to keep perspective Byrne, or you'll truly exhaust yourself with this."

We looked at each other for a moment or two while I sifted through her reasoning. Clearly, she wasn't wrong. She was being serious without being unreasonable.

"Pamela, I hear you," I said softly, "but you know I am not going to give . . ."

"Oh, don't even say it again—I know: 'Never, never, *ever* give up!' I don't want to hear it again. We've been living that mantra since the start of The Warner, when *that* project almost fell apart a dozen different times. After that, we couldn't give up because The Kaempfer Company was in a meltdown. Maybe it's not a matter of giving up, Byrne. Maybe it's a matter of picking which fight to fight. Maybe this time, this is Balladur's fight and not yours."

I was always impressed by Pamela's debating skills when she was on a roll. And right then she was clearly on a roll. Even more impressive was the calmness with which she delivered her most passionate exchanges. I couldn't help but smile.

"Go ahead, honey, tell me how you *really* feel about it."

She smiled as well. She knew she was right. More important, she knew that *I* knew she was right. She also knew I wasn't going to give up on my fight, but perspective was not a bad thing under the circumstances.

"So, we'll have a family outing with the Ernsts on Sunday," Pamela summed up.

"That will be fun," I said with an honest smile.

There were two themes which we honed at those Tuesday morning sessions. The first was that the Balladur *gel* had been specifically designed to stop the growth of hypermarkets, and the McArthurGlen concept was not a hypermarket. We worked hard, even harder than for the Troyes presentation, to differentiate our designer-outlet concept from hypermarkets. We addressed the issue from all perspectives—legal, commercial, and political. It was a theme we developed in great detail, and then in documentation, over the course of several presentations to Monsieur Caton, of the National Commission. At first, he didn't seem too interested in our case. Then, after a few meetings, suddenly he was. Were we that persuasive? Or had Herzog's letter to Balladur had an impact?

The second theme was our clarifying exactly who was fighting whom in this case. This wasn't an issue of predatory Americans invading the country at the expense of small French retailers. Rather, it was a fight about Paris's power, or perceived right, to dictate to the provinces.

As we saw it, the leaders at Troyes had decided on their own that my designer-outlet project would foster prosperity in their region and help create new jobs. They had backed me with unprecedented unanimity. And as soon as they did so, Paris then calmly strode in and quashed their chosen project in a blatant example of brute politics.

The theme of "Paris dictating to the provinces" was a very potent one just then. It was one of the issues being debated in the presidential election campaign under the rubric of "de-localization." For the provinces, it was a sore point that many of the government's initiatives served well in creating more jobs around Paris, but poorly in creating jobs outside of Paris. The provinces felt they sent taxes to Paris, which often yielded no jobs in return.

This was certainly a powerful issue when the press heard about it. And we ensured that the press did hear about it, both in Troyes and then in Paris, just a few months before the presidential elections. Those stories created headlines that no candidate wanted to see just a few months before election day. Certainly, not a candidate like Chirac—Balladur's boss-to-be—who was going out of his way to appear sensitive to the needs of the provinces.

Though my *interlocuteur* Rochefort was no longer attending the Tuesday meetings, we stayed in touch. I would drop by his office from time to time when I was in Troyes, and he would sometimes pop into mine when he was in Paris. During one session in my office Rochefort again stressed that at the heart of the issue was politics, high-level politics. It could be very helpful, he pointed out, if I made a political contribution to the party of Balladur and Chirac—perfectly legally, of course. He could ensure that in this way I could find a sympathetic ear in the right places to at least listen to my side of the story.

Later, when I reported my conversation with Rochefort to Olivier Jamey, he shook his head solemnly. "That will not do, Byrne. You must not make any political contribution through him. At Bouygues, we are real- ists, and we know perfectly well that political parties require support. So we support them. All of them, Byrne—Left, Right, and center. And how we do it is our business, not yours. We have agreements on how these things are handled. We have made our contributions, and this is one of our projects. We are *not* going to make another one; certainly not another one so that Rochefort earns credit from his seniors in the party.

"Rochefort is overstepping on this one," Olivier went on, shaking his head. "You are not to bother yourself with such matters. Leave this one with us; we will explain things to him."

I remembered feeling as though I was witnessing a process which I was not meant to observe. I was happy to leave it to Olivier and to Bouygues to sort it out. For a moment I felt badly not helping out Rochefort after all the help he gave as my *interlocuteur.* But these were intra-French political matters, and my interference could greatly complicate the goal of saving my project. Time was very short by then; I didn't need any more compli- cations.

In mid-December we appeared before the National Commission.

Maître Tavernier and Eric accompanied me to the hearing. We had de- cided that despite my American accent and awkward French, I should do most of the talking. The hope was that I might come across as more sin- cere; it was, after all, an American concept at issue.

The actual presentation went off without incident. We were well prepared, and so were the members of the commission. They had clearly read
the briefs in advance, and we were able to move quickly through the basic
points of our argument. But I had something new to offer them, something that hadn't been in those briefs. Something I had been working out
with Monsieur Caton.

In addition to all the restrictions I had agreed to accept at the Troyes
hearing, I now offered a new and even more potent pledge. I unveiled a
"McArthurGlen Charter," which I promised would become part of the
legally binding lease document between McArthurGlen and all of the tenants who opened a store with us. In the charter, I committed to working
with only manufacturers or brand owners. I committed to offering only
end-of-season stock from those manufacturers, or slight seconds from the
factory production. I was guaranteeing there would be no gray-market
goods or cheap Asian imports. I would certify to the shopping public—
and my tenants would also certify—that we would abide by a series of
rules, which the charter articulated and which no other shopping center or
outlet center had theretofore committed to.

In addition, each tenant and I would sign a framed copy of this charter
and display it in the windows of each store in the outlet center. The cumu-
lative effect of all this was to legally define a new retail concept that had
never before existed in France, and which clearly differentiated the
McArthurGlen concept not only from hypermarkets but from all other
forms of shopping centers. It also exposed us to punitive measures that
could be imposed upon us by the government agencies responsible for
policing the "rules of commerce" applicable to shopping centers. In other
words, I was putting my company's money and reputation where my
mouth was.

When I finished, the president of the commission, one of the esteemed
justices of the French Supreme Court, posed a question to me. By the time
he finished his highly articulate query couched in an arcane, polysyllabic,
and incredibly legalistic French vocabulary, completely foreign to me, I
could only respond with a blank face, a weak smile, and raised eyebrows
while I tried to decipher what in the hell he had just said.

Well now, I thought to myself, *this* is an awkward moment.

In those weekly Tuesday-morning sessions we had succeeded in deciding which tactics to employ when appearing before the commission. But

we had never considered that I could end up speechless with confusion once there.

For a second, as I looked around the table from Supreme Court Justice to Inspector General of Public Funds to the esteemed Appointee of the President of the French Senate, and to all the others there looking back down the polished mahogany table at me—"the American with a new idea"—I could only think, "Oh God, this time I am *really* in over my head. . . ."

Thankfully, Maître Tavernier gracefully stepped in and responded to the question with vocabulary just as arcane and polysyllabic. He then answered the next several questions, and Eric and I fielded one or two easy ones. Suddenly the meeting was over, and we were out of the hearing room, and walking down the steps of the Palais de Justice, not really knowing if we had fared well or bombed out altogether. The three of us chatted on the steps for just a few moments. We all agreed that we had given it our best shot. Not just at the hearing, but everything leading up to it.

I toyed with the idea of heading back to the office with Eric. I realized, though, that there was absolutely nothing for me to do there. Once again, the future of my fledgling company lay not in my hands but in the hands of seven strangers seated in a government building far removed from my world. All I could do was hope.

I thanked Maître Tavernier and Eric for their support, hailed a taxi, and directed it to Rue de Bourgogne, back to our apartment, the apartment still lacking artwork on its walls.

In the taxi I suddenly felt very light. It wasn't so much that a heavy load had been lifted from my shoulders. Rather, it was a realization that there was *nothing left to do*. After so many months—two years, in fact—of struggling to keep up with all that needed to be assessed, analyzed, managed, and presented, suddenly now there was nothing left to be done. Until a decision emerged from those commissioners, any new efforts on my part would be meaningless.

As the taxi pulled up to the entrance of our building it started to snow, the first snow of the year. I buzzed the apartment from the intercom at street level, and when Pamela answered I asked very simply, "How about a walk?"

It was highly unusual for me to be home at three o'clock in the afternoon.

Pamela had been surprised to hear my voice. She'd be right down she said. Our housekeeper, Mely, would stay with the kids.

While I waited I marveled once more at Pamela's parking expertise for our seven-seater Renault Espace. Pamela was becoming quite Parisian: The car was placed just ten feet from our door, angled three-quarters onto the sidewalk and one-quarter onto the street, smack in the middle of a NO PARKING zone. So, too, were the fifteen or so cars behind her. Like nearly all the other cars there, Pamela's sported a fresh *billet*, a parking ticket, on the windshield, just as there had been twenty or so other *billets* in the last month, and every month. Collecting parking tickets is almost a sport in Paris. No one pays them.

Why?

Because President de Gaulle had once unexpectedly forgiven all unpaid parking tickets as a *geste* to ring in the New Year. Instantly it became, in the minds of the French public, an *acquis sociaux*: a privileged right. Once given in France, beware ever try taking away a benefit. It is *acquis*: acquired. Hence, early in January of every year the presidential decree arrives that all have been banking on the prior twelve months: parking-ticket amnesty. We must have had over 150 tickets by that time, testimony to the difficulty of running a growing household in the tight confines of Paris.

When Pamela arrived downstairs she gave me a kiss, and a hug, and then looked at me expectantly. I could see she wanted to ask how the presentation had gone, but somehow, intuitively, she grasped my mood, and said nothing. In return I just gave her a shrug, then a hug, and she understood.

We walked down the Rue de Bourgogne and around the Assemblée nationale to the Pont de la Concorde. The snow was light but steady and was just starting to stick on the roads. Paris was looking beautiful in her new blanket. It was a fabulous moment for a stroll through her streets.

We turned right after crossing over the Seine on the Pont de la Concorde, and walked down along the river's embankment. We spoke mainly about Paris and our living there, and how was it possible that it had already been so long—two years—since I had left our new house on the first flight to Paris. We walked up a ramp from the Seine to street level again, and crossed over into the Jardin des Tuileries. By now the snow had blanketed everything and the distinctive shapes of the Parisian street lamps, the benches, and the carousels stood out. Everything was still. Very, very quiet and still. The scene reminded us of images from the master photographers who had lived and worked in Paris: Robert Doisneau, Brassaï, and Henri Cartier-Bresson. We spoke especially of Cartier-Bresson's images from right around that particular area: the banks of the Seine and the Tuileries. The soft northern light was the same as fifty, sixty years before when those images were created. Very much of the scenery was, in fact, exactly the same. Despite its own adversities, Paris endures.

We had been walking arm in arm and still hadn't discussed the hearing. We just chatted about things we'd like to see and do while we were still living there.

We emerged from the Tuileries, turned left, and walked along the Seine again until we reached the Pont Neuf where we crossed back over and changed course, drifting back toward home. The wind had come up, and Pamela and I walked together as a tight unit in the cold. The streetlights were flickering on in the white city streets and I started to relax. Pamela noticed.

"I picked up the airline tickets," she said. We had long since finalized plans for what was to be an important Christmas with my parents.

I nodded. And then, finally, I said, "I think we did well this morning. We'll probably know the decision before we leave."

"That's good," she said.

EIGHTEEN

The Call

One of the many indulgences that France has invented for relieving stress is a regime called "thalassotherapy," or water therapy, conducted at a seaside spa. Using seawater, seaweed, sponges, minerals, mud, and other forms of nature's aquatic life, thalassotherapy has a specific treatment for whatever ails you and many more just in case.

One of the professed benefits of thalassotherapy is that it is particularly well suited for women who have recently given birth. Deciding that "when in Rome . . ." Pamela and I, accompanied by newborn Cara, decided to retire to the beautiful island of Belle Isle off the coast of Brittany to a well-known thalassotherapy spa. It was famous for hosting celebrities, including many times hosting President Mitterrand during his annual *cure,* a three-week immersion of seawater and mud during the August recess.

As an American entering the spa for the first time I was struck by the prevalence of nudity. Clothes, apparently, clog up the process and so, the thinking went, why interfere with nature? In the treatment rooms the very polite women attendants wait expectantly until you disrobe. Then starts the mud application, or the salt rubdown, or the mineral bath, where they delicately scrub those microbes into your skin, all over, so that you needn't cause stress doing it yourself.

I assumed, given the reputation and professionalism of the spa, that all the treatments were clinically administered in the same way, with the same process, to all clients, time after time. So it was a bit odd when I emerged after the sea-mud treatment to discover a variation in the treatment from Pamela's to mine, both with the same young attendant, one after the other. After being painted with thick sea mud all over my body, forehead to ankle, I was left coccooned in a NASA-style thin aluminum blanket that prevented any air from moving in or out of the "wrap." After thirty minutes of perspiring profusely inside the blanket, thereby permitting the mud to enter my pores, I arose to be de-wrapped. I then stepped over to the shower in the treatment room to wash the muddy remains from my body.

"Oh pleez," offers the young woman from Brittany, "I assist you with that . . ." as she reaches for a sponge and softly wipes me down.

"That's funny," says Pamela when we compare notes afterward, "she didn't offer to sponge it off me . . ."

Hmmm, I begin to think, and Mitterrand stayed here for three weeks at a stretch . . .

Later, in my rotation of treatments, I visited what was dubbed "the hose room." It was a thirty- to forty-foot long, low-ceilinged room, completely tiled in white on all walls, floor, and ceiling. It felt like a quasi-tunnel, with the far end closed off. Coiled at the near end was a hose, two inches in diameter the type that can withstand highly pressurized water coursing through it.

Upon entering, I studied the setup for a moment and was thinking that whatever went on in that tunnel was certainly not for me, when a short burly middle-aged madam entered and, without a smile, firmly pronounced "*Allons-y*" ("Let's Go").

I began to explain, "*Pardonnez-moi,*" that I was taking a pass on this one, when she came over with some determination to help me disrobe. Thinking that actually I might be safer just doing as I was told, I hung up my robe (keeping my back to her) and strode over, in my *au natural* state, to the far wall. Only when approaching it did I notice two steel rings bolted into the wall up high and to both sides for my hands to grasp onto while I faced the wall.

I was reflecting that perhaps this seemed a bit too medieval for me when *Spooshh!*—a jet stream of seawater slammed into my lower calf muscle with a vengeance. Madam then slowly edged that two-inch high-velocity jet stream up the back of my left leg, up my left thigh to my bare left buttocks, over a few inches (*steady* there, I silently signaled to her, *steady*), and slowly back down the right leg, staying fairly close but not perfectly on the meridian line of my leg as she navigated. When she finally arrived down to my right ankle I breathed again.

But *Spoossh!*—she was off on another slow tour of lower limbs, and after that up to my upper torso and arms. The power of the seawater stream was so strong that when it hit my back it became difficult to breathe. It was the strongest massage I had ever experienced. After what seemed an hour of having Niagara rush at me it suddenly stopped. I had survived, and was just beginning to reflect that in fact it wasn't so bad when madam pronounced in coarse English *"Turn 'round . . ."*

Turn *around?* For a frontal assault?? Thoughts about the safety of my manhood raced through my mind.

Silence in the quasi-tunnel while I meditated on the command.

"Turn 'round . . ." she repeated.

I glanced over my shoulder to see her standing with legs squarely on the floor, hose held waist high with both hands. With some impatience she waved an arm in a swirl, signaling a turn-around motion.

I eased up my grasp on the rings and began slowly turning to face her. Just as my back was flat on the wall behind me I heard the *Spooossh!* and could swear I saw a slight smirk on her face just before I closed my eyes, just before the jet stream tore into me.

I was in a meeting with Jim O'Rourke, the president of Ralph Lauren/Europe, when his secretary poked her head in.

"Excuse me, but there's a phone call for Mr. Murphy. The gentleman said it was important—that I should interrupt you."

Jim had been president of Ralph Lauren/Europe for four or five years at the time, and he looked and acted the part: a handsome man, projecting great self-confidence, and dressed in an elegant Polo herringbone jacket with a spread-collar shirt and his trademark gold cuff links. Jim had engineered a remarkable turnaround for the brand during his years in Paris. He and the core team he assembled—including Brenda Bertholf, Elizabeth de la Nue, and others—had made the Polo brand so strong that everyone in Europe wanted work with it. He could afford to be highly selective with whom he chose to meet. He certainly was not accustomed to having visitors taking calls in his office, chewing up his valuable time.

"This will just take a second," I said apologetically to Jim and his colleague Philip Favre. "I don't know who would be calling me here." I was immediately concerned that something was amiss with Pamela and the girls.

"Hello, this is Byrne," I said when I picked up Jim's phone from his oversized mahogany desk.

"*Bairn*—Gérard Tavernier. Sorry to disturb you. Can you speak now?"

Gérard. My lawyer. No family problems then. Still, something was urgent. It was the Monday after the make-or-break hearing at the Palais de Justice—presumably his call was in connection with that.

"It's not really a convenient moment, Gérard. May I call you in ten or fifteen minutes time?"

I didn't relish hearing whatever news was so urgent in front of the two most important people at one of my most important potential customers. A bit unseemly to puncture the Polo air of serene elegance with either moans of despair or shouts of glee.

"Yes, yes. Please call when you can," Gérard was saying. I didn't like the gravity in his voice.

It took an effort to remain focused on the meeting with Jim and Philip, but I finished up as dispassionately as possible. I didn't absorb much of what they were saying as I replayed Gérard's voice in my mind, searching for hints of the news to come.

When I left Jim O'Rourke's office I didn't have the patience to wait for the elevator, but stutter-stepped down the three flights past the Men's Department, the Women's Department, and onto the ground floor, past the doorman at the double oak doors, and out onto the street. As I hurried down the Rue Royale I stepped into a little café, and ducked downstairs to the public phone in a narrow corridor opposite the washrooms.

"Maître Tavernier, *s'il vous plaît*," I said to the law-firm receptionist.

"*Bairn* . . ." Gérard began, just as the door to the men's room behind me opened and a very audible *sshsluussshhhh* echoed off the narrow walls of the hallway. "*Bairn* . . . where are you *now?*"

"It's a long story, Gérard. What's up?"

"Well, I received a call from Monsieur Caton today," Gérard began slowly. "An unofficial call, you understand. It is not customary for him to do so."

"Yes?"

"Well, it seems, *Bairn,* that . . . well . . ." he hesitated, and then, "you got it! You got the vote—your project is approved!"

I don't remember much about the rest of the call.

Gérard quickly put me on the speakerphone and there were his associates, Antoine and Eric, who were just as excited as I was.

I asked Gérard, was this the end of the process? No more appeals?

"Oui, bien sur," he confirmed. "Well, technically something is still possible, but I have never seen it in twenty years. Consider yourself clear."

I thanked them again and again, and finally hung up. I took a breath, leaning backward on the wall just behind me, and stood still, eyes closed in that narrow, dimly lit hall for several moments, alone with the news. Alone with the result of all that angst and effort, once again reduced to one short phone call.

Then, I started slowly back up the narrow staircase and out the café to the sidewalk. This time I didn't have the euphoric, jump-to-the-sky reaction I had when I heard the news of the approval in Troyes. This time I only felt deep, deep relief. Just relief and thanks that the last round of the fight was over. I was a little more seasoned by then. I had survived, and apparently I had won—barely—on points.

I walked slowly along the street, wanting to keep the news to myself a bit longer. What an incredibly long struggle, I thought to myself. I hoped, desperately, that this was the last ledge to climb.

I walked into the nearest wine store, bought three bottles of Veuve Clicquot champagne, and burst open the door to our office, spraying champagne as far and wide as possible, purposely aiming it at the resulting shouts and squeals inside.

NINETEEN

Responding in Context

The regional newspapers in and around Troyes quickly spread the news about McArthurGlen's unlikely victory in Paris, as did the national press that had been following the controversy and our on again/off again tribulations.

Two days after the press wrote of our victory came the counterattack that I had hoped to avoid. A newly formed retailer association in Troyes named Mercatus announced to the world that it would appeal the latest decision in our favor to the French Supreme Court. (On the phone to Gérard Tavernier, I sputtered in exasperation: "Gérard—the *Supreme Court?* My little regional zoning approval is worthy of the *Supreme Court* of the Republic of France?!" Gérard glumly intoned his response: "This is the technicality I mentioned, *Bairn.* I admit, this is a rarity . . .")

And then barely one week later, there was another unwelcome surprise. Two new approvals were granted to outlet projects in Troyes. One of them was for a small project, but the other was substantial, and would have an impact directly on my project. Marques Avenue, the existing outlet center and my prospective strongest competition, received approval for a large extension that would ensure it remained at least twice as large as McArthurGlen (presuming, of course, we were ever allowed to build). Clearly, the local politicians wanted to ensure that the homegrown favorite remained twice as large, with twice the number of brands, and, therefore, twice the drawing power for the shoppers choosing which center to visit. The increase in size was a major competitive advantage for Marques Avenue because there wasn't time enough in one day for a shopper to visit both locations. The market rules of supply and demand, of competitive advantage and disadvantage, were being decided in the backrooms of politicians' offices. I began to recall that memo which François and I found on the train about the "dangers of McArthurGlen's arrival . . . and something must be done." Something, it seemed, was being done.

At first, the retail association Mercatus threatened to fight these two new approvals as well as ours. In March, though, they suddenly announced they were not going to appeal the new approvals at all. Marques Avenue and the other project were free to develop as soon as they wanted. Construction started the next day in what appeared to be a well-coordinated move.

In a second step, Mercatus clarified that it had indeed filed an appeal to the French Supreme Court against the December decision in Paris, but only against McArthurGlen's project. The other two French projects, which had been a part of the original appeal, had been silently dropped from the protest.

So the score then stood as follows: Of the five projects approved over that six-month period, four were French-sponsored, and one—McArthurGlen—was not French. All four French projects were now suddenly free to proceed, and only McArthurGlen remained subject to an appeal to the French Supreme Court.

Hmmm.

Of the five projects approved, only ours had received a unanimous vote in its favor. Only our project had carefully defined what it would do to protect the local retailers, and to assist the downtown hotels and restaurants in attracting the millions of out-of-towners to their front doors. Only ours had placed limits on the types of stores it would allow in its center, the merchandise it would carry, the type of food it would offer. Only ours had promised to make all these commitments in legally binding documents, which were to be publicly displayed for all to see.

The pattern was clear.

And then, in the middle of March, we discovered we had yet another legal battle. Not only had our zoning approval been appealed, but our building permit was appealed as well.

At that moment it would have been easy to ascribe all of my difficulties to straightforward anti-Americanism. Simple (but naïve) analysis would have contended that the French reasoning went as follows: "The Americans failed at Disney and created havoc there for all concerned. Why should we support them here in Troyes?" Such an argument might have comforted my self-esteem, but it would have no success in the public forum. I didn't need sympathy, I needed a solution. Cries of xenophobia would have solved nothing and inflamed a lot of people I didn't need inflamed.

I had to remind myself again that it was I who had come into their country with a new concept. It was *my* company, but it was *their* culture. I had made the decision to plunge forward in France, even after all the French companies declined to be my partner. I had accepted the risk of working there, and it was then simply too late to give up on France. I had invested too much time and money, and frankly, I was too close to success. Clearly, this was not just my opinion—my opponents knew how close I was to succeeding. That was why their opposition was so intense.

I decided that as long as I needed to play within the context of the French culture and as long as I had to abide by rules which they had written, then maybe I could start interpreting those rules the same way as they did—to my own advantage.

During one of my repeated visits to Troyes during those months I bumped into Rochefort as he exited the Chamber of Commerce. I hadn't seen much of him since I had disappointed him with the news that I wasn't making contributions to his political party. Since then he had been notably absent in playing the role of my *interlocuteur.* When I had later asked the appropriate person at Bouygues what they had done about the issue of Rochefort's solicitation, he just looked at me and, without a word, smashed his right fist into the palm of his left hand, and twisted it aggressively back and forth, implying they had, with some roughness, put the offending party back in his place. The fist hit the palm with such a *SMACK!* I winced at the implications. Clearly, Rochefort had been embarrassed inside his own party. At the least, he wouldn't be too terribly happy with me. I wondered: Was it possible that he might now be assisting, if only through benign observation, the mounting opposition to my project? Now, as I faced him at the doors of the Chamber of Commerce, I wondered could it be that Rochefort, who had once been my staunchest ally, had been so infuriated by his embarrassment that he was no longer backing me?

"Ah, Monsieur Murphy," Rochefort said with a broad smile across his face. "I hear you're having some difficulties with your project. Those retailers certainly know how to fight, eh?"

"Yes, Monsieur Rochefort, they certainly do. And you know? I don't think it's just the retailers. I think there are others around Troyes who know how to fight as well," I responded with steady eye contact right back at him. "As you advised me at the outset, there are many unseen forces when it comes to politics. And I have learned that in France most new business initiatives involve politics."

"Yes, especially those which require public approvals."

"Exactly," I responded evenly, "but what I find interesting is that the rules of the fight sometimes change, even in the middle of the fight."

"Yes—that is the essence of politics . . . the building and rebuilding of coalitions as the fight evolves," Rochefort continued, smiling as he spoke of his favorite topic.

"Yes," I agreed, "but sometimes there are surprises. Sometimes the rules of the fight are rewritten by those who are least expected to do so. Sometimes, as we say in English, 'turn about is fair play.'"

Rochefort continued smiling for a second, and then adopted a slightly puzzled look. I smiled back and walked on to my meeting.

"So let's make a summary of all our research," I said to the conference room full of advisers.

The Tuesday-morning team was now reassembled with a similar mission but under different circumstances. Bouygues was again represented by Jean Dumont, their in-house political adviser, Rene Albert, the head of the Bouygues Division for central France; and, of course, Olivier, my constant guide. Gérard and his colleagues, Antoine and Eric, were attending from the law firm. Maurice Herzog was there, too, joined by François, Eric, and myself from McArthurGlen.

"Well," said Gérard, "we have confirmed that the appeal to the Supreme Court has definitely been lodged. However, it will take a year and a half to two years before the court can hear the case."

"And you say that this appeal actually does *not* prevent us from starting construction and moving ahead with development?" I asked.

"That's correct," Gérard confirmed.

"And if ultimately the Supreme Court hears the case and rules against us, they would have the legal right to force us to demolish the center, even if it had been built and opened for, say, six months or a year?"

"That's also correct," Gérard again confirmed.

"And they could do so even if there were two hundred people working there and we had invested twenty million dollars in the development?" I pressed.

"Legally they would have that right," he repeated grimly.

That was the bit I didn't find terribly encouraging.

"And what do you make of the merits of their arguments against us?" I asked.

"Well, I do not agree with them. They argue that the commission did not properly take into account the effect the McArthurGlen center would have on the downtown retailers. While the decision issued by the commission does not directly address that point, it does generally say it has reviewed the information before it, and found in favor of McArthurGlen. That information would include all the impact studies you were required to submit."

"Do you think that's enough for us to win our case?"

"*Bairn,* while I think so, it is not I who will be making the decision. One cannot predict what nine justices of the Supreme Court shall decide."

Silence for a moment as we all let that soak in.

"Okay, Rene, what about the building permit?" I said, turning to the counselors from Bouygues.

"For the building permit I can confirm that it was issued three weeks ago, in conformity with our application, that is to say, in conformity with the design that we submitted. However, as you know, an appeal has been lodged against the building permit. The people who filed the appeal followed the procedures precisely, so it has to be seriously considered by the Troyes authorities."

"And the grounds on which the appeal was made—do they have merit?"

"Even if they did, it would only be on technical grounds. We're quite sure we can work with the authorities in Troyes to amend the building permit so that eventually we can proceed." Rene said with a calming sense of authority. Clearly he had seen similar tactics many times before.

Then I asked what was for me the key question.

"And does the appeal against the building permit legally prevent us from starting construction?"

"No, it does not."

"Well," I said, "I'm beginning to understand how the game is played here. We've followed all the rules, pursued all avenues of appeal where and when possible. And still there is opposition to us, organized and efficient, with almost no fingerprints left behind. We alone are stymied, while all the other projects are moving forward."

I paused for a moment. There was very little time to debate the action plan. For outlet shopping, there were two peak sales seasons of the year, each dictated by school holidays. Sixty percent of outlet sales in Troyes were earned during the Back-to-School season in October, and then the spring break in March. We were aiming to meet the critical October opening date, just six months away. If we failed to open by October 5, we would have to delay the opening another six months to the following March. The months in between were slow and couldn't justify the expense of opening a center during that period. That meant we had only six months to grade the thirty acres of land, lay in the sewer, water, and electric lines, build forty-three shops in 150,000 square feet of construction—the equivalent of building approximately four to five city blocks of retail. Then, after we finished construction, the stores would need to complete their own internal construction, load in their inventory, and hire and train 180 to 220 staff, people who had never worked in an outlet center before. All this, of course, presumed that in the meantime we'd be able to sign up forty-three different brands at terms we'd accept. As we sat in the conference room, with all the chaos of the appeals, bad press, and rumors, no brand was willing to sign anything. Most wouldn't even agree to meet with us. All were taking a wait-and-see approach to the fate of McArthur-Glen.

But by then I knew much more about the context in which I was operating. I had followed all the rules. But it was time to fight back.

"It seems that the only way we're ever going to get McArthurGlen up and running in France is if we start construction right now," I declared, "so I'm going to sign the construction contract, cut loose all of sales and marketing programs in order to open next October 5. We'll fight the appeals, but we'll construct at the same time. What we're up against at this point is nothing short of bullying and harassment. I have no doubt there will be more of the same—more rule-bending and more extraordinary attempts to keep us out. But if we don't show confidence in ourselves and in our project we'll never open in France, and that could mean we'll never get going on the Continent.

"Gérard," I went on, "I appreciate the fact that you can't guarantee us victory in the courts two years from now. But if there's anything I've learned about France, it's that the entire culture and economy is about job *preservation* and not job *creation*. It's about enjoying the status quo and protecting what is already there. I don't blame them for that, but now let's finally turn that to our advantage.

"If you tell me I have two years until the Supreme Court renders a decision, I'm telling you that by then we'll have invested twenty million dollars in the local Troyes economy, opened the center, and created approximately two hundred French jobs. We'll have generated three million shopping visits per year, and our estimate is that a third of those will go to downtown Troyes for restaurants, hotels, and more stores. I don't believe the political environment—much less common sense—will permit our center to be closed down and the jobs to be lost."

There was a noticeable shift in the room's atmosphere. Nearly all acknowledged their agreement with a nod of the head.

"So," I said, "we start tomorrow. Rene, let's get your crew mobilized on site and cut loose the construction. Gérard, let's work all legal angles on the current appeals. When the next appeal is thrown at us, we'll work that one, too. In the meantime, we press on regardless. We're moving on."

TWENTY

Getting Underway

I was just climbing out of the taxi next to the construction trailers when suddenly, *BAM!,* the flimsy aluminum door of the nearest trailer came flying open. I saw a familiar black-stitched-leather cowboy boot that had just kicked it open reach down to the wooden step below. An instant later its black-stitched twin joined it. John Nicolosi was in Troyes, and I couldn't help but chuckle at the sight. It was a long way and a long time since our last project together—The Warner, a hundred years ago in Washington.

"Hey, John! It's a beautiful day in France, isn't it?" I shouted over, goading him.

John looked over, as his hands wrestled a Winston cigarette from its box.

"Buzz *off,* Byrne. You got me into this mess."

"Ah, but John, whatever mess you're in is a *bee-u-tee-ful* mess," I responded with cheer. "It's a much more beautiful mess than the mess that I've been in for the last two-and-a-half years. At least now we are actually under construction," I said in an upbeat tone. "Cheer up—it's happening now, John. It's *act-u-al-ly* happening!"

John Nicolosi, The Kaempfer Company's head of construction now commuting to France to help me, was a stocky five-feet seven with jet-black hair, balding on top, a permanent suntan, and deep dark eyes that missed nothing. John came at you with his wise-guy accent, colorful language, razor-sharp wit, and, if you were lucky, a big smile. John grew up in a Brooklyn world of ten city blocks, with tough love as the guiding principle.

"As a kid," John would explain, "you stayed in line cuz if you didn't you were whacked about the head with a rolled newspaper until you fell back in line.

"It was pretty simple," John would continue. "Parents made the decisions and kids followed them. Not doing so had immediate consequences."

Brooklyn in those days reflected the immigration patterns that had shaped New York City for half a century. John's immediate neighborhood and the outer circle just beyond it were full of first- and second-generation Italians certainly, but also Jews, Poles, Lithuanians, and the Irish—lots of Irish. Everyone learned to get along with others but everyone was also intensely aware of their own tribe. Nobody had any wealth. Everything started and ended with your own family. John's first job, as a young teenager, was in construction, carrying cinderblocks around building sites for bricklayers to put into place. He kept on in construction for the next thirty years. His skills, energy, and personality had taken him to a lot of places. Now they had brought him to Troyes.

"Hey, Byrne—you can joke all you want. But what you've thrown me here isn't funny." He paused to light his Winston, his hands cupped against the breeze, and then looked up. "Normally I am in on the design of a project, and I'm the one who bids it out to builders. So, I put the project on my terms. Here, you give me a project that's already designed, hand it over to the biggest construction company in the country, and tell me to work with them. So what's to work? They've got all the fuckin' leverage— they even *own* the subcontractors! And you give me five measly months to build what should be a nine-fuckin'-month job. Big thanks, Byrne! *Big* thanks."

He looked around the site and shook his head a little.

"Normally," he continued, "this type of job requires a lot of give-and-take. Those French SOBs in there," he said, indicating the nearest trailer, "they are giving nothing and are takin' every-damn-thing they can."

John pulled one last drag on his cigarette, then threw it on the ground, and stomped on it with the point of his right black-stitched boot.

Just having John around made me smile. We had worked so closely together during the years in Washington, especially on The Warner project, it was comforting to have him at my side again. He was always gruff, and foul-mouthed, and coming at you with his Brooklyn attitude. But in fact, he was all heart, and if you treated him honestly and fairly, he would never let you down. Never. Just at that moment, though, I decided not to tease him anymore. It was his turn for adjusting to Gallic ways.

I was three hours late in arriving in Troyes that day because my lawyer had told me the Palais de Justice had requested my presence. It seems someone had just taken note of my application for a *carte de séjour* and a *carte de commerçant,* the permits to live and work in France, the applications which were submitted two years before. The examiner wanted to *"faire le point,"* to touch base with me. In the hourlong interview he asked me almost exactly the same questions which a woman examiner had asked me two years before. I knew better than to upset the *fonctionnaire,* as the all-powerful government workers are called. I diligently answered all questions as though they were sparkling with originality. After much shuffling and a bit of Xeroxing, he pronounced the interview over, that the Palais de Justice would be in touch, and that I was free to go. It hadn't occurred to me that I was anything other than "free to go," but I thanked him with somber eye contact and a nod, and off I escaped.

The typical layout of a McArthurGlen center was a horseshoe-shape of some forty or so shops facing in toward a parking lot. It is called an "open plan" design. Large plateglass windows provided for a full display of merchandise at each store. The design ensured that when a shopper arrived and stepped from their car they could see all the brand names overtop each store's entrance. As they approached the shops the large window displays of stock from Polo Ralph Lauren, Nike, Versace, Timberland, and a few dozen others invited them in. As the shopper moved around the horseshoe, walking around what we called "the edge," the design ensured that the shopper retained a line-of-sight view of nearly all the stores' signage and the display windows. The shopper was thus invited to continue along that edge to see what their next favorite brand was offering.

John and I were standing in the middle of the horseshoe a few months into the construction process when Philip Morin, the head of our Paris construction department, asked us casually, "What about ramrodders?"

John and I looked at each other dumbly.

"What are ramrodders?" John asked.

"They are thieves—dangerous thieves who operate with stolen cars or trucks."

With a sweep of his arm he indicated the horseshoe layout.

"Ramrodders will love this open plan design. All of the shops have plateglass windows facing the parking area. Ramrodders will steal a truck and drive it at high speed through the storefront window. Then they snatch as much merchandise as they can, and escape in another stolen car or truck waiting at curbside. Total operation usually takes five minutes or less."

John and I glanced all around the horseshoe, all along the edge—the edge designed to maximize the merchandise display through those very large plateglass windows. Windows that were large enough to drive a truck through. Philip was right: It was a picture-perfect design for ramrodders.

"They especially like sportswear," Philip added.

We then glanced over to the larger units, the ones we had already earmarked for Nike, Reebok, and Puma. Other stores were reserved for Levi's, Polo, Aigle, and Timberland—all sportswear brands whose merchandise ramrodders would have no problem selling on the black market.

"Okay, Philip, we get the message," said John with his Brooklyn get-to-the-point approach. "What's the answer?"

"We have to build a barrier between the shops and the parking area. Something strong enough and big enough to stop a truck, yet low enough to give customers a clear view of the shop windows. Something like a string of steel bollards, twelve inches in diameter, jutting perhaps a meter high above the ground, but two meters deep into the ground."

John began rolling his eyes at the cost, a figure which clearly wasn't in his budget.

"Yes, I know," Philip acknowledged, "it's expensive. Very expensive. But it'll save us a lot of money in the long run. And it will be good for our reputation. It will not help the launch of our new concept in France if it becomes known as 'McArthurGlen—Ramrodders' Favorite.'"

John was looking down at his boots, toeing the brown earth where the bulldozers had scraped off the topsoil. Construction in France, he was learning, was a bit more troublesome than in America.

"But more importantly," Philip went on, "we must also protect ourselves from gypsies."

"*Gypsies?*" John and I exclaimed in unison.

"Gypsies are a problem here?" John asked.

"Gypsies are a problem anywhere where there are large parking lots," Philip responded. "A big problem and a dangerous problem."

There are some six or seven million gypsies in the world, most of them in Europe, where they arrived from India in the Middle Ages. They still live in nomadic bands and wander from place to place as the spirit moves them. Oftentimes they travel in Winnebago-style caravans, though some still wander about in colorful horse-drawn carts in smaller groups, with their children and dogs in tow, campfires burning away. Through the centuries gypsies have proven to be a serious challenge to civil authorities because they don't stay put, they don't pay taxes, and they can be vicious in defending their chosen locations for encampment, often with the help of attack dogs and long knives. In France, the police have no desire to wander into their campsites with eviction notices. In their own way gypsies are defending their *métier*.

Public authorities have determined that setting aside some land on the edge of towns for gypsy use is one way to "accommodate" their wanderings. But that hasn't stopped the larger groups of gypsies from settling down on wide-open parking lots, which can accommodate them more comfortably. When they find a parking lot that suits their needs they will bring their caravans onto it, break out the cooking fires, and settle in for anywhere from a few weeks to a few months. Such mass squatting is not a major problem in America, where the concept of private property is sacrosanct. Most state laws allow the local police to roust out trespassers and, if need be, prosecute them accordingly. But in modern Europe, with its very high density of population and its more liberal outlook on accommodating everyone's needs, the remedy to the gypsy problem is much more nuanced. In France, for example, police cannot arrest squatters unless it can be proven that the squatter caused "damage upon entry" into any given place.

Because our designer-outlet concept involved enticing shoppers to drive much longer distances than they normally drive to go shopping, we wanted to make a gracious statement of "Welcome" to them from the moment they arrived. The architecture, the landscaping, and the amenities were all designed with this in mind. There were no gates, no barriers to impede entry, no strongly worded signs warning of dire consequences. Having a gypsy encampment, with campfires burning and barefoot kids hustling for loose change, didn't seem in keeping with such a welcome. We discovered the answer to keeping them out of our parking lots lay in the definition of "damage upon entry."

For the entrance design we had intensive plantings, low brick walls, and attractive signage. In order to discourage the gypsies we also placed thin poles on either side of the entryway, and stretched a thin plastic tube between them, one which was almost invisible to the arriving shopper who would be looking straight ahead to all those brand names. The tube was set high enough off the ground to allow our customers' cars to pass easily under it. But it was set low enough so that a gypsy van would inevitably smack into it and break it, thus causing "damage upon entry." Such a broken tube could be used as evidence of illegal entry in a French court. This was not a solution unique to McArthurGlen. In France, nearly every shopping center, conference center, or any other building with large open parking lots invokes the same solution.

What made our site particularly vulnerable to gypsies was that it was situated in a thirty-acre open field, with sixty more acres adjacent to it. The gypsies could avoid the main entrance altogether, and just drive over the landscaped areas of grass and flower beds to access the parking lot and not cause any "damage upon entry." They could even approach the site by charging over the farmers' fields next door. A high-perimeter fence would have kept gypsies out, but it would also have made our shoppers feel penned in. Instead, we went to the nearest quarry and purchased nearly six hundred tons of huge but attractive white boulders and spread them along the three-quarter mile perimeter of the site. We ensured the placement of the boulders appeared casual and unplanned, but in fact they were carefully sited to ensure that no car or van could drive between them.

The solution created a problem for John's budget, but from opening day onward we never had a problem with gypsies or ramrodders. Boulder by boulder, we were learning our business in Europe.

It was late June, just before France started its summer holidays in July and August. I was having lunch at Maxim's on the Rue Royale with Bertrand

Vole, retail manager for the Biderman Group, manufacturers of Yves Saint Laurent and Kenzo, two of the strongest brands in France. Vole was as sophisticated as the brands he represented, usually sporting exquisitely tailored suits with crisp sleek lines, set off with glamorous YSL silk ties. His company was a strong believer in outlet stores, and for over a year we had been having conversations about his signing up for our center. So far there had been no commitment on his part.

"Construction's already half completed," I said, showing him recent photographs of the site. "We're right on schedule. Within two months our clients will start stocking their outlets and begin staff training."

Bertrand studied the pictures thoughtfully and nodded. I had hoped that he would cease with the thoughtfulness and start with the action. He had been an early supporter of ours but had been on the fence for months now. The strength of the Yves Saint Laurent brand in particular would lend enormous credence to our center, and induce other brands to follow. But recently, Vole was either losing interest, or was playing hard to get. Exceedingly hard to get. He already had a store with competitor Marques Avenue across town, and I suspected he was under real pressure from them not to sign up for our center as well.

Vole claimed his main objection to our outlet was the rent. We charged an 8 percent share of the total sales from each store. Considering what we brought to the table—the critical mass of brands, the ambience, and amenities for the shopper, the very targeted marketing program, and so forth—I thought it was a fair price. Bertrand, though, had rejected it out of hand.

"We're one of the great brands, *Bairn*," he explained, with a hurt expression. "You need to make a *geste* for us," he had told me at an earlier meeting.

So Marie-France Marchi, our Director of Sales, and I reworked the numbers and came back to Vole with a complicated, scaled-down formula that would start at 8 percent for the first $250,000 of sales, dropping down to 7 percent for the next $250,000, and so on.

Again, Bertrand turned it down flat, dismissing it with a wave of his hand.

Now I was back with still another offer, but before I had the chance to present it, he said, "*Bairn*, I want to ask you a question, okay?"

"Of course," I responded genially.

He leaned toward me conspiratorially and asked, "How many brands have you signed up so far?"

My heart sank. It was exactly the question I was afraid he might ask. I certainly wasn't going to answer it.

"Bertrand," I said evasively, "you know perfectly well that's privileged information."

"Do you want to know how many manufacturers I *think* you've signed up so far?" he asked.

"How many?"

"None."

I laughed. "If that were true, I wouldn't be steaming ahead under construction, would I?"

"*Bairn,* do you know why it is my belief you haven't signed up any brands?" he continued, ignoring my reply and still leaning forward.

"No, Bertrand. Tell me why."

"Because at this point, I'm not at all sure you're going to open. Ever."

He had touched on my greatest fear: Could it be that after all the negative publicity and all the setbacks we had encountered, we had lost credibility in the market? The brands we wanted—the brands we really needed—had heard so much negative news they were laying back to see what happened next, just when I needed them to step forward and sign up with us.

"And if you're not going to open, it doesn't make much sense to sign up with you, does it?" Bertrand went on.

"Bertrand, when I first approached you, you were enthusiastic about my concept. What's happened to change your mind?"

Another airy wave of his hand.

"It was a wonderful concept, *Bairn*. It *still is* a wonderful concept . . . but that was before Balladur, before *le gel*. That was before any of us concluded that the whole French government seemed to be against you . . . that they simply are not going to let you open your project, no matter how good an idea it is. It seems the opposition will always find another trick to use against you."

"Oh, we're going to open, all right," I said with bravado, "and we're going to open by October fifth. And those manufacturers smart enough to have signed up early will enjoy the full benefits of the massive grand-opening marketing campaign, timed to coincide with the annual back-to-school shopping rush. The brands that hesitate are going to miss all that."

As always, we were maintaining a very pleasant, even jocular demeanor in our conversation. But there was real tension at the table. Time was passing, and now that we were under construction, time was not my friend. If we opened the center with too few stores fitted out and ready for business, then those shoppers who arrived would be disappointed by too little choice. The brands that were open would be disappointed by too few sales. Immediately, the word would go out to the fashion world that McArthurGlen's "new American concept" didn't work, so it wasn't worth new brands signing up. A vicious circle could easily develop. Too few brands led to fewer shoppers, which led to no more brands signing up, which led to a downward spiral in sales. All this could lead to a failed center. That could imply not just a total write-off of all the time and 20 million dollars for the Troyes project, but also a serious setback for more centers on the Continent.

My back was to the wall. I needed to lock in the brands, but the upcoming summer break meant that most of the decision-makers at the brands—the people with whom I had to conclude my deals—would be absent for a month or more. YSL was a flagship brand. If I could land Bertrand Vole, that would help me recruit others. It was time to get past the pleasant decorum.

"Seriously, Bertrand, what would it take to change your mind? How can I persuade you that being there for the opening would be a major win for YSL?"

Bertrand put on a pensive face for a moment, and then beamed brightly, as if suddenly struck by a happy solution to our dilemma.

"I tell you what, *Bairn* . . . why don't you agree that you will charge us nothing—zero percent of sales—for our coming to your project? That would be a very attractive offer to us. I think we might even be compelled to seriously consider such an offer."

It was an outrageous proposal, but I pretended otherwise. It wouldn't do to laugh in his face.

"Let me see if I understand you," I said, forcing a smile. "You are suggesting that McArthurGlen subsidize your participation in our project. You propose that every French franc you take in at the cash register goes right into your company's pocket. And no francs go into ours. Is that what you are suggesting?"

"More or less. But, of course, if you were successful, we would be contributing enormously to that success. You know just how strong Yves Saint Laurent and Kenzo are in France. And they are strong attractions not just to the shoppers who will be coming to Troyes looking for bargains on famous brands. Our brands are also leaders among the brands—the brands which you are seeking to come to McArthurGlen. Announcing our agreement to join you will provide a much-needed shot of confidence when you seem to need it most—right now—before the summer holidays."

Bertrand Vole could have been reading my mind, but, in fact, was just letting the facts speak for themselves. I had to work to maintain my look of casual interest in his analysis. He knew and understood my vulnerability. I couldn't admit he was right for fear he would then spread the word to all his colleagues in the industry. Zero percent of sales for him would soon be the rallying cry for others.

"Bertrand, you're a pirate. But, of course, that's part of your charm. I think it best for our friendship's sake that I pretend you never made such an outrageous suggestion. It will be our little secret." I signaled the waiter for the bill.

We parted amicably on the sidewalk and I was left with the reality that I had fewer than one hundred days until Opening Day. And Bertrand had it right. We had not signed up a single brand.

On the gauge of risk measurement, the needle was steadily pointing toward the red zone of Very High.

TWENTY-ONE

Family

Dad had fought an incredibly valiant fight for thirteen months. As the cancer gradually took its toll, he kept fighting harder, not so much from a fear of dying, I think, as from a love of living. It was very primal.

And when the cancer finally won, we were left with an emptiness soothed only by memories.

I remember Dad raising his voice just a few times in my childhood. His was always the calm approach, studied and reflective. He was a lawyer, and it was his style to always leave the door open, to allow the kids to come in. When we did come in, when we finally asked, however obliquely, for counsel, then, he figured, then we would really listen.

It would be convenient to claim that my upbringing was one of overcoming great adversity and impoverishment. Convenient, but inaccurate. Demographers would describe my background as somewhere in the solidly upper-middle-class spectrum. By heritage, it is certainly solidly Irish American. Murphy, O'Hagan, O'Connell, O'Byrne, and Moriarity are all limbs on our family tree. There were five of us kids—four boys bracketing the one girl—and though we enjoyed a comfortable lifestyle it was clear to all that Dad and Mom were earning that lifestyle one day at a time. There was no secret family trust, no monthly dividends. Dad had attended college on scholarship. Mom's family had weathered tough times during the Depression. To keep the operation moving ahead, lawyer Dad had to keep clicking off increments of six-minute billables, and Mom had to stretch those six-minute receivables into two-hour spend-ables.

When we entertained at home, the cardinal rule for the kids was FHB—Family Hold Back—on all the steaks, desserts, fresh orange juice, and the like, until the guests had finished. We all had jobs early on, which grew into bigger jobs over time. Newspaper routes after school started at age twelve. Summer jobs painting houses and cutting lawns started at age fifteen. At college, two or three part-time jobs were needed to hold up our part of the deal: parents paid for room, board, and tuition; kids paid for travel, books, and social life. It was, in effect, a team effort, with each member of the family playing his or her part.

My younger brother Clarke and I designed Dad's memorial service. When we asked Father Rafferty at Our Lady of the Chesapeake for his consent to bring a four-piece jazz band into the church, he laughed. "That'd be a first!" he replied.

Dad loved jazz, especially high-energy Dixieland jazz, and he loved to play it on the piano. It just seemed natural, we thought, to have "When the Saints Go Marching In" pounding through the church rafters at the end of his memorial service.

So we had jazz music, and, of course, we had readings and eulogies. And we had jokes. Clarke rose to tell one of Dad's favorites and he wasn't a dozen words into it when I heard behind me, family friend Tim Cullen lean over to his wife Liz, and whisper, "Listen to this—it's a classic . . ." I twisted around to smile at Tim, and he nodded in return. And indeed it was a classic, especially as told by Dad, many times over the years.

But Dad's dry sense of humor wasn't limited to telling jokes. It was a basic part of who he was. At the service his very close friend and neighbor Jack Garrity told of a note that Dad had left upon Jack's return from a trip the prior winter. Jack lived across the street and had asked Dad to watch his house while he was away. Dad dutifully did so and reported back to Jack in a note tacked to Jack's door:

> *Dear Jack,*
>   *As I promised, I watched the house while you were gone.*
>   *I watched the ice fall off the roof and watched the back gutter fall off with it. I also watched the ice fall off the front roof and as I watched, the drain spout fell off. I kept on watching and another drain spout fell off the front roof. I gave up watching.*
>
> Your friend, Andrew

By the time of the service I had received numerous letters and calls from friends, acquaintances, and work colleagues in France, many very touching. Some surprisingly so. And it helped me feel that maybe France wasn't quite so far away from home.

We spread Dad's ashes across the Chesapeake as he would have liked. Back to his beloved water setting. It was a bitter, windy cold day in March 1995. Only immediate family attended in what was a very relaxed atmosphere, just as Dad would have wanted it. Pamela was wearing his Harvard sweater, inside out and backside to—also just as he would have wanted.

The hardest part was getting back on that long overnight flight to Paris, back to the politics and the never-giving-up attitude. Back to the foreignness and the sheer fatigue of starting up something completely new—new to me, new to the country, new to the politicians and to the customers; something new but in a foreign language, in a foreign place, with people who didn't think like I thought. That was hard, and very hard under the circumstances.

TWENTY-TWO

Cheshire Opening

We had hoped for crowds. We hadn't expected throngs.

When Cheshire Oaks, our project in northwest England opened in April 1995, the stores, the police, and our teams on the ground were very nearly overrun by the onslaught of cars and shoppers.

It had been a year since the infamous orange juice incident at The Goring, known affectionately as "Orangegate." The resolution of the Joey/BAA friction was that Joey had agreed to be more sensitive to BAA's corporate governance needs and Barry Gibson had volunteered to be Joey's point of contact at BAA. The rationale was that Barry's retailing background was a complement to Joey's real-estate background and perhaps it would be easier to achieve a strong working relationship. It worked. Much had been achieved in the year leading up to the Cheshire opening.

There had been a friendly race between the McArthurGlen team in Paris and the one in London to determine which could open their respective center first. By that point each was a fully staffed office which could act independently of the other. Joey, John, and I were the common denominators between the two. Eighty percent of the brands that we were targeting for each center were from the host country; the large international brands, mostly American, made up the balance.

With Cheshire's official opening scheduled for 10 AM, Joey and I arrived by 8:30 to take one last walkabout, and to witness the first shoppers rolling in. We were too late by a wide margin.

There were several hundred cars already in the parking lot, their owners silently waiting for the stores to open. Adrian Wright, Liz Bradley (Managing Director, and Director of Sales for the United Kingdom, respectively), and John Milligan were also already there, checking on the readiness of their clients' stores. At 9 AM, we gathered just outside the management office to hear the center manager, Paul Atkins, run through a checklist of last-minute preparations: stock levels of the stores, parking coordination, the festivities, delivery routines, and staff training—all the usual items for a center's opening. But for Joey and for me, the most important item wasn't on the list—Cheshire's Grand Opening was going to beat the opening of Morgan's Bicester Village center by a full month. Even with Roger's nine-month head start, here we were, thirty days ahead of him, and fiercely intent on making the most of it.

Roger's team and ours had both been lobbying the British and international brands, trying to persuade them to choose our respective centers, each of us pointing out the weaknesses of the other's site. We underscored again and again that Roger's site in Oxfordshire, just thirty minutes up the M40 highway, was too close to all the full-price stores in London. We cautioned the brands that they would be taking a massive risk with their largest retail accounts by offering goods—even end-of-season goods—at deep discounts so close to London. The retailers' retaliation could be swift and severe, we warned, including dropping the brands from their stores.

In turn, Roger and his team were denigrating our site for being so far off the beaten path, forty-five minutes west of Manchester and, more importantly, just thirty minutes south of lowly Liverpool.

"It's a *Liverpool* site," Roger's people would sneer, referring to the town's down-market image and the impression that its prosperous years seemed well behind it. "Do you want your high-end fashion brand to be part of a *Liverpool site?*"

The pressure on the sales front heated up fast, stoked in no small way by Joey's and my urging our sales team to never lose a deal to Roger's center, and certainly never even consider losing the race to open first. Cries of protest ("It's *not* a Liverpool center! It's in the green rolling hills of Cheshire!") degenerated into blunt accusations ("They're *lying!*") It was during this phase—when real money was at stake, scores of millions of dollars of real money—that the rivalry took on a sharper edge. On those rare occasions when Roger's and my path did cross, we didn't attempt polite conversation. We just didn't speak.

But at that moment on Opening Day, when Joey, and I, and the sales team were gathered together just before the shopping began, there was no talk of Morgan or his site. We knew we had won the race, or at least the first lap of the race, and now an even more important test was about to begin.

For months we'd advertised the coming of a new style of shopping, one featuring a new format and new value proposition. But in deference to the traditional retail stores we didn't advertise the brand names we'd be offering. "Famous Brands at Reduced Prices!" was as far as we went. When the shoppers arrived on Opening Day there was no inkling as to what items would be on offer. We knew that the merchandise on the shelves would change weekly, sometimes daily, depending upon which excess goods the traditional stores shipped in. To address this odd style of shopping we'd designed the experience to be a mixture of spectacle and treasure hunt. Our message was, "We have many items you could want at greatly reduced prices. We just can't tell you in which store to find it, or even on which day." So we asked the shoppers to take a risk: come with friends, spend the day, and hunt for the nuggets that awaited you. Find incredible bargains on branded goods, in an elegant, comfortable setting—in essence a treasure hunt. In 1995, that was standard fare for Americans, but nonexistent for Europeans. Until we opened at Cheshire Oaks . . . thirty days ahead of Bicester.

We had Burberry, Jaeger, Mexx, Viyella, Levi's, Timberland, Nike (not many true luxury brands signed up in the early days), and twenty-five more brands on offer that first day, with parades, jazz bands, jugglers, and singers for entertainment. There were treats and sweets for kids, coupons for adults, and marquee tents and refreshments where our VIP guests could retire. We were out to drum up excitement. We were, however, woefully unprepared for the mass of humanity that found its way to Cheshire that morning, or the fact that the crowds brought their own excitement with them.

From before 10 AM, an endless line of cars, packed with three, four, five people each, already lined the adjacent roads and highways, waiting to get in. We had built 1,200 to 1,300 parking spaces, and it was hopelessly too little for the 5,000 to 6,000 cars that descended upon us throughout the day. We had to direct them past the end of the paved parking lot and onto the graveled area intended for the parking lots of Phases 3 and 4. We quickly realized a major problem: the shoppers weren't shopping the way they normally did, with a thirty- to forty-five-minute visit to the local shopping center. Here, thanks to the treasure hunt strategy, they were exploring for up to two-and-a-half to three hours. So their cars stayed in the lot four to five times longer than usual. Result: logjam.

In accordance with our site criteria, Cheshire Oaks was located in a semirural area. The local residents were amazed at the onslaught to their slow-living countryside. The enterprising sent their children from car to car, selling cold drinks. Others pulled up a lawn chair and watched the show. Inside the cars, shoppers endured their ordeal in proper British style, stiff upper lip, waiting politely for their turn, even when there were 112 cars ahead of them. (*"Mustn't grumble."*)

The store managers were as taken aback as we were by the masses. Most had scheduled stock deliveries for once every other week. Many were nearly out of stock before the end of Day One. Their frantic hurry-up calls for fresh merchandise were only partially successful as delivery vans were caught in the surrounding gridlook.

Inside the stores the pace was torrid. Tired and bargain-hungry shoppers scoured through the shelves and pressed forward at the checkout, often overwhelming the just-hired and newly trained sales staff. Regional managers who had come to observe the festivities found themselves folding clothes and manning cash registers for eight to ten hours at a stretch. Other staff, who thought they would just come for the day found they had to stay on for three days or more simply to help out. In many stores the pressure was too much. The staff just quit. Walked away. The stress wasn't worth the pay.

In an effort to ease the logjam of cars waiting for spaces we created "space spotters," armed with large blue flags. They would run up and down the aisles looking for empty spaces and, upon finding one, stood there waving their flags like semaphore officers, signaling the next car in.

Shortly after the lunch hour, Adrian and I found it increasingly difficult to maintain our professional decorum as we watched the cars, shoppers, and wallets continue to roll in. Decorum gave way to grins, and grins gave way to giddiness. Finally, Adrian could contain himself no more.

Adrian had started life as a British bobby, complete with training and experience in traffic control. As the scene grew increasingly chaotic he whipped off his coat, rolled up his sleeves, and joined the fun in the parking lots. Running, and waving, and shouting, he grabbed a walkie-talkie and assumed control of Lot A, the large one nearest the entrance, with a capacity of eight hundred cars or so. He was having a glorious time pointing at cars and waving them along. But alas, it had been years since Adrian had sprinted about with such abandon. He ran a little too far and a little too fast and suddenly—*Snap!!!*—he pulled a hamstring in the line of duty. Down he went with a groan. Instantly, he was surrounded by spotters waving blue flags protecting him from cars. And just as instantly, the multiple flags attracted multiple cars, which screeched to a halt around Adrian, each desperately seeking the promised parking space. The Cheshire Oaks opening was fast, and furious, and wildly successful, and had just claimed its first casualty. Several of us ran out, lifted our fallen colleague and handed off his walkie-talkie to a more fit security guard. The cars kept coming, the shoppers kept shopping.

For all the waves of shoppers, not every store was a runaway hit. Most notably, to offer a wider choice (and to help fill unleased stores), we imported a few French brands which had never before opened stores in England. And, as it turned out, they might never again.

For one of these brands, the head office in Paris sent over experienced staff from their French operations. While they were surely experienced and well trained, they spoke no English. Rendering effective customer service proved somewhat difficult.

In another store, the French manager had forgotten to supply the cash register with spare money with which to make change. It was a bit awkward when the customer was asked, "Could the store keep the change?"

In a third store, the French staff weren't familiar with standard British electrical design. They didn't recognize the light switches on the wall, and so assumed there were no lights in British stores. The French staff sat there in the dark for hours, wondering why so few customers came in. That certainly made for awkward service when the six bored staff members pounced on the one poor customer per hour who actually did venture in.

Perhaps the grandest faux pas of all involved the French brand named DIM, part of the Sara Lee conglomerate, which, in addition to owning the famous cheesecake, also owned many textile brands in the lingerie sector. The regional manager for all of Sara Lee's British and French lingerie brands was an enthusiastic Parisian who was supportive of our outlet concept. He not only wanted to sell the Pretty Polly and Wonderbra brands well known in Britain, but in order to increase his UK market share he also wanted to promote his French brands that were not so well known in England. His first choice for this was "DIM," a well-regarded men's underwear brand in France.

In an effort to promote the brand to the English public he branded the store DIM, with huge letters on the store's fascia. But DIM, as a brand, was totally unknown in England. And in England, "dim" unmistakably means "stupid." So it was a bit difficult for British men to walk into a store with the word "DIM" emblazoned over the door, which sells French-style skimpy underwear. To the shopper strolling past, it seemed almost a joke or a trap, perhaps something set up by *Candid Camera* to see just how stupid some Brits would be. Not many were willing to take that test. Not even in the excitement of Cheshire Oaks's opening hours.

Late in the afternoon, after walking in and out and around the thirty-three stores heaving with shoppers, I joined Joey and John Nicolosi next to the playground area. We were tired from the excitement and from being on our feet all day, but overall satisfied beyond words.

John was looking at the thousands of shoppers around the center, and the dozens of kids in the playground in front of us, and began shaking his head. He looked over to us. We were all thinking the same thing. Only two and a half years before, we had stood together at the opening of another project, The Warner. It had been a glitzy, fabulous night, a night to always remember. But it was also a night that had marked an end to our development days in Washington. At the time we weren't sure if it marked the end of our development days anywhere.

But now here we were, after two and a half years of high adventure but also high risk. With our houses and meager bank accounts on the line, and with an estimated 40,000 shoppers flooding into Cheshire Oaks that opening weekend, we knew we were not at an end. We were, once again, at a beginning.

The hordes and hordes of shoppers that arrived that day in Cheshire clearly demonstrated that, in fact, the British public did want bargains on famous brands. The pundits who harrumphed that the American concept wouldn't work there, who said that Brits don't shop at discount ("One just doesn't . . ."), were proven wrong. Egregiously wrong. Joey, John, and I couldn't have been happier.

Thirty days later Morgan's Bicester center opened. Joey and I had always secretly felt that Morgan was essentially "just an investor," and not really a creative developer, as we were. Then Bicester opened. It was not only a huge retailing success on its opening weekend, but an architectural success as well. In fact, because we had forced overselves (with very strong encouragement from BAA) to build Cheshire Oaks as efficiently as possible, Bicester was a more attractive end product than Cheshire.

We had beaten Morgan to the first finish line, but it suddenly was clear it was going to be a long race.

TWENTY-THREE

Opening in Troyes

During the final week before the Troyes's opening I remained in the Paris office, monitoring the last-minute preparations by phone and fax. I arrived on site the evening before Opening Day, all pumped up and full of anticipation. Within seconds I was nearly speechless.

"Marie-France, what in the *hell* is this?" I snapped as my Director of Sales walked up to greet me, her warm smile on display as always.

Chaos was everywhere. Not lightweight-but-under-control chaos, but pure, unadulterated, brink-of-disaster chaos. It wasn't just that there were several dozen construction workers still there, nailing up signage, laying sod, and planting trees. That activity, as well as the bulldozers, backhoes, and pavers still rumbling around the site, were to be expected.

"*What are they doing?* Are they *kidding* me?" I snapped again, sweeping my arms across the scene around us. Marie-France's smile had vanished at my reaction.

The stores were the problem.

Of the forty-three stores in the center, Marie-France, to her absolute credit, had been able to lease twenty-nine of them. But at five o'clock on the evening before the opening, only one store had its interior shopfit complete, merchandise stocked, staff on hand and trained, ready for operations. That store was Nike. Under the discipleship of VP for Retail, Tim Walley, they "just did it."

No other store was even remotely ready. Every one of them was in one form of disarray or another. Carpenters, and pipe fitters, and shopfit workers were climbing all over each other. Store employees were shouting back and forth to the trucks full of stock waiting outside. Ceiling lights were dangling down by their wires, mannequins were leaning against interior walls or windows out front. Some stores even remained dark, either with no workers to be seen, or worse, with people sitting on the curb out front, sipping wine from thin plastic cups, and calmly munching on baguettes, waiting for who knew what. Cars, trucks, and delivery vans were milling around the parking lot, looking for places to disgorge their merchandise.

In fifteen hours it would be Opening Day.

"Byrne," Marie-France responded calmly and with confidence, "this is normal. In France, it is always this way before an opening."

"Well, not in America," I barked. I had never been harsh with Marie-France, and she didn't deserve it even then. But all I could think of was the train wreck that was about to happen the next day as the hordes of shoppers (we hoped) descended upon twenty-nine stores that would be nowhere near ready for them.

"Byrne," she repeated, "by tomorrow morning everything will be fine. These people will work through the night, just like they always do. *On verra*."

In the two years since Marie-France had been with McArthurGlen she had never been wrong. It was her cool professionalism which had pulled off the miracle of leasing twenty-nine stores in the center, nearly all within the last four weeks before opening. She had done so by focusing on the key brands that would bolster our credibility, then signing up the followers in rapid succession. Yves Saint Laurent had finally agreed to come on board, but only after we caved on pricing, netting a grand 2 percent of sales (down from 8 percent, but better than zero) as rent. From there Marie-France and I locked in those American brands that already understood the concept well and needed outlet stores in Europe—Polo, Timberland, Nike, Reebok, Lee, and Wrangler. They had all fallen into line rapidly once they were convinced we were really going to open. Armed with those names, Marie-France then raced around to land the next rung of brands important to the French, focusing especially on children's brands and women's wear: Petit Bateau, Jacadi, Catimini, and Jean Bourget for the kids, and Cacharel, Mexx, Bally, Gérard Darel, Ventilo, Kenzo, Kookaï, La City for the women. By early September, just three weeks before opening, the brands finally (finally!) started calling in to Marie-France instead of her constantly calling out.

One of the brands that called in was Disney. Apparently, they needed an outlet for the excess merchandise from their theme park located an hour north of our site. Because of Disney's controversial image in France, Marie-France and I debated whether or not to accept them. In the end we did, in part because we had so many empty stores to fill, but also in part because of my family's friendship with the family of then Disney president Steve Burke. Later on, it turned out, that relationship would manifest itself in other ways.

In the final run-up to opening, my main focus was on the incessant bad press we were still receiving. The local newspapers in particular seemed to delight in covering all the bad news they could find about McArthurGlen. Our negative image in the press was so persistent—an image of the carnivorous American leviathan invading the hometown of defenseless small French retailers—that I worried the shopping public wouldn't even bother to come see for themselves.

Finally, the press became too overbearing and unfair. Enough was enough, and Eric, charged with marketing and public relations, scheduled a visit with the editor of the two local newspapers. Significantly, one company owned both of the regional newspapers: one for the politically left-leaning readers, and the other for readers on the Right, a mirror image of daily life in France. The same man edited both.

Eric went alone, pointedly leaving me, the American, behind. Eric presented our concerns, highlighting the consistent factual errors and overall negative tonality in so many articles over the prior months. He ended up by asking for no more than evenhandedness in the coverage of McArthurGlen.

"But why should I support you when you do not support me?" the editor shot back.

Eric looked puzzled.

"You are placing full-page ads in newspapers in Rheims to the north, and in Dijon to the south," the editor explained with indignation. "You are even taking out ads in the Metro stations of Paris. Yet, you have not bought one ad in my newspapers here in Troyes."

"Is *that* the problem?" Eric responded, feeling relieved. This, he thought, would be an easy matter to clear up.

Eric explained that that our hands were tied by a carefully negotiated ac-
cord with the Troyes Chamber of Commerce. A key provision was our agreement not to advertise locally. The chamber had been worried that our ads
might divert shoppers who would otherwise patronize downtown merchants.

"That is not my problem," the editor huffed. "I am also a merchant in
this town. I'm also a member of the Chamber of Commerce. My problem
is that you are not supporting me. So I cannot support you."

One week later, after a frantic series of meetings, conference calls, and
much wagging of French fingers among the internally conflicted members of
the Chamber of Commerce, the first of a series of full-page McArthurGlen
ads appeared in both local newspapers. The very next day front-page articles
appeared extolling McArthurGlen's efforts to ensure that the economic benefits of our arrival in Troyes would be bestowed upon the Troyenne citizens,
including the two hundred new jobs. Flattering quotes about McArthur-
Glen's outreach from locals already hired were sprinkled throughout the stories. The following week, another article highlighted our hiring the local
architectural firm Téqui-Pointeau, complete with a prominent photo of
Jacques Téqui and me unveiling the center's design. As long as those ads
were purchased according to schedule, fair and accurate articles about
McArthurGlen were written. It made me wonder what "might have been" if
I had understood the relationship of commerce and the press from the start.

A more serious distraction in those final days were persistent rumors
about a massive protest against McArthurGlen, scheduled to occur on
Opening Day. Word on the street was that a newly formed alliance claiming to represent all the regional and downtown retailers was organizing the
shopkeepers to close their stores and to march through town, chanting slogans and carrying placards protesting McArthurGlen. The march was to
end with a rally at the main entrance of our center, where the 250 or more
demonstrators were to stage a massive sit-in, thereby blocking any cars,
and hence shoppers, from entering our site.

We first learned of the plot via a friendly phone call from the Office of
Information (*Bureau de Renseignement*) within the Prefecture. The "Office," I
learned, was intensely secretive in nature, something akin to the local FBI.
So secretive, in fact, it didn't even formally report to the powerful *Préfet*
but rather only to "superiors in Paris." Armed with this alert, I turned to
the police for help.

"Yes, we have heard those rumors," the police lieutenant confirmed over the telephone. But no, he said, "there is nothing we can do if they organize a rally."

"But that is a public road that they would be blocking," I argued. Eric was across my desk from me, scribbling notes of support to my line of reasoning.

"Yes, but everyone is entitled to use a public road," the police lieutenant pointed out calmly.

"I agree. But roads are meant for transit purposes, not for staging protests and blocking transit," I countered with some logic.

"But Monsieur Murphy, everyone is entitled to free speech, including downtown retailers," the lieutenant continued.

"But I am not trying to prevent or censor their free speech. They've been exercising free speech at my expense for the last year and I haven't tried to prevent them. I am only trying to exercise my right to free commerce. If they stage a sit-in on that road, they will be taking away that right," I pressed on as calmly as possible, given the urgency of the matter.

"Monsieur Murphy, no one has done anything wrong yet. One must not worry too much until something has actually happened. *On verra.*"

"Monsieur Lieutenant," I countered in a slightly firmer tone, the muscles stiffening up the back of my neck. "I am not asking for preventive action on your part, but I am afraid I can already see what will happen. I'm only asking that, should a mass sit-in take place on the road in front of my entrance, the gendarmes will take action to clear the road so that the cars of shoppers may pass."

"Monsieur Murphy, as I said, they also have a right to use that road."

There we were, right back at the beginning. The Gallic circle of logic had been completed. I dropped my forehead down to my desk in defeat, holding the phone up above my head like a white flag in case Eric wanted to give it a go.

The next morning, Opening Day, and two questions were answered with finality right off.

First, Marie-France had been right. By 9 AM, an hour before opening, twenty-eight out of twenty-nine stores had their interior construction complete, their shelves stocked, cash registers loaded, ready for business. By 11 AM, the last store would join them. The nearly 150 store personnel who had worked through the night looked it. I only hoped they could last out the day. When Marie-France cheerfully greeted me that morning I could only offer a kiss on each cheek in relief and gratitude, and a request for forgivenesse for doubting her.

Secondly, the rumors of a mass protest proved to be legitimate. There, in both regional newspapers, were full-page ads featuring a macabre announcement and details of when and where to meet in protest:

DEATH ANNOUNCEMENT

The Troyes Region is for Sale

The Members of the Department Commission for

Commercial Space ("CDEC") & their Friends

Announce with Great Sorrow the Death of:

500 Traditional Retailers & their 700 Employees

The Funeral Ceremony will be Held on Friday, 6th October, 1995

At the American Crematorium (McArthurGlen) in Pont-Sainte-Marie

Subsequently a Solemn Meeting will Take Place, to be Attended by

The Unemployed: Those Cast out of the Region's Economy

When I read the ad I could only sigh, close my eyes, and sigh again. It was another ledge, another hurdle, though one whose intensity I could not yet gauge. At the bottom of the ad were the names of the organizations that formed the coalition to organize the protest, and, we later learned, posted hundreds and hundreds of fliers with this announcement all over the storefronts in central Troyes. There were four names in the coalition, one of which was a new one to the debate: National Union of Textile Manufacturers. How incredibly odd: Our concept was conceived to increase the profitability of textile manufacturers, and yet this group was not only opposing us, but was doing so without ever having met us. As a national organization they would have the resources to fund the opposition against us, including the opposition from the very start. But who would have organized them to do it? Who, really, was our key opposition?

I was too pressed by the logistics of Opening Day to unravel that mystery just then. I needed to focus on the implications of the protest.

I knew better than to waste time by calling the police lieutenant. We decided instead to face the protesters with our own security staff, the security personnel we had hired for the opening. Originally, we had contracted for three dozen personnel. When I saw the ad I requested two dozen more. Though they were trained for parking and crowd control, and not dealing with angry protesters, they were the best I could find.

I didn't really know what actions we'd take until we saw the size and aggressiveness of the protestors, but I had laid down two principles with the chief of security that morning. First, there was to be no violence; that would be worst-case scenario for all concerned. But secondly, shoppers *were* going to get through the sit-down protest even if it meant a ring of security escorting each car through, one at a time, shopper by shopper.

An hour before opening I gathered the team together into our "HQ" in one of the empty stores. Everyone from the Paris office was there, as well as the half-dozen new people hired to run the center, and more still from the UK team. Our in-house team was some fifteen or eighteen in total. In addition, Eric had another thirty or so entertainers and marketing personnel on hand. We reviewed one last time who was responsible for what, ranging from parking control, to working with the stores, to liaising with the emergency medical team. We were all clustered around uncovered picnic tables. When we broke up from that tight cluster there was a spontaneous shout from everyone, which quickly transformed into a whooping, whistling rush of people spilling out into the center like a hyped-up football team running onto the field. It was a silly reaction in a way. It was only a shopping-center opening, of course, but for our people it was much more than that. The median age of Team McArthurGlen was mid-twenties. I was thirty-six but was clearly one of the old guard. Few of our people had ever experienced a center opening before, and certainly not one which had to overcome so many obstacles. The excitement of the opening was strongly reinforced by the team's youthful energy. That energy was in turn reinforced by an incredible sense of achievement, and all of it was welcomed by a bright, gorgeous, clear sunshiny day.

At 10 AM sharp, Eric cut loose on the entertainment. A massive hot-air balloon, ten stories high and emblazoned with McArthurGlen logos, lifted off majestically from one end of the parking lot and took its place two thousand feet above the center, signaling our presence for miles around. Brightly colored banners and flags snapped gaily in the morning breeze. We flung open the entrance gates, the bands played, and dozens and dozens of clowns, magicians, dancers, jugglers, singers, and mimes poured out into the parking lot to greet the arriving shoppers. In true Gallic tradition, beautiful women, sporting the fashionable designs of the center's various brands, circulated among the shoppers with whistles and candy for the children, and coupons of savings for their parents.

The first of the fifty-five-passenger tour buses was waiting at the entrance well before 10 AM, and another dozen arrived shortly afterward. Fifteen more arrived in the following hour, and yet more the hour after that. The first bus was from Normandy, some four hours' drive away, having left before dawn to ensure a timely arrival before the gates opened. Buses came down from Lille in the north, near the Belgian border, and up from Lyon in the south, nearly five hours away. They had been organized by church groups, social committees, and tour-bus operators, most of whom had learned about the center from those articles in the national press about the "McArthurGlen controversy." The negative press had proved to be not so negative after all.

Where were the protesters? I wondered with some nervousness. When we opened the entrance there was no sign of them. At 10:30 we heard rumors they were gathering downtown, ready to march. Then, just before noon came the report that fewer than half a dozen people had gathered at the designated assembly spot, only to be left standing there by themselves. No other protesters arrived. No downtown retailer closed in protest. Not one placard was being carried to our entrance. The grand protest of the coalition claiming to represent all the downtown retailers, the one that had resources enough to buy expensive full-page ads in both papers, had fizzled. There didn't seem to be such a coalition after all. I could only smile.

At half past noon I climbed up to the roof and looked down at the just over half-full parking lot. We could tell by reading the last two digits of the cars' license plates that nearly a third of the seven hundred cars there had driven the one and a half hours down from Paris. It was a strong showing, though hardly the wild crush of shoppers we'd seen at the Cheshire Oaks opening. I could take comfort from the fact that the tills were ringing and the store managers were happy, so it clearly was a success.

I watched Marie-France make the rounds of the stores, checking on her clients, asking about the level of sales and the quality of the shoppers. When I called down to her she waved and shouted up to me, "*Mickey* is looking for you! Watch out for *Mickey!*" She laughed as she said it, and walked on, but we both knew she was halfway serious.

As a sign of support for our opening, and as a gesture of friendship, Steve Burke, president of Euro Disney, had sent the theme park's Mickey Mouse character, in full costume, to entertain the crowds. It was a rare honor—from their perspective—as Disney management barely ever permit Mickey Mouse to entertain outside the theme parks. When I heard word of this "gesture" from Steve I almost choked. All I could think of was the potential for a PR debacle. The press was all over our center that morning, with newspapers, magazines, and three TV stations covering the event. All I needed was for them to capture "Mickey and Byrne" on film, and all sorts of poisonous analogies would be brought into play. Eventually, we prevailed on the staff of the Disney outlet shop to limit Mickey's activities to the pavement immediately in front of the store. But Mickey had been directed by the powers-that-be at Disney to "find Byrne and offer support" on Opening Day, and he'd been seen wandering about on the lookout for me. I decided to stay hidden on the roof until Marie-France managed to usher Mickey back onto his own turf.

I used the opportunity to call Pamela, and caught her just as she was leaving for Troyes.

"We are *in* business *in* France," I exclaimed over the phone. "It's happening, Pammie—cars and buses are arriving; shoppers are shopping. The bands are playing, the protesters never showed. The stores are happy. It's all happening! *Finally!*"

"Incredible! 'Finally' is right, after all that was thrown at us. Thank God," she said. "I hope you feel good about this. What a struggle!"

"I am feeling all right at just this moment," I confirmed. The stream of new cars arriving had nearly stopped completely by then. The lunch hour had started.

It was one o'clock when I headed over to the luncheon marquee for the McArthurGlen team. All those from the Paris and London offices were there, as well as the clowns, the musicians, and the press. Luckily, Mickey was nowhere in sight. It was a high-spirited meal with much joking and shouting. Though not as overwhelming as the Cheshire Oaks opening, Troyes's opening was still a strong one. I wasn't euphoric, but rather feeling a calm satisfaction. Marie-France, seated at the end of a table with a clear view of the center, remained guardedly upbeat.

Then, just before two o'clock, she let out a delicate whoop and called me over. "Yes, here we go. I thought so—Byrne, come look at this! Come look! Look at the cars!"

I stepped over to where she was sitting, with the center's entry in view, and there was the sight I'd been hoping for all day—a line of cars, bumper to bumper, with more behind them, waiting to get into our parking lot.

Behind me, the center manager began talking with animation into her walkie-talkie. The security people on the roof had radioed her. The line of cars, they said, was unbroken. It led out of our center and back into the industrial zone on the other side of the railroad tracks. The line continued all the way through the zone, back out to the main road on the far side of the site, and continued on, leading to the ring road around Troyes. He couldn't see, the man said into the walkie-talkie, how far it went along that ring road.

Suddenly, there were shouts and cries from all directions as other security personnel called for help in the parking lot. Everyone jumped up from the table first to take a look, then to run to their stations.

And that's when Troyes's Grand Opening really started. That endless line of cars kept on coming, and coming in one continuous wave. They came into our parking lot as fast as the road design would permit them: at the rate of another car every seven seconds.

"This is it, Byrne," Marie-France exclaimed. "This is the real opening crowd!"

"But what is *it?*" I asked, not taking my eyes off the cars. "Why so many cars now?"

"Because this is France," Marie-France replied. "In France, shopping in the morning is never heavy. French people like to start their day out slowly, not rush. Then it's time for lunch, a relaxing lunch. And after lunch, right then, that is the time to go out, to make an excursion—to go shopping. And here they come!"

And were they coming! Over the next two hours, more and more cars and buses arrived. Four hundred and seventy cars during the first hour after lunch, four hundred and fifty the next. The parking lot filled to its 1,300-car capacity within seventy minutes, and hardly any cars were leaving. The line of cars backed up for a mile to the ring road and for nearly another mile after that. When the cars were backed up at the Cheshire Oaks opening, the Brits waited patiently and politely for their turn to enter the lot. Not so in France. Drivers started pulling off the road and parking on the adjoining fields, sometimes plowing across the fields to get as close as possible to the stores before getting out to hike the final distance. In the industrial zone adjoining the center, the road was nearly choked off completely as cars were left, at odd angles, along the curbside. It all happened so fast, in a blurry endless rush, that we couldn't get our parking coordinators out there quickly enough to organize it.

Inside our parking lot, cars pulled up on curbside, and often into the landscaped gardens. In turn, this didn't leave enough room for the buses that had arrived in the morning to then depart. The buses were stuck, but the passengers didn't seem too concerned. They clambered back out and resumed shopping.

In the midst of this two-hour tsunami of cars, a police lieutenant came rushing up to me, the same lieutenant I'd spoken to on the phone a few days earlier. This time he was considerably less calm.

"Monsieur Murphy. This is *out of control*. You *must* stop so many cars from coming. This is not correct."

I looked out at all the cars, and at the crowds of people who had left their cars and were walking across the fields to start shopping. I looked back at the lieutenant, offered him the very best Gallic shrug I could muster—chin thrust slightly forward, shoulders hunched up, hands a bit outstretched and turned up—and said, simply and in a calm voice, "How?"

The lieutenant stared back at me blankly.

"You know, Monsieur Lieutenant, everyone has a right to use the roads," I added with a sincere smile.

Inside the stores it was pandemonium. Lines at the tills were often ten or twelve people deep. At Polo, the line grew to thirty people and would have extended out the store had the manager not feared that people might give up waiting and just walk off with the merchandise. When I entered the store for YSL and Kenzo, there was Bertrand Vole, perspiring behind the cash register, a mountain of clothes on the counter in front of him.

"*Now* do you think we'll ever open?" I shouted over to him. He looked over briefly and shook his head in disbelief, sporting a grin for just a second before resuming the shirt folding and bag stuffing.

At the store for La City, a trendy brand for young women, they had stocked up with merchandise enough for the entire three-day Grand Opening weekend. Or so they thought. At four o'clock they were placing frantic calls to their warehouse begging for another truckload that evening.

In other stores, weary staff, especially those who had stayed up all night stocking the shelves, began walking off for some rest. The fifteen-foot-wide sidewalk running in the front of all the stores was one unbroken wave of shoppers. It was jostling, and slow shuffling, and constantly turning to find your companion as you progressed, with the clowns and entertainers on hand to keep up the smiles and the laughter. Mickey Mouse could barely move in the crowd; the risk of the dreaded photo op drowned away in the masses.

As it approached six o'clock, the scheduled time for the center to close, we thought there would be a revolt from the shoppers if we tried to do so. Too many thousands of people who had invested too many hours of waiting to arrive at McArthurGlen were still strolling from store to store. I could see men and women walking to their cars carrying several bags each, loading them into the trunk, then turning around and heading back for more. We postponed closing till 7:30, and most of the stores wearily accepted the decision. Others closed at six or earlier anyway, their exhausted staff flopping down to the floor in surrender.

There was a McArthurGlen celebratory dinner and dancing that night, in downtown Troyes. Despite exhaustion from the day's activities, the spirit and morale were sky-high, and the dancing was intense. By 10:30, Pamela and I called it a night. As I left, I nearly begged the younger team members to please not stay out too late. I reminded them in a somewhat fatherly tone we had two more days of Grand Opening. I needn't have wasted my breath. The fun went on, and on, and—apparently—on until the wee hours. I didn't realize how much fun was had until three months later when Jeanette, a very attractive and bubbly young member of our marketing department, bounced into my office to joyfully announce her pregnancy. The father, and current boyfriend, was the chief jester among the clowns.

By the end of Sunday, over 55,000 shoppers, 18,000 cars, and fifty tour buses had descended upon McArthurGlen. No protesters had appeared. In fact, the downtown merchants—stores, restaurants, and hoteliers—had experienced very positive effects from the opening. All reviews were warm and upbeat.

Of particular satisfaction was that on Monday, Marie-France received phone calls from both Cerruti and Armani, two of the super-brands we had unsuccessfully tried to sign up. They had never even granted us a meeting. Now their people were on the phone. Did we, they asked Marie-France, by any chance have room for them?

The Grand Opening's press coverage was extensive and complimentary. It was heartening to see so much coverage with so little negative comment. The national business magazine *La Tribune* continued to follow the McArthurGlen saga closely. Their story, in the form of an interview with me, was printed under a double headline: WARRIOR'S REFLECTIONS ON THE OBSTACLE COURSE was placed just over a quote used as the second headline: NEVER NEVER *EVER* GIVE UP.

TWENTY-FOUR

The Big Prize

For the entrepreneur who introduces a new concept there are two stages of particularly high risk.

The first is when you and your financial backers have taken the plunge and invested large sums of money, hoping—but not knowing—that the new concept will work. Before the results of Cheshire Oaks and Troyes started rolling in, BAA McArthurGlen had invested 60 million dollars. We had bought the land, designed the centers, and built the buildings. All on spec. Ours was the field-of-dreams approach: Build it and they will come.

In addition to financing those first two centers, we had also invested another five million dollars to acquire control of other sites around the United Kingdom and France, hoping and preparing for the moment when Cheshire Oaks and Troyes proved successful. When they did, in fact, do just that, we then hit the entrepreneur's second moment of high risk: Competition arrives. At that point much has been learned and proven about the new concept, therefore, the risk is much reduced. Inversely, the potential for profits is greatly enhanced. Potential competitors start gathering along the sidelines—watching, noting, calculating. We knew that and didn't like it. So we did something about it.

Because we had already invested five million dollars to control the next round of sites, we had an immediate pipeline of future projects on which we could begin development. By marshalling our assets and springing forward the moment we felt our concept had been proven we could open an even wider gap between ourselves and any potential competition. It meant reducing the risk of facing competition by taking more risks through spending more money. That's why we persuaded BAA to authorize another 40 million dollars to develop more sites as soon as the initial results were in.

Our strategy was to build an insurmountable lead through market dominance. And to achieve it, we now had a 100-million-dollar gamble on the line.

But we weren't going to be satisfied by market dominance in just the United Kingdom and French markets. We wanted to dominate Europe— *all* of Europe. We believed in our bones that this outlet concept was *our* concept. It was *our* idea to bring it to Europe; it was *our* 65 million dollars, and then 100 million dollars, that was at risk. We believed in our future and we invested in it; no profits were distributed. Everything was recycled back into the company. It was *our* industry to dominate, and if possible, to own. We were very driven and very hungry. Perhaps, at that point, we were also a bit arrogant.

With that goal in mind, I created a new team of local consultants and advisers for the Spanish market, and began scouring the environs of Barcelona, Madrid, and the Costa del Sol. I did the same for Portugal, focusing on the northern corridor between Lisbon and El Porto, and south along the Algarve coast.

Simultaneously, we mapped out the lowlands of Belgium, Holland, and Luxembourg. My advisers and I drove the highways, checked out the exits, ran the demographics, and met with the politicians, Chambers of Commerce, developers, consultants, brand owners, retailers, mayors, members of parliament, old experts, new experts, wannabe experts. I carried a powerful calling card for my meetings. First, I had the credibility of our Cheshire Oaks and Troyes successes in hand. Secondly, I was backed by the undisputed strength of BAA, our six-billion-dollar gorilla.

And with that financial strength we went on to Sweden, Norway, and Denmark. Others in the company were scouring the highways and byways of Switzerland, Austria, and Germany. We cast the site-searching net very far and very wide. And we did so with incredible energy and ruthlessness, and an endless appetite for more information and more meetings in less time. There were more flights, and more hotels, and more highway drive-bys. Several of us were in a constant state of exhaustion and managed to press on only with a constant inflow of espresso and endless little triangles of Toblerone chocolate. For Joey and for me, our state of health was always a little shaky during the early years of the startup, but especially so in this period. But we were going to jump ahead before the potential competition even knew our concept existed, much less that we were already in their backyard.

Our efforts to expand on the Continent produced promising results. We had offers of joint ventures from some of the world's most august names in retailing. We were in advanced discussions with Ikano, the sister company of IKEA. They were eager to join forces in Scandinavia, and perhaps for all of Europe, for locations where they had existing IKEA stores. In Germany, I was having very seductive meetings with the head of Kaufhof, Germany's second-largest department-store chain, and one of the key divisions of the mighty Metro Group. Metro was, and is, the number-two retailer in the world, second only to Wal-Mart, with annual sales of 34 billion dollars. Preliminary conversations were being held with El Cortes Inglés, the very dominant department-store chain in Spain. In Portugal, we were being aggressively courted by the country's largest and most successful retail developer, Sonae. Our concept was fresh, exciting, and had demonstrated great potential. The best and brightest of the European retail and property world were suddenly willing to speak with us. We were the new kid on the block and the flavor of the month.

But it soon became clear to us that as hungry as we were for market dominance throughout Europe, even we, with our American zeal and with the massive financial resources of BAA, could not spread ourselves across all of Europe like that. The key to our early successes in France and England had been our laserlike focus and determination, and we would need to maintain that energy and single-mindedness to re-create them in other markets. And as this realization began to truly sink in, nurtured along in no small part by our very corporate, very methodical BAA partners, we began turning down these alluring options.

"But how can we turn down IKEA? Sonae? El Cortes Inglés?" we asked ourselves, with the reluctance of an alcoholic backing off from the bar. We kept saying to ourselves that it would take one very powerful force to distract us from those prizes. And it did.

That very powerful force was Germany.

Before signing off on a major expansion program BAA wanted us to attend to some corporate housekeeping. When we first formed the joint venture with BAA two years prior to the opening of Cheshire Oaks and Troyes, Sir John Egan had promised that if our concept proved successful, BAA would back our rollout across Europe. By early 1996, the results were in. The two projects were not just successful, but wildly so. It was time for the expansion.

Not surprisingly, BAA wanted to ensure that the execution of this expansion strategy was as well-managed as possible. Perhaps with images of flying orange pulp in their minds, BAA requested that I move from Paris to London, and oversee all the projects, not just those on the Continent. What they wanted overall was a little less pure entrepreneurialism and a little more structured approach to the program.

When I was first approached about the move, I gently said thanks but no thanks. Despite the frustrations of France, Pamela and I were happy in Paris. But when BAA politely signaled that a change in the management structure was, in effect, a prerequisite to their nearly 500-million-dollar funding of the McArthurGlen's growth, it seemed prudent to reconsider.

In the wake of Troyes's opening in autumn 1995, it would have been natural for me to move to London for early 1996. But something interceded to postpone that, something which can only be ascribed to "country risk."

France has a long history of strikes, mostly by public-sector unions to protest government attempts to rein in the generous terms of their contracts. For several decades those initiatives have withered in the face of strikes, which, of course, have only encouraged more strikes. In the autumn of 1995, the new Prime Minister Alain Juppé announced a series of reforms, ones meant to signal a new level of determination by the government. The unions took action shortly thereafter.

Strikes are so prevalent in Paris they are woven into the fabric of daily life. After living there for nearly three years Pamela and I remained composed when they occurred. Pamela was then pregnant with our third child, and went about her daily routines and having her checkups as scheduled. I continued on with expanding the company.

The '95 strikes started out innocently enough—a one-day strike in late November by the railroad workers, *les cheminots*. They were upset that the Juppé government was proposing to trim their right to retire at age fifty with nearly full pay thereafter. At the same time a strike by university students demanding smaller class sizes and more subsidy was also underway. The marchers arrived in Paris about the same time. They clogged the streets, chanted slogans, and filled cafés, hoping to be noticed, which in fact they were: by other unions. In an act of support the Metro workers suddenly went on a wildcat strike, followed shortly thereafter by the postal workers, and finally, the telecommunication company France Telecom. In less than ten days Paris was brought to a complete standstill. No railroads, no subway, no phone assistance, no mail. Paris was a mess.

Pamela and I carried on with our lives as best we could. Eventually, as with all the other strikes, these too, passed, and life seemed to return to normal.

It was a shock, then, when Pamela received an urgent call months afterward, in late March, when she was in her ninth month of pregnancy. A nurse was on the phone requesting that Pamela rush to meet her doctor at the hospital. They had just reviewed test results from several months before, indicating she had toxoplasmosis.

Toxoplasmosis is a bacterial disease, which in the States is most commonly associated with germs spread by cat litter. In France, the usual carriers are fresh fruits and vegetables. The French have a built-in resistance to the microbe just from growing up there. Visitors do not. Every foreign pregnant woman is tested regularly throughout her pregnancy. If toxoplasmosis is detected early in the pregnancy, antibiotics are an easy remedy. But if left undetected for too long, the risks are high. Toxoplasmosis can cause brain damage and possibly congenital blindness in the fetus.

I was out of the country when the call came in. Pamela and I agreed she should wait to see the doctor until I could be there the next day.

We were sitting in the hushed, low light environment of Dr. Rolet's office at l'Hôpital Américain in Neuilly, as he outlined for us the gravity of the situation. He sat across his desk wearing his white medical coat and wireless glasses, his hands folded in front of him. Unfortunately, he explained in a soothing tone, an amniocentesis exam would need to be performed right away. The risk of piercing into the placenta with a long needle to extract fluids carried such risk that it was usually not performed so late in the term. But this was not a normal situation. He needed to know as soon as possible if there were, at the least, gross abnormalities in the baby. He went on to explain what other procedures were required.

We agreed to the program he outlined, but I remained confused on one point.

"Why did the situation become so serious. Why couldn't this have been detected sooner?" I asked.

"I am sorry for you both. I really am very sorry," he responded in the same soft tone. "It is because of the strikes."

Pamela last had a toxoplasmosis test just before the strikes broke out. The results, unfortunately, had been lost in the chaos of the mail strike. Lost, even, for several months until the aftermath of that chaos was sorted out. The report had just arrived in the doctor's office the day that the nurse had urgently called Pamela.

It was when we were walking out of the hospital on that gray winter's day that we felt sharply once again that we were foreigners living in a foreign land. Surely, we thought, this was not a situation we likely would have faced at home. When moving to a foreign culture you sometimes take risks of which you aren't even aware.

The amniocentesis test did confirm the presence of the disease in Pamela, but could not confirm its presence in the baby. Gross abnormalities were not ruled out, but were less likely. Only at birth, when a test on the baby's blood could be performed, would the results be certain.

Our third daughter, Erin Byrne Murphy, was born on April 18, 1996. She came out bellowing, appearing cherubic and healthy. The blood tests confirmed she had, in fact, escaped the reach of toxoplasmosis.

It was an especially joyful moment.

Three months later we gathered up that bundle of joy, and all our other precious belongings, and moved to London.

TWENTY-FIVE

Fallingbostel Ambush

Germany's numbers always jump off the page when you analyze European markets. The JLW studies we commissioned stated that with almost 90 million people, Germany accounts for nearly 30 percent of the total population of continental Europe. A high percentage of their wealthy population is concentrated in urban areas—ideal for our outlet concept. In the mid-1990s, the German market accounted for over 35 percent of total European retail sales and, most important, it was the largest market for the total amount spent on clothing and footwear.

The statistics went on and on, and were, by retailing standards, mouthwatering. The German market not only contained the most attractive urban concentrations in Europe but also fewer shopping centers than all the other major countries. Germany actually had less shopping area per person than France, the United Kingdom, Ireland, Austria, The Netherlands, Switzerland, and Spain. Significantly, it had only one-fifth the total floor space of shopping centers of either France or the United Kingdom. And yet it had 40 percent more population, and a much wealthier population per capita.

Our concept needed large population centers. Germany had four of the top ten metropolitan areas in Europe. We compared population and spending power per capita by city. We sliced and diced all the demographics, the shopping patterns, the traffic counts, and no matter what figures we turned up, the message was always the same: Germany, Germany, and Germany. It was clear where we needed to be. Germany was Europe's greatest prize, and became our number-one expansion priority.

Germany was going to be tough. Just how tough, we weren't sure. But early on I received a hint.

On one of my early reconnaissance trips to Germany I was told a story about the type of welcome reserved for outlet stores there. It is a story that I subsequently heard many times in various forms. It obviously had been passed around from brand to brand, both German and non-German. It became legend. And the story involves one of the greatest global brands: Nike.

In the early 1990s, Nike was already a world powerhouse in the athletic shoe and sportswear market. With total global sales of 12 billion dollars, its famous swoosh was a familiar icon throughout the western world as well as in developing countries. Its phenomenally successful "Air Jordan" ad campaign was in full swing, and Nike's shoes, shirts, shorts, and socks were seen in nearly every stadium and on every sandlot. Combining the shoe category with the sportswear segment, Nike had a dominating global market share of approximately 33 percent to Adidas's second-place position of 20 percent.

Germany was a tougher market than most for Nike. It was the home market for Adidas and Germans were loyal to their own brand, especially in the very visible, very important soccer shoe category. Adidas had an overall market share of approximately 40 percent, perhaps twice as Nike's. But Nike was focused on the German market, and was coming on strong. Total Nike sales there had risen from 80 million dollars in 1990 to 140 million dollars in 1991. Nike was becoming the hot "fashion sportswear" brand in Germany.

Overall, Nike's sales in Europe were approximately 500 million dollars, and like all brands, especially those growing fast in new markets, Nike had an excess stock problem. With excess stock running an average of 10 percent a year, that was a 50-million-dollar annual problem and climbing. Nike decided it needed an outlet store in Europe adhering to the same principles as those in America, namely, to protect the retail accounts and to enhance the brand while also liquidating excess stock. Thus, it announced to its retail accounts that it was contemplating opening an outlet store somewhere in Europe. The response from the German retailers was quick, clear, and unequivocal: They told Nike that an outlet was a bad idea, a very bad idea.

As far as the German retailers were concerned, the opening of an outlet store by such a major manufacturer was little short of an open declaration of war. Even if the outlet accounted for less than one-tenth of 1 percent of the total Nike sales in Europe, for the Germans it was the principle that mattered. The rules were simple and inviolate: Manufacturers manufactured, retailers retailed, and consumers consumed. Any infraction of that formula jeopardized the entire system, and was, therefore, strictly forbidden. An outlet store connected the manufacturer directly to the end consumer, and that could not be allowed. When it was pointed out to retailers that there were already quite a number of existing outlet stores connected to factories throughout Germany, in fact hundreds and hundreds of them, the retailers countered, "Yes, but even one more outlet store would tip the system into disequilibrium." When it was also pointed out that the outlet stores enabled the manufacturers to clear their excess goods, keep their operating costs down, and enable them to focus on the sales of new seasonal designs, all of which would benefit the retailers, the response was indignation.

After some reflection, Nike—the great almighty Nike, unquestionably the strongest sports brand in the world—decided that yes, they really *did* need an outlet store, but no, they wouldn't open it in Germany. They decided instead to open it in the midpoint of their European logistics system, which meant in the Alsace region of France, just over the border from Germany. It seemed to them to be both a diplomatic and an efficient solution that would work for all parties. Nike would get its needed outlet store, and the German retailers could claim victory, having thus prevented any more outlet stores from opening in Germany.

The German retailers were not persuaded and they discarded diplomacy. They told Nike in no uncertain terms that it had better not open that outlet store, not even in France.

Nike considered their threat, and then opened the store anyway.

The German retailers, coordinated through their powerful German Retail Federation, decided that this act of defiance could not be tolerated. They consulted by phone, by fax, by word of mouth, and they organized a swift response to the great and mighty Nike. In effect, the retailers went on strike. For the season following the opening of the French outlet store, orders from German retailers to Nike fell by *over 50 percent* from the year before. They had told Nike "No," and they had meant it.

Nike heard the message and found religion. The company closed the French outlet store soon afterward.

I was told this story by a senior German executive, sitting in the headquarters of Escada, a very successful and well-known German brand. I countered that there was similar opposition when I had first arrived in France, and that our outlet center in Troyes was by then perceived to be a grand success for all parties, including retailers. The German leaned forward, looked at me intently, and said in an almost hushed tone, "Yes, but there is a difference between the Germans and the French. In Germany, *we are organized.*"

And that was the message the German Retail Federation sent not only to Nike, but all the other brands selling in their country. It became painfully clear that cracking the German market would require an enormous effort for acquiring the appropriate sites and securing their zoning approvals. We would need someone on it full-time. Joey turned to the one person in America who had over the years spent more time acquiring sites with Joey than anyone else, an old friend of his named George Bennett. Joey and George would together focus on Germany. At the same time, I moved to London and focused on the expansion in the United Kingdom and France.

Bennett is a formidable figure. At six-feet-four and 250 pounds, he is large enough to deserve the name Big George. Raised in Kansas, he is quintessentially American: loud, visible, and meat-and-potatoes in his views. But George knew and loved the finer things in life: grand opera, well-engineered cars, and hand-rolled cigars. His passion for music was impressive. He could identify obscure arias after hearing no more than the opening bars. But like everyone else in real estate, George took a hit in the S&L debacle, and thereafter his access to that good life was significantly constrained. When Joey approached him about spearheading the German project, he jumped at the chance. At age fifty-seven he saw it as an ideal opportunity to get back on top. All George needed to do was find the right sites, get the zoning approved, and let the bargain-starved Germans take care of the rest.

Simple enough. By March of that year, Big George had located a site that not only met but far exceeded all the key criteria of the McArthurGlen formula. The site was a town named Fallingbostel, located in the northwest shoulder of Germany, approximately halfway between Hannover and Hamburg. Situated adjacent to the A7, the highway that winds like a river the length of Germany from north to south, Fallingbostel is small but proud. Over a thousand years old, it has aged gracefully. Set amid rolling countryside, the town center is marked by the tall, austere spire of the Lutheran church, which dominates all the other buildings huddled around it. This is farming country, and the neatly plowed fields run right up to the edge of town. Though it has only twelve thousand German residents, Fallingbostel has a history of outsiders coming to its township. In 1936, the outsider was Adolf Hitler, who took over a vast area surrounding Fallingbostel for an army training ground. From 1939 to 1945, it became Stalag XIB, housing Allied and Soviet POWs. Since World War II, Fallingbostel has also been home to twenty-five hundred members of the British forces and their families, mostly the Seventh Armored Brigade. Outsiders who came and who stayed.

The fact that Fallingbostel is so small and sleepy seemed ideal. It had no retail fashion trade that would be upset with our new discount concept. And besides being sleepy, Fallingbostel enjoyed a front seat along that A7 river highway, over which 70,000 vehicles pass per day—almost twice the car count we needed for effective advertising of our presence. Fallingbostel is also in the middle of a region of 6.2 million people, a population approximately twice our criteria. Fallingbostel had the right kind of land, the right access to it, and most important, the right attitude toward our proposal.

As in nearly all towns in Europe, the town fathers of Fallingbostel had no idea what our concept entailed when we first knocked on their door. Big George visited the mayor and introduced our designer-outlet concept to him. The mayor, middle-aged, soft-spoken, and polite, was as straight and dignified as the Lutheran steeple visible from his office window. His formal manners spoke of his German heritage, and his rough hands and cracked fingernails made it evident that he was a man of the soil. He made appreciative noises at George's proposal, and then passed him along to the town planner who arranged for a full presentation to the planning staff, followed up by presentations to the City Council. For all its modest size Fallingbostel did not lack for officials, all of whom had to be included in the process. Initially, none of them really understood the concept. How could they? They had never seen anything like it. But they got the message of new jobs by the armful and of visitors by the millions. Visitors who otherwise wouldn't stop there. Visitors spending millions in this little local economy they wouldn't otherwise spend there. The town leaders were won over. By the spring of 1996, Fallingbostel decided that the outlet concept was one they could back. They agreed to start work on a formal agreement. We began to feel optimistic.

We shouldn't have.

An odd thing happened in the summer of 1996. Early in June, Big George placed an urgent call to me in London to relate how, out of the blue and totally without warning, our rivals, Roger Morgan and his people from Fashion Retail, had suddenly appeared on the streets of little Fallingbostel. They were asking for meetings to discuss building a designer outlet. Roger Morgan! How on earth had he found our little Fallingbostel, our number-one priority site in our number-one expansion market? I asked George two or three times, "Are you sure? Are you positive it's Morgan?" Keeping our site selection secret was of paramount importance, and I couldn't believe it was simply coincidental that he'd popped up at such a critical moment. This wasn't the first time Morgan's people popped up on the scene of a site we were secretly analyzing. It had happened elsewhere in Germany, and in Belgium and Holland. I felt a mixture of rage and dark foreboding. Rage that he was stalking us in Germany, after we had saved him from being double-crossed by the sleaze-ball gazumper at Bicester. It was foreboding because I knew what a tough competitor Morgan was, and how much more difficult it would now be to close our deal in Fallingbostel.

Meanwhile, Roger ran his own analysis of the site, concurred with the merits of the location, and decided to pounce. While we weren't the least bit surprised that he, too, liked the site, we asked ourselves over and over again, "How in the *hell* did he know we were in Fallingbostel?" It was a question that was to haunt us for some time, in that location and others.

The town fathers of Fallingbostel couldn't believe their good fortune. In the flurry of just a few months, not only had a new concept been sent to them from heaven, complete with foreign investors to finance it and to create hundreds of jobs for their small town, but in addition—in an incredible addition to that—now there were *two* foreign companies knocking on their door. In fact, they were *beating* on their door, *begging* for the right to create that tourist attraction. So what would any upstanding, God-fearing, mayor of a small provincial town do in such circumstances?

Naturally, he would hold an auction.

And suddenly all the exhausting months of education, presentations, all the lunches, dinners, and visits to our centers in Cheshire and Troyes for the Fallingbostel locals that George had organized, were as nothing. Our chances of success now depended entirely on whether we could come up with the most competitive bid. Emotions rose to a new level in the McArthur-Glen–Fashion Retail rivalry, especially for me. The sheer gall of Roger's behavior was what really hurt. Friendships gone bad can produce stormy reactions. I wanted to strike back, and strike hard. And as it turned out, I had stronger financial reasons to do so than I even knew.

As we began analyzing the ongoing results of Cheshire and Troyes, it became clear we had bigger successes on our hands than we had previously imagined. And we envisioned an even bigger success in Germany, where the shoppers had more income and less choice. We estimated that the Fallingbostel project could create up to 35 million dollars in value, maybe 40 million dollars. And for that amount we weren't about to give into a competitor. And certainly not to one who was encroaching on *our site* with *our concept.* This time, we decided, Morgan had gone too far.

It began to appear that all of Big George's prior lobbying and good relations were not completely for naught. The mayor quietly let George know that the town fathers preferred McArthurGlen, if only for the fact that we had been there longer and had established real relationships. When Morgan and Co. swooped into town, and made presentations and promises, we usually heard the details of their offer within a few hours. We'd work out the numbers and be ready to respond immediately. George would then go back in with our new ideas and new proposal. Morgan promised to pay for a municipal pool, a 500-thousand-dollar windfall for the town. So we promised the same thing, and threw in a million dollars more in road improvements. Morgan matched us and added another million for road improvements. Over the frenzied weeks of negotiations millions of dollars of new "add-ons" kept materializing. I could only imagine the mayor's pulse rate as the heaven-sent goodies kept piling on.

During the week when the final bids were due the wires were working overtime. Just before bid day, Joey and I were sitting by our telephones in

Washington and London, waiting for news from Germany, the mayor of Fallingbostel called up George and said he needed to have a chat. Something important had come up. George dutifully arrived at the mayor's office and went in for a closed-door session.

"It's come to the township's attention," said the mayor, looking even more formal than usual, "that the chief executive of McArthurGlen, Mr. Kaempfer of Washington D.C., and his firm, The Kaempfer Company, apparently has a checkered past in regard to financial stability back in America. Is this true?" Pause. "Can you shed any light on the matter?"

George sat there stunned. Of course, Joey had run into difficulties! So had virtually every other developer in America, and all as a direct result of the S&L crisis. In fact, Roger's own fledgling investment company had faced severe problems because of the S&L mess. Why was this coming up now? Now it was George's pulse that started to gallop, as he explained what the S&L crisis was all about.

When the final bids were unveiled Morgan's offer trumped ours by a wide margin, by many millions of dollars. It was a margin that caused us to pause before trying to pursue a last-minute counterbid.

Joey, George, and I held a painful meeting in London to decide whether or not to continue with this bidding war. We calculated that if we topped Morgan's offer we would dramatically increase our risk of never seeing profits in Fallingbostel. After all, this was to be the first outlet center in Germany, and nobody really knew how it would perform. How much risk should we take? With the entire continent open to us, with approximately 350 million Europeans available elsewhere to welcome an outlet to their region, and with the incredible profitability we had on our hands in Troyes and Cheshire Oaks, we couldn't see a compelling business reason to continue battling over Fallingbostel. There were, however, emotional reasons to keep fighting. Testosterone is a tough thing to ignore in any competition. Ultimately, we decided that if Morgan was willing to overpay just to get into the game, and was happy to accept marginal returns, then we shouldn't be dumb and play according to his rules. We wanted to play smart.

So we let Fallingbostel go.

It made my stomach churn, letting "our" McArthurGlen site become "their" Fashion Retail site. After the meeting I left the office and walked glumly around the backstreets of London for an hour or so. That night Pamela noticed I couldn't eat.

We knew that Morgan and his cohorts would be high-fiving each other all the way to the signing ceremony. We decided that the old adage, "Don't get mad, get even," didn't apply here. We were mad *and* we intended to get even. The Fallingbostel Ambush, as we called it, marked a turning point in our relations with Fashion Retail. It was becoming a bare-knuckle brawl. And so, the following week Big George climbed back on the plane, and flew back to Germany, and drove back to Lower Saxony, and, in fact, went right back to the same A7 highway. He then drove two junctions up the highway to the neighboring town of Soltau. It was a bigger and more-recently developed place than Fallingbostel, and lacked a lot of the historic charm of our first site. In a certain light, Fallingbostel could look like a pastoral Christmas card. Soltau did not. It had suffered badly in World War II, and almost all the buildings were new and not as picturesque. The good news was that Soltau was in the same region, on the same highway, with the same demographics as Fallingbostel, and all at a price tag that was almost fifteen million dollars cheaper. And it was located just a few short miles from Heide-Park, one of Germany's largest and most successful leisure parks, replete with miles of hiking trails, bicycle paths, woodland lakes, and millions of vacationing visitors per year. (Leisure activities are a natural complement to outlet centers.) Within a month George had found us a new site at Soltau. Even at that point, even with our very limited experience in Germany, it was clear to us that the two sites were so close together that only one of them would ever receive final approval. When we announced our Soltau site to the world, I had visions of the Morgan people stopping their high-fives in midair and looking over their shoulders, mouths open and eyebrows raised, to Soltau.

I dined very well that night. The battle for Germany had only just begun.

TWENTY-SIX

Spooks

Secrets are a critical part of many business operations, and maintaining them was certainly vital to our rollout across Europe. When expanding a successful new retailing concept, being "first to market" in a region can mean the difference between becoming the dominant player there and languishing as the also-ran. We had to keep our expansion plans hidden from our competitors for two reasons. First, it prevented them from barging into the target market and initiating a bidding war for the chosen site. Second, in the instance when a competitor was too late to buy the site themselves, then keeping the site's identity secret could stop them from stirring up the local opposition to the approvals we needed.

In the year following Roger's smash opening and ongoing success at Bicester, we tracked his every move via the brokerage market, the trade press, and circulating rumors, to figure out his next step. While our McArthurGlen team raced about the country searching for subsequent sites to Cheshire Oaks we repeatedly crossed his path in the west country around Bath, down south toward Plymouth, and all over Scotland. It seemed that Fashion Retail had run into difficulties in securing their next site. Eventually, Roger made a startling announcement: Fashion Retail's new strategy for Europe, he said, would be to develop one key center in each chosen country, starting with Bicester in the London market. In other words, Fashion Retail was finished developing in the United Kingdom.

It took us a while to fully appreciate that Roger's change in strategy was a move of colossal importance to us. It essentially left us without meaningful competition in what would emerge as the most welcoming, most profitable market in Europe. Over the next three years, thanks in part to Fashion Retail's withdrawal from the UK scene, McArthurGlen expanded Cheshire Oaks three times and developed six more UK projects, with completed values totaling 600 million dollars.

At that time Joey and I wondered whether in fact Roger could be induced to throw in the towel for all of Europe. If we could buy Roger's Fashion Retail and his Bicester center we would absorb our only meaningful competition not only in Britain, but on the Continent as well.

Eliminating the competition by purchase wasn't such a farfetched idea—we had already done just that by taking out, at a very low cost, another UK competitor, the U.S.-based development company called Prime. Prime's British partner, the Richardsons—a very successful family of developers from the Midlands—were the owners of three highly promising sites in the United Kingdom. We had sensed discontent on the part of the Richardsons with their partner. Smelling an opportunity, we instigated a series of clandestine meetings at Heathrow Airport, where I flew in from Paris to meet with the Richardsons, and our adviser, John Milligan. Those initial sessions led to further, more serious talks, which in turn led to larger, more formal meetings, attended by Joey and the BAA principles. Within eight weeks terms were agreed: Prime was out and we were in as the Richardsons' partner. We became not only the first developer in the United Kingdom to open a center, but we were then clearly the largest developer in Europe with the largest pipeline. The combination of our open centers and our sites in development suddenly made us larger than Fashion Retail by a ratio of eight to one.

We knew we'd never succeed with that sort of blindsiding tactic against Roger; he was far too smart for that. One of his great strengths lies in his self-control and discipline. He knows how to listen a lot, question even more, remember everything, but reveal nothing. In other words, he knew how to keep his secrets. I knew this aspect of his character well, and after we became business rivals my initial instinct had been to follow suit. I would keep a smile on my face but keep my mouth shut. But in time the tactics changed on both our parts. We then mutually began a subtle campaign of disinformation. In those rare instances when we did speak we would each drop nuggets of information intended to throw the other off. I would drop hints about visiting eastern Germany when in fact we had no interest there. I felt he did the same, for example mentioning where other developers were targeting sites when I think he actually didn't have a clue.

Matters on this front came to a head not long after the Fallingbostel Ambush when, during an ostensibly friendly encounter in London, Roger stated that McArthurGlen's constant harassment in shadowing Fashion Retail's moves was proving a major distraction to them.

"It's become a real issue, Byrne. Every morning my guys start their day asking: 'Where's McArthurGlen? What do we have to do to defend ourselves?' And it's getting a little crazy. It seems to them that you keep showing up in markets where we are just trying to find a site and get started."

Listening to Roger made me think he was expressing my concerns about Fashion Retail's moves against us—only in reverse. It was *his* team who kept turning up in our hard-found new sites, such as Fallingbostel. Was this, I wondered, another disinformation move on his part?

"Frankly," Roger went on, "we're wondering if you've tapped our phones to know what we're doing next."

"What? Tapping *your* phones?" I retorted.

Had we now entered into a new level of competition, one akin to a game of chess?

I move my rook up to take your knight . . .

This new chess match included a series of new moves, one of which was the *faux*-move, like a head fake on the basketball court. Make it seem you're moving to the left just to force your opponent to move to his right. It occurred to me that Roger might have just done a head fake. He may have been projecting onto McArthurGlen team what in fact we thought he might be doing—stalking us in every way possible, electronic and otherwise. Maybe by suggesting we were committing that sin, he was trying to deflect suspicion from himself.

Because in fact we had just started taking steps to protect ourselves against that of which he had accused us: eavesdropping. We had begun sweeping our offices for bugs. We were wondering, especially after Fallingbostel, if Roger and his team were spying on us. We had taken our first tentative step into the gray world of corporate espionage only days after we first spotted Roger's people on the streets of Fallingbostel.

"Well, what are you guys doing to protect yourself?" Terry Lenzner asked us over the speakerphone. Terry was the founder and managing director of Investigative Group International ("IGI"), one of America's leading security firms. With him on the phone was IGI's Director of International Operations, Terry Burke, a former Director of the U.S. Drug Enforcement Agency. Both knew their way around all kinds of intelligence risk. Their clients ranged from some of the largest multinationals to the wealthiest and most socially prominent families, American and foreign. Lenzner worked with the Clintons in trying to manage the Monica Lewinsky affair. Later IGI worked for Oracle in its famous garbology spy case against Microsoft, another client of the firm's.

"Do you have any security practices in place?" Lenzner asked.

Joey and I looked at each other and shrugged our shoulders.

"The usual things," I offered. "We lock the office at night. We have passwords on the PCs. We restrict access to our server."

"Listen," Joey said, "at the end of the day we're real-estate developers. We're not some hotshot software firm with a new breakthrough code to protect, or a Wall Street firm with a secret IPO in the works. I've never had to protect myself from spies."

"Are you using paper shredders?" Burke then asked, ignoring Joey's comment.

"No—no paper shredders," I responded.

"What do you do about trash? You just put it all in the wastebasket next to your desks, and it's collected at the end of the day, right?"

"Yep, just like every other normal office in London or New York or wherever," Joey explained.

"Yeah, but your company may be both less and more normal than you think. What about your working papers: Do you leave a lot of them out on your desk every night? Or do you lock them all away, out of sight?"

"On the desk," we both responded, matter-of-factly.

"And would your two desks contain nearly all the vital information needed to understand in what direction you're steering the company?"

We looked at each other across the speakerphone and shrugged again. "Yes," we both responded in chorus.

"Do you have a temp agency that supplies temporary help to your office, whether as secretaries, receptionists, or the like?"

"Sure. But we've used the same one for the last few years without any apparent problem," I responded.

"Finally, is there real money to be made if someone knew what to do with the information laying around your offices?"

"Of course."

"Millions to be made?"

"Well, that depends on just how much they want to do with it," Joey came back. "But millions? Easily. Hundreds of millions in asset value if you know how to develop real estate and implement the outlet concept."

"Okay then. Oldest trick in the book," Burke summed up. "All that your competition has to do is pay off the janitorial staff or the temp agency and they've got direct access to your business correspondence, your memos, company strategies, everything. And I presume your competition knows how to develop real estate."

So we started looking over our shoulders every day. We cleared our desks and locked away our files every night. I arranged for unscheduled sweeps of all our offices around Europe. We checked for miniature transmitters no larger than a Lincoln penny. We ran all throwaway papers through our shredders, and cycled out all temps in the office. And we changed the locks on our doors monthly.

And now Roger was telling me his people were doing the same.

I move my knight over in line with your king—check.

We never found a bug, or a spy, or any indication of how our secrets had leaked out. Nor could we prove that anyone had been spying on us, whether associated with Fashion Retail or any other competitor. Maybe leaks happened through the brokerage community, where agents had a history of not keeping their mouth shut.

But clearly the intensity of the competition and the stakes at risk had been ratcheted up even further. McArthurGlen had come a long way from that lonely hotel room in Paris, back when there was nobody to call.

TWENTY-SEVEN

Royal Walkabouts

Britain is a relatively small country with a relatively large population, and some of the world's most beautiful countryside. The British take a fierce pride in that countryside and display an equally fierce determination to ensure it isn't spoiled. In that respect they have erected endless legal and regulatory barriers meant to discourage development. Developments such as, for example, designer outlets.

And it was those stringent barriers that forced McArthurGlen to search for new ways to develop an outlet center that would attract the public while at the same time abide by the letter and spirit of the preservation laws. It had been those barriers that had prompted us to arrange the clandestine airport meetings with the Richardsons to explore taking over the sites they had targeted for outlet development, each one of which had already made some measure of progress toward approval. As soon as we had secured those sites, we focused our attention on the one in Swindon, Wiltshire, just a little more than halfway between London and the city of Bath.

Swindon is a town with an industrial heritage and, somewhat unfairly, a down-market image. For 160 years it has also been the home of a sprawling old Victorian monster, the Great Western Locomotive Works, a factory opened in 1843 by the engineering genius Isambard Kingdom Brunel. He produced there massive railway steam engines that helped propel Great Britain into the Industrial Age. Few Americans even recognize the name of

Brunel, but in Britain he is a national hero. As recently as 2002, he placed second only to Winston Churchill in a BBC poll of the 100 Greatest Britons. It was his Swindon factory that produced the first steam-powered locomotive to break the 100-mile-per-hour speed barrier.

Because of its important role in Victorian Britain and because of its distinctive architecture, the factory had been designated a National Heritage landmark. That had saved it from destruction, but when we arrived on the scene in 1996, the factory had lain empty since its closure some ten years before. If we were to redevelop it, every brick wall, steel pillar, broken window, and rusting crane had to be restored and preserved. The factory would be a distinct departure for our concept. We would have to adapt to an existing structure instead of building our own. Moreover, it was on the edge of a town that boasted a vibrant retail core, instead of being located in some isolated spot away from town centers. Most worrisome of all, it would be hard for out-of-towners to find because it lay several miles off the highway and required navigating seven different rotaries to get there—a potential disaster for a retailing operation that depended on motorists.

But the factory had a number of positive attributes as well. The demographics were strong, and importantly, the historic buildings, after laying vacant for all those years, stood a very good chance of winning approval for restoration and conversion to a commercial activity. Though historic preservation and restoration projects are inherently riskier and much more costly than constructing new buildings, our company had been through even more daunting restoration projects before, notably The Warner in Washington. We weren't turned off by regeneration; in fact, we saw it as a bonus. Instead of fighting the preservation restrictions at every step, we embraced it, as we had at The Warner. We decided it was better to robustly celebrate the railroad and factory heritage in such a way that the restoration became an attraction in itself. The fact is the British public has a very active and nostalgic love affair with the old railways and trains. There had already been some efforts undertaken to open a railway museum in Swindon, adjacent to the factory, featuring such famous original steam engines as the Puffing Billy and the Flying Scotsman. As is often the case, insufficient capital had stalled the museum project. Our conclusion was: Why not be the catalyst to make all these projects viable? Why not be the founding sponsor for the creation of the Railway Museum, restore the factories, open up an outlet center, and create hundreds of jobs in the process? The hardest part would be in working with the existing downtown retailers to ensure our retail offer was complementary, and not competitive, to theirs.

Under the very able direction of our UK Development Director Gary Bond and his colleague Candace Valunias, we spent nearly two years restoring the factory to something which perhaps surpassed even its original glory. It was a three-dimensional puzzle meshing together two distinctly different cultures: Victorian manufacturing and modern retailing.

By the end of the process, we had refurbished 99 percent of the factory's original fabric, left in place an active railcar repair shop, and created 120 shops carefully fitted into the existing structure. We had also built in an interesting reversible feature. Years into the future it would be possible to remove all the stores, and the original factory would be revealed in perfect condition. That was one of the litmus tests of true historic preservation.

In order to incorporate the various separate factory buildings into a single commercial center, we designed a continuous shopping path, which meandered in a loop through the disjointed factory buildings. Shoppers didn't have to make any decisions about turning left or right inside one of the old buildings only to find themselves lost. Instead, they just sauntered along the one route we created for them. We painted the old steel columns in a color-coded scheme to signal where you were in the center. We reclaimed original features when we could find them: nineteenth-century cranes built to lift multiton engines from assembly lines to finishing areas were remounted overhead; original sections of track were relaid along the former assembly line, now the center of the mall area; the chassis of hundred-year-old railcars were placed on the tracks. You could read the history of Britain's growth and power during the Industrial Age and the factory's role in it as you walked about.

In one of Joey's more creative moments, he insisted on making the nexus of railway heritage and modern-day shopping more sensual and more interactive than merely undertaking a factory restoration with a museum tacked on at the end. He wanted the sights, sounds, and smells of the railway to come alive again for all to experience. At one end of the center, adjacent to the Food Court, where all visitors were sure to pass, we designed an all-glass structure with forty-foot-tall, removable glass walls. Inside we laid down a 150-foot section of real railway track that could hold a full-size steam engine. Then we began exhibiting, in rotation, Britain's most famous locomotives, which we were able to set onto those tracks via those removable walls. Because the steam engines we selected were all in working order, every hour the engine's whistle would sound off, steam would billow out, the floor would shake from the power of it all, and shoppers and babies would sometimes jump or scream if they weren't ready for it. You could stand so close to the massive steam engines you could feel the heat and smell the axle grease.

The first steam engine to go on display arrived before the center even opened. She was the famous Flying Scotsman, and five thousand train buffs and a small army of reporters gathered to watch her installation, standing by all day long in admiration.

The development of the Swindon center was just the beginning of our rolling out the concept across Europe. To assist with the massive effort which the rollout required we began staffing up with the talent needed. As part of that staffing effort three people moved to London from America.

Patience O'Connor joined us to head up the marketing and operations departments. Patience brought with her more than twenty years of experience with the Rouse Company and the Mills Corporation, two cutting-edge retail development companies in their respective niches: urban redevelopment and off-price retailing.

The second person was John Nicolosi, our true blue Brooklynite. John had been helping out part-time, flying in as needed, until we knew if the first projects were going to succeed. The projects were a success and John moved over.

The third person to move over was Peter Nash. Peter took on the critical role of project finance, working closely with BAA and outside providers of capital to fund the several hundred million dollars needed to finance the rollout.

I was two weeks into my new office in London when a call came in from Paris. It was from the young immigration lawyer, Philippe, who had been ushering my applications for the *carte de commerçant* and *carte de séjour* through the fog of the French judicial system. He worked for a different firm than my other lawyers, and so was not always aware of the latest McArthurGlen news.

"I have good news, *Bairn*. Both your *carte de séjour* and *carte de commerçant* have been approved. You now have permission to live in France. In addition, you have permission to work in France, *and* start up a company. Eh?" he asked, obviously happy to have good news for once.

"Well done, Philippe," I responded, "It's been a long struggle I know."

"Yes, it has. Now, you must merely go to the Palais de Justice with your passport and pick them up. Congratulations!" Philippe concluded.

"Thank you, Philippe, thank you very much. May I now update you with some news of my own?"

"But surely, of course, you can," Philippe said cheerfully.

"Well, first, the McArthurGlen center opened in Troyes eight months ago, after we secured many different government approvals. We've created about two hundred jobs there already, with more to come. I guess it's a good thing the French government has now decided to grant me permission to work in France, no?"

Philippe was young and earnest, and didn't quite know how to assess my humor.

"Well, yes, *Bairn*, it's good. It took some time, of course . . ."

"Sorry to interrupt, Philippe, but I should update you on another item," I said politely.

"Yes, what's that?"

"My family and I moved to London a few months ago. I am still president of the French company, but based here," I explained.

"Oooh. Oh. Hmm. I am sorry, *Bairn*, I am sorry. But both the *carte de séjour* and the *carte de commerçant* do not allow for that. It allows only for you to live in France, as described on your application. . . . The French government hasn't agreed to those conditions."

Two days later an even more illuminating call came in.

"Byrne," said Claire Quill, our Director of Human Resources, "your assistant Penny is on the line. She seems a little agitated."

I picked up the phone.

"Penny, is everything all right?"

Penny was my secretary in Paris—American by upbringing, but Parisian for the last fifteen years or so. She did not like matters to be out of order.

"Byrne, the *huissiers* are here—they're right here in reception, two of them in uniforms!" Penny burst out, trying to keep calm.

Huissiers (pronounced "HWEE-see-ays") are the French equivalent of sheriffs of the court, sent out on judges' orders to enforce rulings of the court.

"Okay, Penny. *Huissiers* are there. What do they want?" I responded slowly and calmly, in hopes it would help to keep Penny calm.

"Well, they want to take *all* the office furniture. And they want *all the computers!* They say they'll start with the computers *now*. Take the computers today, and come back with movers for the furniture tomorrow . . ."

"Whoa—whoa—whoa," I responded. This did sound a bit serious. "On what grounds are they saying they have a right to take the computers?"

"Well, because the tickets weren't paid," Penny gushed over the line. "The tickets."

"What tickets?" I ask.

"The *parking* tickets!"

"Parking tickets? You mean for the Renault Espace??" I asked with incredulity.

"Yes, the Espace, the one Pamela drove around. They say there are over fifty thousand francs of fines outstanding. They say it's from over four different years."

And then I started laughing, a good, strong, deep laugh.

"Byrne, I'm not kidding. *Seriously,* they're out front," Penny implored.

I laughed even more.

"Byrne? Byrne?"

"Sorry, Penny, sorry."

The irony was too much.

For two and a half years the French government, at virtually every level, had expended enormous energy handling actions meant to stop me. In that time I managed to start a company, create over two hundred jobs, invest 20 million dollars, and build a highly successful project. After all that, and after three years of processing a few pages of a single visa application, paperwork arrives to finally permit me to actually live in the country and manage a business. It does not, however, permit me to live outside the country and manage the business.

Now, after three successive New Year's presidential pardons for parking-ticket holders, it *suddenly* becomes clear those pardons were only meant for French offenders, not foreigners. It also becomes clear that in a unique and wholly uncharacteristic spasm of incredible Gallic efficiency

that same government has determined that a foreigner owned the offending car; that the foreigner is president of a company in Paris (whether or
not he has a permit to be so), and that money can be squeezed from the
foreigner-parking-ticket-holder-who-is-a-company-president merely by
threatening said company by the same Palais de Justice, which is deliber-
ating whether to permit said president to manage a company from outside
the country, whether or not that company still has computers in its office.
   Mon Dieu.

The festivities of Opening Day at Swindon were all that Cheshire Oaks
and Troyes had been and more, thanks in large part to Patience O'Connor. She brought all her experience to bear, transforming the opening
into a Norman-Rockwell-comes-to-England celebration. There were
high-school marching bands setting the pace for the local Rotary Chapter, and a few hundred other marchers who followed. Both the U.S. am-
bassador to the Court of St. James, Phil Lader, and the future CEO of
Sony Corporation, Sir Howard Stringer, offered opening remarks to the
gathered thousands. Given our experience at Cheshire Oaks and Troyes,
we thought we were fully prepared for the crowds this time, but when
the center's doors opened the stores were as nearly as overrun as before.
The Flying Scotsman's whistle shrieked, steam issued forth, shoppers
shopped and gaped, and the historic halls of Isambard Kingdom Brunel's
engine factory was alive and vibrant once again.

   The public loved it. The press loved it. Patience secured coverage not
only in all the local and regional press, but also on the BBC, in *The Times* of
London, all other broadsheets, and eventually CNN. Suddenly, McArthur-
Glen was not just offering a whole new style of shopping, but one which,
if carefully executed, was good for the retailers, the manufacturers, the
shopping public, and now the environment as well. It was, we hoped, a
harbinger of things to come. If we could make those old factory buildings
come alive as an outlet center, the possibilities for converting abandoned
structures throughout Europe's Old World were nearly infinite.

Joey was euphoric the night of the Great Western Opening, much more so
than at Cheshire Oaks and Troyes. Euphoric because Swindon was more than

just another outlet center. It had been a difficult historic restoration project, presenting complexities not only in design and construction, but also in its leasing, financing, and marketing. It was the type of project at which The Kaempfer Company in Washington had excelled. It was the type where Joey's design talent came to the fore in using architecture to both speak for itself while also forming a profitable solution to a development challenge. Like our earlier Warner and Investment Building projects, the Great Western project had taken years of restoration efforts, and the results were stunning. Amid the champagne, the music, and the hundreds of well-dressed VIPs who came as our guests to view and maybe to shop, the star of the show was clearly the factory itself. As with the rest of us, Joey beamed in its reflected glow.

Among Joey's many idiosyncrasies is his impulsiveness. His personal lifestyle includes a staccato penchant for fads and fashion: now he's smoking—a lot . . . now he's not smoking—at all. Now he's exercising—a lot . . . now—not at all.

At the time of the Great Western opening, Joey was deeply into his latest fad: rollerblading. Despite a few notable falls he was pretty good at it. Toward the end of the opening celebrations, Joey realized that one of the greatest venues he'd ever seen for rollerblading was right before his eyes—the Great Western Outlet Center, with its smooth, polished concrete flooring meandering all around the center, in one long lazy loop, coming right back to where it started. Infused with sufficient champagne to conclude he had a brilliant idea, Joey, then aged fifty, decided to go rollerblading, then and there.

The only hitch was that Joey did not have his $249 double-ball-bearing Nike rollerblades with him. Thinking quickly, he realized that what he *did* have was a shopping center full of merchandise, including one store that specialized in rollerblading. Simple enough, Joey concluded as he marched off in his dashing new Polo chalk-stripe suit, he'd just borrow a pair of blades and some equipment from the store and off he'd go.

The evening was already late. The band musicians were packing up. All the stores in the center were closed, their security grills rolled down and locked to the floor.

No problem, thought Joey. He was in a McArthurGlen center, he was head of McArthurGlen, ergo this was *his* center. He searched for a security guard to unlock all those bothersome security obstacles, so he could choose his rollerblades and equipment.

The security guard was duly located, Joey outlined his scheme, and when the guard suggested a little testily that it was not a good idea, Joey pulled himself up and asked pointedly, "Do you know who I *am?*" Whereupon the security guard radioed for his manager.

Sometime later, as the party wound down, departing VIP guests asked me, "Where's Joey?" I had no idea, and after questioning Adrian and John, it was clear that they didn't, either.

Just then the remaining partygoers were treated to the sight of a crouched Joey whipping around one of the corners of that meandering shopping route he'd worked so hard to design, his chalk-stripe Polo jacket missing, the top of the rollerblades jutting boldly over the fashionably tailored cuffs of his trousers, and his head jammed into a navy-blue helmet emblazoned with a streak of yellow lightning. With his five-foot-six-inch figure bent low for speed, he looked like a wannabe Harry Potter on wheels. He had just navigated a sharp corner, and was leaning perilously to his left, with his right leg off the floor and his arms spinning frantically to maintain balance. He was on the brink of a spectacular wipeout as he passed by the Hanro Lingerie Outlet and zigzagged toward the Thorton Chocolate store. Two security guards, huffing and puffing as they vainly tried to keep up with him, looked embarrassed and increasingly distressed as they encountered the amazed looks of the VIP crowd. In Britain, embarrassment is the most painful of all forms of social distress. To suffer embarrassment in the line of duty was particularly cruel.

The incident ended with a not-amused Adrian Wright, ex-policeman and former BAA director of Airport Retail, marching up and explaining to Joey that entering locked retail stores, even if we were the landlord, was "just not on." The next day calls were made, notes of apology written. Shoppers came back shopping, the incident blew over, and McArthurGlen began thinking about expanding the Great Western Outlet Center.

The shopping public came to the Great Western, loved the rail-heritage-meets-modern-commerce experience, and came back again. They spread the word and then came back yet again. To our delight, sales in Swindon's downtown department stores, specialty stores, and restaurants all increased. It was emerging that our outlet concept, if carefully executed (balancing a town's existing retail with our outlet retail), was a catalyst not only for re-generating abandoned old structures but also in helping to increase sales and vitality in existing downtowns.

With her decades of experience in public relations and retail projects, Patience knew that we had something special on hand. The combination of urban regeneration, innovative retailing, and a restored Victorian factory with a unique role in British history was highly unusual. Who better to truly appreciate these successes, Patience thought, than those whose inter-ests had been best served by the factory in its heyday—the descendants of Queen Victoria herself, namely the Royal Family?

The British have a mixed-message relationship with their monarchy. The tabloid press hounds the Royals mercilessly, sniffing for stories of con-troversy which the public happily buy and read. Yet, there is also genuine affection for the Royal Family, and a royal endorsement for a private sector project is observed with respect. Patience concluded the mix of our center with royal causes might just be a symbiotic one. The Royals, it soon became apparent, agreed.

The first member of the House of Windsor to visit us at Swindon was Anne, the Princess Royal, daughter of the Queen and sister of Prince Charles. Princess Anne, whose royal duties included serving as patron of many historic British institutions seeking new life in the modern world, was intrigued by what she had heard about our Great Western Outlet Cen-ter and came for a "Royal Walkabout" to see for herself. Arriving in her chauffeured Daimler, with her ladies-in-waiting and her Lord Lieutenant escort, she alighted from her car to be greeted by a receiving line of local dignitaries, ending with the somewhat less dignified Barry Gibson and me as hosts of the tour. Princess Anne was presented with a posie of flowers by my six-year-old and four-year-old daughters Avery and Cara, thereby peak-ing early on their lifelong exposure to royalty, though leaving them with a story to tell.

After her walkabout, during which she inspected the historic features and talked with retirees who had worked in the factory, Princess Anne must have been impressed enough to mention it around the family dinner table at Buckingham Palace. That may have been why the Prince of Wales, or at least his staff, was already intrigued by our project by the time Pa-tience contacted his office.

For all the critical press coverage showered upon Prince Charles concerning his idiosyncrasies and foibles, there is no doubt about his keen interest in British history and his love of traditional architecture. At the time of our Great Western project Prince Charles was in the process of establishing his Regeneration Through Heritage initiative, a campaign to preserve historically important but outmoded structures by creating new uses for them. Our Swindon project, the prince apparently concluded, was exactly the sort of thing for which he was campaigning, and he wanted to learn more about it. In fact, the prince decided to take the initiative.

We were invited to meet privately with him at St. James's Palace, his in-London residence, just prior to the reception he was hosting to formally launch the Regeneration Through Heritage campaign. He met with us in a salon alongside the main reception. Charles walked up to greet us while, in one of his telltale royal mannerisms, he tugged gently at his cuffs from under his buttoned deep-blue double-breasted jacket. The carpeting was so thick there was not a sound as he approached.

"Very kind of you to join me this evening," the prince said extending his hand. He told us he was particularly intrigued by the fact that ours was the only fully private sector initiative featured that night.

Shortly after our meeting, the prince's office called to propose a private visit by His Royal Highness to our Great Western project. No press invited. Inevitably, word leaked out and the town of Swindon found itself suddenly receiving more royal attention in a few months than during the prior hundred years.

The prince came, toured, listened, and liked what he saw and heard. So much so, he decided that the project needed to be highlighted, to be held up as an example of what was possible, especially without government support. Furthermore, we were informed, Prince Charles wanted to highlight it himself. He wanted his Regeneration Through Heritage Trust to host a symposium at Great Western to showcase our project. However, his personal staff made it clear that the event would have to be controlled by the prince's office. There would be, *cough-cough,* no crass commercialism associated with the event. Just speeches, a tour, and, naturally, for the chosen ones, tea afterward with HRH.

We politely demurred, reflected upon it . . . and then jumped at the offer. Who needed unseemly commercialism, we thought, if we could arrange for some of our most important customers to have tea with the Prince of Wales?

For the few months leading up to the symposium, we made it a practice to casually drop a word to our most valued clients, toward the end of an otherwise humdrum meeting, along the lines of, "By the way, we're hosting a small gathering with Prince Charles down at our Great Western project— care to come along for a cuppa?" That usually caught their interest. Suddenly, discussing surplus stock, outlet stores, and rental figures didn't seem so dry.

Unexpectedly, during the months leading up to the prince's symposium, another royal invitation found its way to McArthurGlen. This one was from Prince Philip, the Duke of Edinburgh, consort to the Queen, who was hosting a dinner in honor of those retailing companies which over the years had made a particularly significant contribution to the nation's general welfare. The invitation was mainly due to Barry Gibson's achievements in the industry. But, as Barry was then chairman of McArthurGlen, and because the Great Western center was causing such a stir, there I was, walking up those same steps on that same plush carpet in St. James's Palace as I had done a few months earlier, this time to meet the father of the man who had invited us last time.

When the Duke of Edinburgh arrived at my place in the reception line, escorted along by Barry, he was fairly well briefed.

"Ah, yes. You're one of the Americans with a new factory concept. Are you enjoying living here?" the duke said, looking straight into my eye, his silver, combed-back hair seeming more prominent by the offsetting black of his tuxedo.

"Yes, Your Highness," I replied, "my family and I are very happy living here in London."

"But what I don't understand is what an old factory has to do with modern retailing," the duke inquired.

I provided my brief explanation of the outlet concept, and the role of the factory in Swindon.

"Yes, I see," the duke responded, though I wasn't at all sure I was successful in getting him to really see. It might have been my accent.

Prince Charles's symposium went off without a hitch. Many of the high-and-mighty of the British real-estate industry and the intelligentsia of the design world attended, as well as a lot of press. Certainly, the prince was gracious in his comments about our project.

"McArthurGlen should be recognized and congratulated for undertaking this project and delivering it so well," the prince said, evoking oohs and aahs from the crowd during the slide-show presentation he gave on the project.

Afterward was the tea with HRH, the one which I had so casually mentioned in meetings with the sought-after brands. There is an oft-viewed photograph in the McArthurGlen archives of Joey and me together with Prince Charles and Santo Versace, president of the Versace fashion house. There are a few white china teacups in hand, and, notably, a dapper red silk kerchief popping up from the breast pocket of Prince Charles's suit jacket. Santo Versace is beaming a broad smile, clearly enjoying himself as the chatter amongst the four of us unfolds.

Soon afterward Santo signed up for a store in our next UK center, a store in our first Italian center, and a store in the expansion phase of Troyes. Santo liked tea with the Prince.

We figured that Prince Charles's symposium was the high-water mark of the Royals' interest in McArthurGlen's work. By then we had had a visit with or from the Princess Royal, the Prince of Wales (three times), and the Duke of Edinburgh. There aren't many British Royals more senior than those. In fact, there's only one—Her Majesty, Queen Elizabeth II.

It was about a year later when the Office of the Private Secretary for the Queen called. There was interest, the private secretary intoned with proper solemnity, in a Royal Walkabout at our Cheshire Oaks project.

Jackpot . . .

This was in the era in which the advisers to the Queen had concluded Her Majesty needed to spend time "getting closer to her people." Some insightful courtier, apparently, decided that dropping by McArthurGlen was getting Her Majesty close to her people.

Visits by the Queen to any location are carefully scripted out well in advance, as much to avoid missteps as for security. Suffering public embarrassment is painful enough for anyone in British society. Having the Queen experience such a fate is unthinkable.

The visit to Cheshire Oaks was timed out like all other visits. The

Queen would arrive at 2 PM sharp by automobile. The Queen's Daimler is a wide, heavy car, deep blue in color with the Queen's crest prominently featured, jutting up on top where the windshield met the roofline. The car was to drive up the center aisle of our front parking lot, a string of outlet stores on either side for viewing. The crowds would be cordoned off but close enough for the Queen to see and be seen.

The car would continue on for five hundred yards or so, take a right-hand turn at the drive-through of the McDonald's, and slowly return to that same parking lot, where the Queen would then alight for her Royal Walkabout, escorted by Joey and a small squad of others.

The Queen's car arrived exactly on time and proceeded up the parking lot exactly as planned, driving past the several thousand spectators crowded on either side. The Queen was dressed in a bright canary yellow suit, in keeping with the bright spring sunshine of the day. The Daimler continued on to the right turn into the drive-through, also exactly as planned.

And that's where the planning broke down.

Incredibly, no one had thought to measure the width of the McDonald's drive-through to make sure it was wide enough to accommodate the Queen's wide Daimler. Nor had anyone thought to measure the height of the McDonald's drive-through overhang to make sure it was tall enough to allow the passage of Her Majesty's tall Daimler. It thus came as a highly unwelcome surprise when the Daimler glided quietly into the drive-through and suddenly a sharp scraping sound came from above combined with mooshy-rubbery sounds from the sides. The Daimler, and therefore the Queen, became stuck in the McDonald's drive-through, wedged between the take-out window and the concrete column opposite. The world's press was awaiting just the other side of the building. The potential for a royal embarrassment of truly epic proportions, of monumental proportions, was at hand.

Fortunately, the structure of the McDonald's building shielded the scene. No one in the crowds could see the Daimler. The drive around the McDonald's building should have taken twenty seconds at most. The crowd waited dutifully for the anticipated reappearance of their monarch, but to no avail.

Thirty seconds passed and a few security guards glanced at each other with a puzzled expression. Joey, the host-to-be, shifted his weight from one foot to another, hands clasped in front of him, as he looked over to where the Daimler should be coming out.

Nor could anyone, not even the Queen, see the small beads of perspiration break out on the forehead and above the upper lip of the Queen's chauffeur. This was, literally, a jam he had not encountered before.

The chauffeur realized he needed to act quickly, but also calmly and with dignity. He was struggling to ignore images of the next day's headlines which flashed through his mind: QUEEN GETS STUCK FOR BIG MAC AND FRIES.

Finally, after more than sixty seconds—an absolute lifetime to those handlers charged with forever avoiding embarrassing moments for the Queen—her car came gliding slowly around the corner. The potential embarrassment of the Queen being caught at the take-away window of a McDonald's drive-though had been avoided.

It was the chauffeur who had saved the day. He was a pro, naturally. You aren't selected to chauffeur the Queen around unless you know how to avoid problems, and to solve the ones you can't avoid. Only the Queen and her lady-in-waiting beside her had seen, moments before, the chauffeur step quickly out of the car, reach up, and unceremoniously bend, with a haunting screech, the metal royal crest flat onto the car roof, freeing it from the drive-through overhang but also completely hiding its damaged condition from the crowds and press. Nor did anyone else see him, suddenly and expertly, reverse the Daimler, and with an ingenious maneuver ramp it up onto the raised concrete platform, and steer it through the drive-aisle at an angle, with millimeters to spare on either side, saying with calm dignity to the Queen, then tilted at a precarious angle in back, "Apologies Your Majesty."

Smiling and unruffled, the Queen alighted from her car for a successful walkabout with Joey and others as though nothing had happened. Calm and dignified. Never complain; never explain. The Queen's image, and that of the monarchy, had been saved from mortal embarrassment. The "McDonald's Scare" had passed.

Until the next morning.

Splashed across the front pages of every paper in the United Kingdom and many around the world was a photo of Her Majesty and Joey walking along, he in his dark Polo suit with a white kerchief popping out of the breast pocket; she in her canary yellow suit. Over their shoulders, in the background but large and completely legible, was the McDonald's name and golden-arches logo, matching in yellow tones the bright suit of the Queen. The yellow seemed to imply synchronicity. Fortunately, nowhere was there mention of the stuck Daimler or damaged royal crest, nor was there any mention of McArthurGlen. It was all about the Queen and McDonald's, and getting closer to her people. Later, we heard that the president of McDonald's Corporation was traveling in Asia that day, saw the photo in the newspaper, and immediately called his office to have it framed and mounted in the reception of their corporate headquarters. There is, however, no photo of the Queen and McDonald's hanging in the halls of McArthurGlen.

While Britain was proving to be a fruitful (if prickly) market for outlet development, we were finding it increasingly difficult to obtain suitable zoning approvals on the Continent. Then our success at Swindon prompted us to reconsider our expansion strategy. It demonstrated that we could alter our site criteria and still succeed. It appeared as though our outlet concept was so powerful that perhaps we could go into many of the former industrial towns of Europe—the dreary, down-market residue of the industrial revolution—and regenerate them. There were plenty of those towns looking for a new future. I had already been speaking with the mayor of one such town in France, and after Swindon, I decided to have another look.

The town in question was Roubaix in the mining region of northern France, a grimy, downtrodden place with a long history of unemployment and social unrest. Roubaix is a former textile manufacturing town, which for decades had watched prosperity pass it by. Three times the Roubaix mayor had approached me in the hopes that planting a McArthurGlen outlet there would act as a catalyst for the city's regeneration. Three times I had turned him down.

But now I had been wondering whether to reconsider Roubaix. I didn't have an alternative site in France with such a high level of certainty for zoning approval. One Sunday afternoon I asked the entire Paris team to come into the office to brief Joey on the merits and risks of the project. My own opinion was, even upon review, to not go forward. The prospect was

just too risky. But on that particular day I was especially tired from end-
lessly running around Europe looking for new sites. Joey, on the other
hand, was full of energy and optimism, and concluded we were all being
too conservative.

Joey had never set eyes on Roubaix. "Why don't we all go see the site
together?" he suggested. "Right now." And so we did, on a beautiful Sunday afternoon.

Even in the glorious spring sunshine of northern France, Roubaix continued to look as risky as it always had, but wherever I saw problems, Joey
saw opportunities. I began to wonder if maybe I was being too conservative in my state of fatigue. In the end we drafted a long wish list to submit
to the city and to the regional authorities as the quid pro quo for our going
forward. We asked for a purchase price of one dollar for the land. We asked
for the city to pay for all infrastructure, to charge no property taxes for ten
years, to renovate an existing parking garage, and to pay for 50 percent of
all the marketing costs, and other expenses. We asked for as much as we
could to reduce our risk of the project not working. We submitted the type
of requests that the press usually decries as public freebies to a greedy developer. But we weren't being greedy. Roubaix, then, was exactly the type
of downtrodden town that has to pony up a lot of public support in order
to attract outside investment.

The public authorities understood the situation regarding the state of
their own city, and quickly agreed to all our requests. With that strong
vote of confidence we went to work, our hopes high for both a commercial
success and a great contribution to the region's welfare.

The Grand Opening was just that—grand and successful amid much
pomp and ceremony. All the region's political leaders were on hand, including Monsieur Pierre Mauroy, former prime minister of France and the
current mayor of the nearby city of Lille.

And that's where it ended. The center never took off. The crowds came to
shop—once—and never came back. The down-market image of Roubaix,
and the fear of personal risk if you went there to shop, was just too great. One
glamorous shopping center alone wasn't enough to change that.

Joey and I had both made big mistakes. We were both too eager to have
another dot on the map in France. I hadn't stuck with my instincts.

The big mistake was that we shouldn't have believed all of our own

PR. We had done so and had diluted the ageless rule of real estate, a rule which no shopper forgets: location, location, location. Past success, even if phenomenal, is no guarantee of the future. Roubaix is the one McArthur-Glen center in Europe that did not meet our criteria for success. and it continues as an underperforming center to this day.

TWENTY-EIGHT

A Smoke-Filled Room

As always is the case when working in a foreign country, there are some elements of the host culture with which you immediately feel comfortable, and others that never seem to settle in. I never felt comfortable with Germany's intense focus on "the rules." It wasn't the laws per se. It's their country and I respect whatever laws they deemed necessary. It was more the psychology of, "These are the rules. They have been handed down for generations, and so we follow them."

And in Germany there are lots of rules. Rules governing your everyday personal life and rules governing a company's everyday professional life. I remember well when a German friend gave birth to a healthy, cherubic baby. In the ensuing celebrations I asked the mother why she hadn't given the baby the name she had been mentioning to us during the prior several months.

"Oh," she said, "because it wasn't approved."

"Approved?" I repeated.

"Yes, approved," she said matter-of-factly. In response to my stare, she explained, "If the government does not think the chosen name clearly indicates the baby's gender, they will not approve it."

"How can they stop you?" I persisted.

"Oh, it's simple. If it's not approved, then no birth certificate, no registration, and therefore no passport, no identity papers, and no state benefits. You have to register the baby."

I had no response.

"Well, you see, the government protects babies from having confusing names slapped on them like Faith, Sting, Bono, or Bonzo, or worse. So, there is an approval process," she concluded as she excused herself to feed her crying, hungry, properly named, freshly minted German baby.

There are aspects of Germany's live-by-the-rules formality that are also reassuring. For starters, I observed a lot of truly top-rate professionalism in the workplace. Not much humor, but plenty of professionalism. The meetings have set agendas, they start on time, they wrap up with a summary and a list of who is responsible for what. Our chief legal adviser in Germany was a man named Christophe Munche, from Munich. Christophe was always punctual, always prepared, and always impeccably dressed. In four years I never saw him with a wrinkle in his Hugo Boss suits. When Christophe made his first presentation to us on Germany's laws and what they would mean to us, he was so insightful, composed, organized, and measured that when he left the room I turned to Joey and George, and said, "Please, dear God, let's not go anywhere in Germany without him at our side." We met others, many others, like him.

I also felt comfortable with Germany's political system. Much like the American system it's based on federalism. There are sixteen separate states and for most areas of administration each has its own laws that may or may not be the same as the neighboring state. Each state is a powerful entity unto itself, and the minister-president of each—the equivalent of an American governor—is subject to much of the same intense lobbying by special-interest groups as in the United States. One of the most powerful of such special-interest groups is the retailing industry. That industry, comprising 430,000 separate businesses, a total of 2.8 million employees, with annual sales of over 500 billion dollars, is in a powerful position to let its views be known. And it does. It does so through a troika comprised of trade unions, an association of small retailers, and an umbrella organization called the German Retail Federation.

In the early 1990s, a conflict that had been brewing for decades was coming to a head concerning the rules governing opening hours for stores. As more and more women joined the workforce, those new workers found they needed longer shopping hours—including Saturday shopping hours—to complete their household purchasing. But German retailers were reluctant to change their highly restricted working hours. The rules had been set, they insisted, and they were to be followed. One element of the code that was considered sacrosanct severely limited shopping hours on Saturdays. Every shop was required to close by 2 PM. The thinking was that other people didn't work on Saturdays, so why should retailers? The fact that consumers really wanted to shop on Saturdays, and working women really needed to, was irrelevant. The aim was to protect retailers, not to serve customers.

In 1996, a compromise was finally forged, one which was bitterly fought by the unions and smaller retailers. The new rules allowed stores, at their option, to stay open until 4 PM on Saturday. The issue of Sunday openings was so controversial that even discussing it was off-limits. The powerful unions opposed it. The Church opposed it. So politicians avoided it.

There were a few other basic rules on which the retail industry had been built. One governed discounting on prices. Since 1933, discounting greater than 3 percent had been banned.

Why?

Because it was deemed to be unfair competition.

Why?

Because the unions and small retailers said it was.

But not all the rules were so regressive. There were a few signs of progress. While discounts were restricted, some seasonal sales were permitted. The rules stated that sales could start on the last Monday in January, and the last Monday in July, and run for periods of exactly twelve working days. No more, no less. Winter season and summer season. Very organized.

Anniversary sales were also permitted. They could be held once: on the twenty-fifth anniversary of the business. Germans take the long view.

And clearance sales were allowed. But only after a business had declared bankruptcy and its inventory needed to be cleared. Otherwise, apparently, there was no need for a clearance.

But what did these restrictions do for the consumer?

That was not the point.

Another rule was that there can be no money-back guarantees on products sold in Germany.

Why?

Because to do so would provide unfair competition, even if many retailers wanted to offer guarantees.

Why?

Because other retailers might not be offering them. Those were the rules.

This was the German retailing environment in the mid-1990s. Rules set in the early1930s, were still rigidly observed in the 1990s. (Some have been relaxed since then.) The fact that German society's needs had moved on, and women had joined the workforce, and product quality now can often be guaranteed, and Saturday opening hours don't require a new shift of employees, was irrelevant.

There was one last retail rule, the most important rule of all: There should be no retail operations outside of town. In this fight the unions and retailers were joined by the Green Party, which in Germany acts as the protector of the environment, and is one of the most powerful political forces in the country. Its power explains why there is so little out-of-town retail in Germany. It explains why Germany has one-fifth the number of shopping centers per thousand inhabitants as, say, France or the United Kingdom, and approximately one-tenth the number as in the United States.

And so how did McArthurGlen fit into this picture? Very simply: We arrived in Lower Saxony as a foreign-owned, foreign-controlled, foreign-represented company with a new retailing concept. That concept involved an operation that would generate 60 percent to 65 percent of its sales on weekends. It would be located out of town, require the use of a car, and would be based on a discount-sales model. The promise to the consumer would include a guarantee of quality from the brand owner to overcome any perceived image of second-quality goods in the outlet stores. Our concept violated all the established retailing rules. So, in the eyes of the German retail industry and the Green Party, we were dead on arrival.

We were attacking the holy sacraments of the industry, as well as the legal matrix that had grown up around it. It was that infrastructure that cocooned retailers from the volatile pressures of the passages of time, of changed social trends, of macroeconomics, and of internationalization. It was also that infrastructure that had created a chasm between the industry and its customers.

But we were McArthurGlen, the company that had time and again been told "No," and yet had nonetheless stunningly succeeded in England and in France. We now thought—in fact, we *knew*—we were poised for success after success. By that point our innovative concept and successes were well known in the world of retail, and we had offers of help and of joint ventures from some of the very best retailers in the world, including IKEA in Scandanavia, El Corte Inglés in Spain, and Metro Group in Germany. Of course, there were going to be challenges in Germany. Our concept was never easy to implement. But Germany was the prize and this was to be our moment.

We applied for zoning approval for our Soltau site in early 1997. We estimated it would take a year, maybe a little longer, to navigate our way through the process. We learned around this time that the elections for Lower Saxony were scheduled for just over one year ahead. Our development campaign coincided almost exactly with the local political campaign. It turned out the two were on a collision course.

In the arena of public approvals, the situation can become complicated overnight. The town fathers of both Soltau and Fallingbostel were eager to grant approval for their respective outlet applications, but local permission wasn't going to be enough. This was Germany. Final approval would have to come from the state level. And suddenly the showdown wasn't just McArthurGlen versus Fashion Retail. It was Soltau versus Fallingbostel. CONTROVERSY OVER GIANT CENTERS: WILL THE FIRST ONE BE IN SOLTAU OR FALLINGBOSTEL? shouted the headlines in the *Hannoversche Allgemeine Zeitung.* The lobbyists from Soltau and Fallingbostel, fortified with data, renderings, architectural plans, and occasionally accompanied by members of the rival American designer-outlet teams, were directed to the offices of one Herr Frederich Taddon, the secretary for commerce and industry for Lower Saxony. Taddon, whose close-cropped hair, wire-rimmed glasses, and spotlessly organized office spoke of German efficiency, was at the center of the confrontation. It was to his desk that the dossiers of our projects would be submitted for approval or disapproval. It was his phone that started ringing when the issue spilled over beyond the quiet corridors of the town-council offices in Soltau and Fallingbostel.

And the more that each town campaigned against the other, the more opposition appeared against both, and then against the concept. DISPUTE OVER NEW MARKET PLAYERS USING DUMPING PRICES cried the newspapers. OPPOSITION TO GIANT SHOPPING CENTERS IS GROWING. The unions and retailers came out swinging. The Green Party decided that no outlets should be allowed into Germany at all. Anywhere. Ever. And it decided to make it a "key issue in the regional parliament." The Lower Saxony Cities Assembly determined that this fad was an urgent matter of "national importance," and asked the federal government for support. It claimed that "the entire German cultural landscape was under threat." The phone on Herr Taddon's desk rang incessantly. Letters began arriving. Appointments were requested. But it was an election year. Herr Taddon's boss, the minister-president of Lower Saxony, was up for reelection. And Herr Taddon's boss was known for not wanting to make tough decisions even in good years, much less in an election year. Herr Taddon's boss was a man named Gerhard Schroeder, the same Gerhard Schroeder who would eventually arrive on the world stage as chancellor of Germany, for a while the most powerful politician in Europe. But at this point in his career he was still on the way up, and little known beyond the borders of Germany.

Taddon figured if he had to approve one project over the other he was in a no-win situation. So he decided it was best not to make a decision. In fact, why not put it back into the applicants' court?

"Why don't McArthurGlen and Fashion Retail seek a joint solution to this problem?" he asked Big George. "Perhaps create a joint venture on one site or the other. Perhaps one of the companies could locate in Lower Saxony and the other go elsewhere—of course, with some assistance from us."

"No," was George's message back to him.

"Why not?" Taddon asked innocently.

"Because McArthurGlen and Fashion Retail cannot work together," George explained. He felt no need to elaborate, no need to explain that after the Fallingbostel Ambush there was no way we'd ever be able to work with them. Taddon must have caught something in George's tone of voice because he dropped the matter.

The pressure continued to build. The press continued to excoriate us. The phones continued to ring.

And eventually the phone rang with a call that Taddon couldn't ignore. It was from his boss, Minister-President Gerhard Schroeder. The minister-president was upset. He was up for reelection he reminded Taddon, and he was having a little problem with this so-called designer-outlet business: too much controversy. Schroeder also reminded Taddon that his party had only a one-seat majority in Parliament and this was a particularly tight race. He could not afford losing a vote. Not even one single vote in one single district.

Schroeder wanted to know what was a "designer outlet," anyway? And why the hell were the Americans, of all people, involved in his reelection bid? Couldn't Taddon just make the whole problem go away? Soon?

But much as he might have liked to, Taddon couldn't make it go away. We at McArthurGlen were not going to budge. We had a site that was an excellent highway location with brilliant demographics. It was adjacent to Heide-Park with its millions of visitors per year. Our entire corporate strategy was now wholly focused on getting this foothold in Germany. Our 100-million-dollar bet in the United Kingdom and in France had been predicated in part on rolling out the concept across Europe. Germany was the key to that rollout. And Soltau, it turned out, was now the key to Germany.

Fashion Retail wasn't about to budge, either. They had wiggled their way into the game and thought they had a legitimate shot at winning.

As the lobbying process evolved we began to sense that we were the favored party. Taddon never quite told us as much—he was too professional—but the suggestion was there. The tone of voice. The hint of a "we versus them" alignment. We weren't sure if it was because he favored the town of Soltau, or that he just preferred McArthurGlen or the financial credibility of BAA. But we smelled victory.

And then it was Big George's turn for the phone to ring. It was Taddon on the other end. "The minister-president has taken an interest in the merits of your case," he said to George.

"Wonderful," George replied. "We were certain that the merits would speak for themselves over time."

"Would McArthurGlen be interested in presenting your thoughts directly to Minister-President Schroeder, and in turn hearing his thoughts? Maybe, just maybe, there's a way for all of us to find a solution to this problem," Taddon said.

"Well, we certainly think there is," George responded.

"Of course, you can appreciate the delicacy of this matter," Taddon continued, "what with the election coming up, and all. So I'm proposing a small meeting with you and Mr. Schroeder, without advisers from either side."

"Oh yes, yes, of course," George agreed.

"In fact," Taddon said, "we'll hold the meeting in the minister-president's office in Hannover in a week's time."

For this meeting Joey flew in from America, and he and Big George went along to meet Schroeder in the minister-president's imposing office. Great sweeping staircases led up to extra wide hallways with pillars and galleries overlooking the gray-veined marble floors below. Large heavy wooden doors announced the entrance to anterooms, which in turn announced the entrance to large offices, holding very important people tirelessly organizing Lower Saxony according to the rules.

George and Joey were ushered into Mr. Schroeder's anteroom, and then into the great man's office. Herr Taddon was there, too, and the pleasantries began. Schroeder rose and greeted the visitors cordially. Schroeder is a man who projects authority. Charisma is one of the secrets of his political success. In part, it derives from his looks: He is Hollywood handsome, with very thick black hair, and matching eyebrows, and a quick and telegenic smile. His strong support among women voters suggests his appeal. He is neither as tall nor as broad as Big George Bennett, but when the two men shook hands he came across every bit as George's physical equal.

George had done his homework and he knew that, like George himself, Gerhard Schroeder was an avid cigar smoker. George pulled out a Cohiba Lanceros, one of the longest and highest-quality hand-rolled Cuban cigars that money can find anywhere, and offered it to his new friend Gerhard.

Not to be outdone, Gerhard bolted up from his magnificently large, leather chair. "No no no. Thank you, but wouldn't you like one of my Montecristo A cigars?"—one of the only other very long, high quality, hand-rolled Cuban cigars that money can find anywhere. And then some friendly one-upmanship ensued.

George says, "No, no, thank you, I'll stick with my Cohiba. Wouldn't you like to have one?"

"No no, thank you very much I'll stick with my Montecristo. Don't you want to try one?" And at this point both men were standing across Gerhard's enormous oak desk, arms extended, reaching out to each other with these massive ten-inch, high-quality hand-rolled cigars, like dueling barons from another century.

The amiable banter gave way to smiles as both parties sank back into deep leather seats, and, with Joey, lit up their respective favorite hand-rolled Cuban cigars. Taddon was smart enough not to get into this game and sat quietly to the side as the cigar clouds unfolded.

Schroeder asked to hear more about the outlet concept, feigning great interest. Joey obliged, extolling the virtues of the tourism McArthurGlen would generate, the jobs we would create, and the pride that Lower Saxony would have in hosting the first designer outlet in the country.

Schroeder agreed with all the above and complimented McArthurGlen's success elsewhere in Europe, and took a turn explaining his position. It was a remarkably short explanation.

"The elections are coming," said Gerhard to his new friends, Joey and Big George. "And the retail industry and Green lobby are raising a colossal fuss about these so-called designer outlets. I don't need a fuss right now."

"Of course not," said Gerhard's new friends, Joey and George, shaking their heads in unison.

"And so I have an idea for you. An idea that works for you, works for me, and will work for the people of Lower Saxony."

"Okay," Joey responded.

"If you leave your application in, and we start the formal zoning review process we'll have no choice but to kill it. And I promise you," friend Gerhard said with a newfound intensity in his eyes, "*I will kill it.* I'll have to."

"Right," said George, noting the new level of intensity.

"And you don't want me to kill the application and, therefore, your project, do you?" asked Gerhard, in something of a schoolteacher tone.

"Nope. Certainly don't want you to do that," said George.

"This is my idea," said Gerhard. "Why don't we 'freeze' your application until after the election. You don't push it any further; and we don't process it any further; no more questions asked, no more answers given. It simply freezes. There's no news, so the media loses interest, and the story fades away."

"Uh-huh," said George. "I see."

"And what about the application from Fashion Retail in Fallingbostel?" Joey asked.

"Well, I understand that the town of Fallingbostel is reconsidering its position," Gerhard replied.

George, our man-on-the-ground in Germany, couldn't respond other than to leave his arched eyebrows floating high up in midair. This was news to George. Big news. If Fallingbostel and Fashion Retail withdrew, for whatever reason, that only left Soltau and McArthurGlen. And if there was only Soltau and McArthurGlen, then there was dramatically less risk in waiting until after the elections. In fact, it was clear that if we kept pressing our application, it was going to be killed anyway.

"I see," said George. "I see very clearly."

Joey and George told Herr Taddon they would get back to him with a response very shortly. More pleasantries were exchanged, more jokes made, and Gerhard went so far as to invite George to another meeting, this time at the German Chamber of Commerce in a few weeks' time.

Of course, we agreed to freeze our application. What choice did we have? And, in fact, given the options, what risk was there in doing so?

And in an effort to keep the bonhomie between George and his newfound friend Gerhard continuing, George sent along a thank-you note and a large box of twenty-five Montecristos, Gerhard Schroeder's favorite highest-quality hand-rolled Cuban cigars.

We went quiet on our Soltau application for the several months until the election. We called no one, we lobbied no one, we went underground. George did confirm that Fallingbostel eventually pulled out of the contest, though it was not clear why. It certainly wasn't Morgan's decision to withdraw. Big George had very rnuch wanted to be in the room when Morgan found out the game was up in Lower Saxony for Fashion Retail, and that, ultimately, their Fallingbostel Ambush had failed. We were certain that Roger would blame Fallingbostel's withdrawal squarely on us. But that didn't matter. For us, it seemed that our strategy to focus on Germany was the right one and it was about to take a giant step forward.

So we waited. It seemed like a year. In fact, it was only seven months. Gerhard was reelected by a slim margin, but he was reelected. We felt it impolite if not impolitic to call him on the night of victory asking for our zoning approval, so we waited for a week for them to call us as promised.

We waited then for another week, and another week, and then a month until we decided it was time for us to call Taddon and start the zoning process again. Taddon's secretary remembered us, and assured us her boss would get back to us right away. He never did. George continued to call

Taddon's office, and then he had the Soltau mayor call Taddon's office. Taddon wouldn't take *his* calls, either.

Finally, George went over Taddon's head and called the minister-president's office directly. It was not a call that one made haphazardly. At this point the press was buzzing with speculation that the now twice-elected Minister-President Schroeder might well be the leading contender to succeed Helmut Kohl as chancellor of Germany in the approaching national elections. With Germany's recent reunification, it would make him the head of Europe's largest country. Perhaps charisma was about to meet destiny.

When George finally got through to Gerhard Schroeder's personal secretary, he explained politely that he represented McArthurGlen, and that he hoped to follow up our meeting of several months before. She promised to get back to him the next day.

And indeed, with German professionalism the secretary did call George back the next day. The secretary said that she had spoken to the minister-president regarding the request from McArthurGlen and that the response from the Minister-President had been, "Who is McArthurGlen?" In effect, the government of Lower Saxony was denying any relationship or prior dialogue with us.

"You mean he's dumped us?" Joey spat into the phone from his vantage point in Washington, D.C., some 3,500 miles away. "He just left us at the altar? How can he treat us like that?" Joey was aghast. It was a very American response to what he saw as German sleight-of-hand.

"We've been working on this site for over two years! We did what he told us to do! We pulled back! We played by the rules. Who the hell does this guy think he is?" Joey asked.

"Well, I'll tell you who he is," George said. "To start with, he is the re-elected minister-president of Lower Saxony, and he is also perhaps the leading candidate to be the next chancellor of Germany, which will make him leader of the largest country in Europe. That's who he is. And we're Americans applying for a sensitive public authorization from his government who just had our heads handed to us in, I suspect, our first lesson in hardball German politics."

What struck me most about the resistance we met in Germany was not so much that the entrenched interests did not want us there. As in France, that was certainly a contributing factor. But there was something more than protectionism and greed opposing us. The Germans didn't want us there because we represented change, and the Germans, at this point in their history, mistrusted change above all else.

It seemed that this great, powerful nation, which had caused so much trouble with its neighbors in the last hundred years, and which had undergone so much turmoil itself as a result, had now found itself in the comfortable position of having a pacifist and socialist government set up to take care of its own, and never mind the rest of the world. The rules were set and the benefits were good—in fact, very good. Germany provided Europe's most comprehensive social safety net, in terms of highest number of vacation days, most generous pension rules, and other state benefits.

Why, they ask themselves, after all the pain of the last century, should they seek change?

But the German aversion to change isn't only about the comfort of the womb-to-tomb protection of their social system. One level below that blanket of comfort lies a layer of discomfort caused, I think, by a lack of confidence. Many of the men and women with whom I spoke, particularly those over thirty, commented on how openly Americans expressed their patriotism and their confidence in the future. Germans couldn't do that they told me, because . . . well . . . they just couldn't. There was an unspoken need, in light of World War II and prior aggressions, to lay low and let others take center stage. Hence the aversion to change. By the mid-1990s, Germany had turned into what *Die Zeit,* a highly respected national newspaper, described as "a barricaded society . . . which hinders almost any modernization, strangles any movement." In 2002, the World Competitive rating, compiled by the Lausanne-based International Institute for Management Development, ranked Germany forty-seven out of forty-nine major countries when it came to flexibility and adaptability. In a 2004 report by the European Commission, Germans were judged to be the most risk-averse people in the European Union. In an effort to determine why there was so little entrepreneurship in Europe, the study found that 57 percent of Germans believed they should not start a business "if there was *any* risk that it *might* fail." This is not the Germany of earlier decades, the Germany renowned for its efficiency and industrial leadership. This is a very cautious Germany.

Ironically, the Germans' quest to protect themselves from outside change, to preserve their benefits, and to avoid bold action, only set themselves up for the need for greater, more troublesome change at a later date. Because Germany will, in time, change if only because it must. Given current demographic trends the country quite literally will not be able to continue paying out the extensive social benefits it currently provides. (In that sense, Germany is by no means alone, but rather just more exposed.) Germany will also change because the next generation will likely have more confidence in the future simply because they are one more generation removed from the immediate past. Given time, Germany will gain in confidence to the point where it can accept new concepts, intellectual as well as commercial, in ways that it couldn't in the mid-1990s.

But that will be too late to help McArthurGlen. More useful would have been a better understanding by us of Germany's depth of resistance to change. We consulted all the intellectual research we could find, all the demographic, real estate, and financial studies. But what we really needed was something that could answer the question, "How open is that market to change, to new concepts?" Because the answer to that question at that time was that it was nearly closed shut. Admittedly, we did make it much more difficult for ourselves by not taking on a local partner. That could have gone a long way in helping us to better understand the environment in which we were operating.

There was one final response from Schroeder's office that summed up all our efforts in Lower Saxony. Almost two weeks after the fatal word came back from Schroeder's office, a parcel arrived at our London office addressed to George. Inside were the twenty-five highest quality, hand-rolled Cuban Montecristos that George had sent to Schroeder months before. The box had clearly been opened. The cigars were now dry and somewhat broken from the shipping back and forth. They were no good to anyone. Big George stood in the middle of his office just staring at them. For him it was almost a criminal waste of one of life's greatest delicacies. Finally, he simply tossed them in the trash.

TWENTY-NINE

Dolce Vita

One single seemingly innocuous statistic changed everything. It turned me around, it turned McArthurGlen around, and it turned all our plans for our European rollout around.

For five years following my experience at Troyes I never considered Italy in our expansion plans. In fact, when I ordered up a feasibility study for a multicountry expansion strategy from adviser Jones Lang Wootten, I pointedly told them to leave Italy off the list. If France was that difficult, I figured, life was simply too short to attempt Italy. The Latin business climate seemed so different from ours that I figured we could advance much further, with greater return for our efforts, in a non-Latin environment. The result seemed to bear me out. Five years after our initial successes in France and in the United Kingdom, we had created six hundred jobs in France, but nearly six *thousand* in the United Kingdom.

It was those figures—and those prejudices—that helped us formulate our grand strategy for expansion, a strategy that largely ignored southern Europe and focused on Germany for our continental growth. That decision, of course, was made before the Fallingbostel Ambush, before Schroeder dumped us at Soltau, and before the full weight of Germany's traditional retail establishment had stalled us at the border.

And so it was, when our great strategic juggernaut was checked before we even got started, that we were forced to go back to those grim volumes of statistics from Jones Lang Wootten. And it was in those mountains of numbers that I stumbled over a single statistic that gave me pause.

Over the years we had discovered that some of the most meaningful statistics relate to home ownership. Such figures go a long way to helping us define the wealth, stability, and socioeconomic health of a community. When I checked out the home ownership numbers for Italy, I found that 67 percent of the population owned their own homes. I noted approvingly that this was the same percentage as in the United Kingdom.

But then I noticed something odd. Of all those home owners in Italy, only *17 percent* had a mortgage. That was the lowest figure in the whole of Europe. By comparison, the percentage in Britain was four times higher.

How come so few Italian mortgages?

The answer lay in the Italian culture. To a far greater extent than in most other countries, Italian households are likely to be three generational. Many, many people continue to live where they were born and grew up, grandparents, parents, and children, all in the same home. When the grandparents pass away, the ownership of the house moves down to the next generation, and when they pass away it moves down to the next generation, and so on. In the process, mortgages become a thing of the past.

Imagine a country of 58 million homeowners, I thought, where 87 percent have no mortgage payments each month. What in the world do they do with all that disposable income?

Answer: Italians, like all their Mediterranean brethren, like to spend money on *fashion*. Dresses, tops, suits, shoes, and accessories, and the higher the quality the better. Italians spent more of their disposable income on apparel and other textile goods than anyone else in Europe, other than the Portuguese. Italy was nearly five times the size of Portugal, and with a per capita GDP nearly three times larger. Suddenly the choice of where to concentrate my next expansion efforts was no choice of all.

Joey and George Bennett had their hands full trying to unlock the treasure of Germany, so I took the lead on Italy. But I couldn't do it from my office in London. Desktop surveys are of only limited usefulness. What we needed, I thought, was on-the-ground research, cappuccino-tasting, Chianti-sipping, Tuscany-touring research. I was off to Milan within a week.

To a great extent it was like returning to the early days of McArthurGlen—setting up explorative meetings, reading up on the demographics, the highway counts, the purchasing patterns. Only now, five years on, I knew the right questions to ask, the kind of people I needed to meet.

With five centers now operating and several more on the way, we had credibility, cash, and a need to expand. And we knew well enough that if we didn't offer expansion options to the brands, Morgan would.

After several trips to Milan, Florence, and Rome, I was flying back to Heathrow feeling remarkably upbeat. Italy had a culture that offered optimism in contrast to the French pessimism, and openness in contrast to the German dogged close-mindedness. The responses to my normal first three questions in France had always been "No," "No," and "No." In Germany, the responses were always, "The rules do not permit that—end of story." In Italy, I found the responses to those same questions were usually, "Yes," "Good idea," and "Why not?"

Italy was a country, it seemed, where the family unit was not only the bedrock for much of the social fabric (witness those mortgage statistics) but also one of the greatest sources of its business dynamism. There are the endless little family firms that run the bakeries, pharmacies, and hotels in each town. And there are the very large family firms that dominate the business news of Italy—the Agnellis of Fiat, and the Pirellis of tire and real-estate fame. But there is also the in-between tier, especially in the textile and fashion worlds, the tier where one finds the families of Gucci, Prada, Armani, Ferragamo, Versace, Etro, Zegna, Dolce & Gabbana— families that employ hundreds and often thousands of workers, many with worldwide reputations for their designs and collections. Families that told me, when I explained our concept, "This is interesting. Let's explore it. Why not?" Families and, therefore, businesses that expressed an openness to new ideas and a willingness to try them.

These were people who were also intimately connected with every aspect of their business. The Italian textile manufacturer was often the brand owner and the retailer, too, selling their goods through their own shops. They understood firsthand the need for preserving the power of their brand, as well as the need to protect their retailers. When I explained the designer-outlet concept to them they were incredibly quick to understand its virtues, and eager to learn more. Dealing with them was exciting and *fun*.

Almost everywhere I went in Italy I was getting to "yes" remarkably fast. I took my enthusiasm back to London and waxed eloquently to the

BMG board about the potential of expanding in Italy. What I had not yet learned, and what it would take me a year to realize, was that in Italy getting to "yes" was the easy part. Implementing that "yes" was the challenge.

Italy has its own sense of time. It is a country that measures its progress not in decades, not even in centuries, but in millennia. The nobility trace their ancestry back to the Romans. Every project is expected to proceed one longggggg, sloooooow step at a time. Italians like to say "Yes," and they mean it. But their style of implementing that "yes" can drive an Anglo businessman absolutely, completely bonkers. What was important is they had said yes. Figuring out the implementation, to a large extent, was going to be up to me.

One of my first contacts in Italy was David Paulson, of the law firm of Paulson and Meloni, of Milan. David is the product of an Italian father and an American mother, and his personality is simultaneously very much of both. He is enthused with optimism and energy, and loves to work a deal and make connections to it, and to talk and talk and talk.

David listened to my story of McArthurGlen in Europe and loved it. He told me: "Come back, Byrne, come back again, and let me introduce you to the most important people in Milan. The people that you need to crack open this market. Come back again and we shall talk."

And so I came back the following week and true to his word, David had organized a meeting with lots of people eager to sit around the table and discuss the outlet concept with me. Designers, manufacturers, retail distributors, people who knew, they assured me, the head of Prada and even Giorgio Armani *personally*.

"Yes, personally, I tell you, *very* personally . . ."

And that one madhouse meeting with perhaps ten or twelve people around the table provided me with a snapshot of what it really would be like operating in Italy. It should have been a warning, but I wasn't paying attention. I was too confused. Though I was the guest of honor, I quickly realized I was there to observe, not to speak. It was my first experience with the exuberant cacophony of many Italian meetings, with simultaneous conversations, simultaneous negotiations, mobile phones ringing, and mobile conversations ensuing, all competing with secretaries darting in and out, and voices rising to announce new streams of thought, and God knows what else. *Who is in charge of the meeting?* I wondered. *Why am I here?*

All of a sudden David announces, "That's enough discussion!"

"Discussion?" I asked myself. "What have we discussed?" Everyone had been discussing, true, but there had been literally ten different discussions at once, nearly all in Italian, which I didn't understand, and no translations offered. I had no idea what, if anything, had been usefully discussed.

"Let's go for a tour!" David proclaimed. Without warning he led the entire roomful of people into the great, vibrant streets of Milan, to show the visiting American the wonderful potential that Italy and its fashion industry presented for McArthurGlen. He wanted us to see the latest in retail trends, the latest collections, the glamorous new stores—to show how Italians were trying new ideas. Up and down via Monte Napoleone and the surrounding streets we charged, almost as a group. At any given time the twelve was whittled down to one or two or three when mobile phones took over, conversations erupted in the street, or one of our number would proclaim with loud greetings and bear hugs the chance encounter with "my oldest and dearest friend." Other members of our troop indulged in a little shopping or just plain disappeared. I guess David was the leader of the tour, but several times I had no idea why we went in and out of certain stores or what I was meant to learn from the visit. I was utterly beguiled by the Italian optimism. "Yes, this would be a great concept for Milan"; "Yes a great concept for Italy"; "Yes it was bound to be very successful." They wanted to be involved, but then my starchy American intolerance of chaos kicked in, and by the third hour I had a splitting headache, and serious misgivings about my enthusiasm for plunging into Italy. I was beginning to feel concerned. I didn't have a clue what any of these people were talking about, or how to organize them or even how to organize an approach to Italy. Suddenly it felt like my early arrival in Paris all over again.

Despite my misgivings, the pace of my exploration into Italy actually accelerated. On the next trip to Milan two weeks later I let it be known that I was looking for potential partners. I was cautious about launching our concept in what was reputed to be the most opaque business culture in Europe. I wanted a local partner who could deal with all matters regarding public approvals, the politics associated with them, as well as the day-to-day management of construction.

With that in mind I agreed to David's suggestion to meet with a Mr.

Mercardi, owner of one of the largest retail distribution companies in Italy, a company equipped to handle all the details. He was based in the small city of Brescia, east of Milan. Mr. Mercardi turned out to be a man of slight build, with jet-black hair, jet-black eyebrows, and his own trademark dark fiery eyes. As is often the case in Italy, when meeting with the head of a large and successful company, Mr. Mercardi sat at the head of the table, but said little. It was his number two who did most of the talking, even when I directed my questions to Mr. Mercardi. David Paulson had explained to me that the custom was a matter of status. It seemed when the head man believed himself to be truly powerful in Italian business circles, he often let others do the talking.

After forty to fifty minutes of my questions and Mr. Number Two's long answers, Mr. Mercardi, unconsciously echoing many a small-town French mayor, finally interrupted with perhaps the most important pronouncement of the day: "We go to lunch now." And off we went.

Within a ten-minute drive to the west of Brescia we were deep in the Lombardy countryside, where olive groves and vineyards blanket the gently rolling hills that separate Brescia from the lake country to the north. It was an ideal day to travel across the northern Italian landscape—a quattrocento painting come to life—and I was enchanted. We passed dignified farmhouses with red tiled roofs, centuries-old, and immaculately maintained, with smallish windows to provide views looking out, but preventing heat from coming in. The hot September sun reflected warmly on the patchwork quilt of fields, geometric patterns as old as the houses, each field carefully designed to direct the rainwater for maximum use as it made its way down to the valley below.

Our Alfa Romeo pulled into a gate at the top of the hillside and came to rest before a Romanesque villa that commanded a view of the entire region. We were met by the restaurateur who was clearly expecting us, standing at the front door, and showing us to our table in the much darker and cooler interior. The meal was worthy of the setting, washed down with the local red wine throughout, and accompanied by chatter of business but also of soccer, America's poor showing in the World Cup, and the lamentable shortcomings of English cuisine. My host was much looser in this setting than in the office, and at the end of the meal he led me out to the grand terrace so I could experience its glorious view. The bright autumnal sunshine touched me like a benediction. I dipped my biscotti into the *vin santi,* gazed out on all those olive groves and vineyards below and beyond, and said to myself, "Yes . . . expanding into Italy is beginning to look like a very, very promising idea."

Word of our arrival in Italy spread within the retailing and development circles. Without question, Italians were very interested in our concept. I was receiving as many calls in as I was making calls out. One caller seemed particularly interested. His name was Rossatti. Mr. Rossatti found me very early on, and never let go.

I met him for the first time in his office in northeastern Italy. When I arrived the great man was not there to greet me. Instead, it was his number two, Marco, a particularly nervous type. He ushered me into Rossatti's offices to await his arrival. Everything in the room was decorated in tones of brown, tan, and sand, reminding me again that I was in a different culture. Sandy-colored curtains were drawn shut, completely blocking out the afternoon's bright sun beyond. A darker brown shag carpet ran throughout the sprawling office. Rossatti's vast desk, dominating the room even from its corner location, was a thin marble slab with tones of brown and white veining throughout. One wall was covered by dimly lit mirrors, with two-tone brown framing. In the far corner, opposite his desk, was the chocolate-brown sofa where I sat waiting, surrounded by more brown furnishings.

Eventually, Marco returned to announce that Mr. Rossatti would arrive shortly. Marco's English was excellent but his presence was unsettling. He never seemed at ease and as soon as his boss entered it was clear why.

"He doesn't have coffee!" Rossatti complained in Italian. "Tell Simona to bring in the coffee immediately!" He snapped his fingers peremptorily, gesturing toward us as Marco skipped hurriedly to the door. Mr. Rossatti was a man used to getting his way.

He was in his sixties, I judged, still vigorous, with a full head of silver hair plastered down and swept back with gel. His clothing matched his office. Oxford brown shoes, a three-piece burnt umber suit, a café-au-lait shirt set off by a taupe necktie. He leaned forward in his chair when he spoke to me, eyes slightly squinting, despite the dimly lit office. (Why, I wondered, if he had eyesight problems, did he keep the office so dimly lit?)

Mr. Rossatti started our meeting in halting English. "I—am—a—successful businessman—and—therefore—do—not—need—to—speak—much." He spoke in a hoarse, scratchy voice that came from the back of the throat. It reminded me so strongly of Marlon Brando as Don Corleone that I almost smiled.

Mr. Rossatti, with the help of Marco's translations, came right to the point. "I know that you are coming to Italy with your concept," he hoarse-whispered to me. "I know your concept. I have already decided that I will do that concept in Italy and I will be your partner. Because you *will* need a partner to work in Italy. Trust me. Italy is different. It is different, different, and different from where you come from. You need a partner," he continued as he leaned forward almost onto the conference table, "and I *will* be your partner."

Mr. Rossatti was a successful developer in Italy, where it is tough to do business and you need to be tough to be successful. Mr. Rossatti, from all reports, was very successful.

"Well, thank you, Mr. Rossatti, for your kind words about our success," I led off. "I've just arrived in Italy, and am meeting with lots of people." Blah blah blah, I went on with background chatter, looking him unflinchingly in the eye, leading up to my primary message: "I'm not at all sure if we will need a partner for Italy, at least at this point," I concluded.

Mr. Rossatti, asking his assistant with every ten words of English, "What did he say? Tell me faster!" and as soon as he understood the thrust of my response he cut me off and responded.

"The outlet concept will work here. I know that. I am going to develop it here. I know you know how to do it, but you need a partner. I am going to be your partner. Let's talk about that."

Maybe it was the Corleone voice, or maybe it was Mr. Rossatti's looming presence in this bizarre setting, with the closed curtains and door shutting out the outside world. Or maybe it was his message. But for the first time since landing in Paris five years before I was getting a little nervous. Nervous like maybe I was getting in a little over my head. How did developers operate in Italy? Was this a threat? And were such tactics a matter of daily business? I had been involved in enough partnerships to know that fear is not a particularly effective means of building a successful relationship.

I bobbed, and weaved, and was profuse in thanking him for his confidence in us and his interest in our project. But of course, *naturally,* as he could understand, it was too early for me to determine what our strategy would be in Italy *if, in fact,* we came to Italy (try to throw him off with that one, I thought). As I drove away from his building it was clear to me that Mr. Rossatti was definitely not the partner that I sought in Italy. That should be the end of that, I thought.

But I did not know Italy so well. Or at least I did not know Mr. Rossatti. Because "that" certainly was not the end of "that." *That* was just the beginning.

My courtship with Italy developed deep, and fast, and furiously that autumn of 1997. I'd like to claim that I decided whether or not to launch into Italy with a cold calculating, analytical approach. What were the risks involved in setting up an Italian operation? Would they entail as much bureaucracy and backroom dealing as I had once feared? Was there, in fact, a Mafia alive and well, and looking for fresh meat arriving over the borders? Or was I just imagining things?

What really tipped the balance was the fact I *liked* visiting Italy. I looked forward to the cuisine and the rolling, historic countryside. I enjoyed the optimistic atmosphere; I loved the people. Pamela and I had spent our honeymoon in Italy, and all the romantic visions that Americans have of Tuscany, *Cinque Terra,* and the Amalfi coast were already hardwired into me. I could easily support my decision with references to that 17 percent mortgage statistic, the disposable income spent on fashion, and the like. But for all the demographics and financial analysis, for all the hard-won business-school dispassion and acumen, the truth was I wanted to keep coming back to Italy. I hoped the analysis backed me up.

THIRTY

Serravalle

There was that voice again.

"Hello, this is Rossatti," he would announce in his Marlon Brando voice. "When are you coming to Italy? I am going to be your partner."

Mr. Rossatti was, if nothing else, persistent. The calls kept coming, sometimes to my hotel room in Italy, sometimes to my office in London.

Mr. Rossatti was a forceful man, a man with a strong personality, which was easily felt even over the phone lines. Property development is a high-wire act, and requires a high degree of trust between partners. I wasn't ready to entrust my Italian operation to a partnership with a person who made me uneasy.

At the same time, I had to consider Mr. Rossatti's impressive track record. His development projects stretched nearly the entire length of Italy from Milan to Rome, and points farther south. Maybe I shouldn't overlook the very palpable help he might be able to bring to the table? To check my instincts about Mr. Rossatti, I turned to IGI, the same investigative firm we had consulted earlier. They specialized in background checks anywhere on the globe.

"You mean you want to see if there's any criminal or other unsavory activities in his past," Terry Burke summed up over the phone from Washington.

"Well, I wouldn't exactly put it that way," I started to respond.

"I would," Terry said, cutting me off good-naturedly. "We do this all the time with corporate ventures in foreign lands, including those in southern Europe. We find out all sorts of history, and pretty fast, too. Tell me how much you want to know."

That stumped me. How much *did* I want to know?

"Well . . . I don't need graphic details about anything."

"You only want a plain vanilla character check then—with enough details for us to back it up should you decide to know more. Is that about right?" Terry concluded for me.

Terry was back to me in just a few days because it had been easy to confirm my suspicions. "Careful here," he said before signing off. I didn't need any further warning.

So I stalled and evaded, and tried to brush Rossatti off whenever he called, but he would not go away. He must have heard of my meetings with the fashion brands and, therefore, knew I was serious about coming to Italy. He was equally serious about being my partner.

But if I wasn't making much headway in terms of finding an Italian partner, I made a major leap forward in terms of finding a potential site. It was near a tiny village named Serravalle in the Piedmont country, thirty minutes drive north of Genoa and fifty minutes south of Milan. The site was on the edge of a small industrial zone, with nothing around it. No other retail, no city center, and seemingly no people. And incredibly, it had already been granted a *nulla osta*—a zoning approval for retail development. As in so many European countries, zoning permissions for retail in Italy normally take years to secure. It wasn't uncommon to hear tales of ten years spent negotiating a *nulla osta*. And here was one, in place, right where I wanted it. Our research showed that the approval had been granted in part expressly because there was so little development in the region, in the hopes the approval would attract just what we brought—hundreds of jobs.

There was, it turned out, a hitch. The zoning approval was for the wrong type of shopping. It was for a traditional, grocery-anchored retail, not for outlet retail. I asked my lawyer in Milan if it would be difficult to obtain a change in the approval to accommodate our concept. My question elicited a large smile. No problem, Mr. Murphy, simply a formality. It shouldn't take more than three to six months to complete.

There it was again, that wonderful Italian enthusiasm. By that time I'd been in Italy long enough to curb my own optimistic assessments. I'd learned to respond to the ubiquitous "yes-yes-yes," with a hopeful but skeptical "When? When? When?"

Rossatti's calls didn't stop. As I was in a sensitive negotiating stage with securing the Serravalle site, I decided it was tactically prudent to keep stalling him, buying myself time before giving him the definitive "no." I wasn't sure if he knew of our activities in Serravalle, but with his long record of having secured favorable zoning decisions, sometimes under very difficult circumstances, he clearly knew the system. If he knew how to win such approvals, he certainly knew how to block them as well. I didn't need a skilled enemy out there on my first foray into Italy. So I continued to talk. And Rossatti continued to assure me that he, and only he, was going to be my partner in Italy. As long as I brought the brand names and operating team to the project, Rossatti said, he would do the rest. Unfailingly, around this point in our conversations he would lean forward and say, for the seventy-second time, "There is much to be done that you do not know about. I will do it," he would hoarse-whisper. I didn't want to know what he thought had to be done. I certainly didn't want to know how he did it. I just wanted to be left alone.

One morning in London I received a call from Marie-France Marchi, our Director of Sales in Paris. She informed me that Calvin Klein were eager to sign on in Troyes, but they were only willing to pay a very low rent, a paltry 2 percent of their sales, when the standard was then 10 percent.

"That's ridiculous," I said. Only Yves Saint Laurent, which had beaten me bloody in their negotiations as the first brand to sign, was paying 2 percent. "Tell them to forget it. They pay the standard rate. Take it or leave it," I huffed.

"Okay, but Byrne, that is exactly what the Calvin Klein people told me," Marie-France responded. "It is time you gave them a try."

The people who held the European licenses for Calvin Klein were the Fratini brothers of Florence, and I agreed to see them on my next trip south. Prior to that meeting I researched their backgrounds, and it was apparent that they were deeply entrenched in the world of global fashion. The brothers, Corrado and Marcello Fratini, were the driving force behind a family business that was one of the largest denim manufacturers in the world. They had factories in Italy, North Africa, Eastern Europe, and the Far East. By the time I met them they had launched several of their own jeans brands in Italy, including Cotton Belt, Rifle, and others. They also supplied denim to most of the higher-end luxury brands and were the owners of the European and Asian license for Guess? Jeans. In addition, Corrado Fratini had just concluded a joint venture with the Richmont Groupe of Paris to buy the luxury jeweler Van Cleef & Arpels. Recently the Fratinis had started to focus on real-estate development.

I arrived for my 9:30 appointment to discover that the interest in luxury seemed limited to the brands they sold. The Fratini offices occupied the third floor of one of their mills north of Florence. The only access was via an outdoor bare steel staircase from the parking lot below.

Marcello Fratini met me at the top of the stairs, and was as direct and unassuming as his office. He was a sturdy, no-nonsense man in his late fifties, who glided about his premises with little wasted effort. I marveled that his shoulders remained level no matter what his movements. He was bald on top, with deep blue eyes that never blinked as he stared right at you. I never saw a smile during the ensuing negotiating session.

Marcello was polite but pointed. There was nothing deferential about him, and since it was I who had asked for the meeting, he let me do most of the talking. His English was excellent, but I quickly learned that his favorite refrain was, "No, not possible." Marcello didn't bother with a number two talking for him. He handled things very ably by himself.

I described our success story at Troyes, but he seemed convinced that the power of the Calvin Klein name would be stronger than the power of McArthurGlen in drawing shoppers to the center. He made it look as if he had all the leverage, and, with a brand name as strong as Calvin Klein, maybe he did.

By eleven o'clock the 2 percent rent had risen gradually to 3 percent where it seemed stuck. I had run out of angles. Where, I wondered, was I going to go from here?

At that moment, Marcello's brother, Corrado, strolled in. Marcello unfolded from his chair and the brothers embraced with a kiss on either cheek and a strong pat on the back, looking at each other straight in the eye.

"Va bene?"

"Tuto bene. Bellissimo."

The brothers had lived and worked together for over fifty years and there was a palpable bond of trust and respect between them.

Corrado was the taller of the two, and had an air of being more subtle and less direct. Like all Italians, Corrado spoke with his hands, moving them in graceful circles. Marcello gave him a brief update on our discussion—in English, so that I could understand—and Corrado nodded and eased into an empty chair. I carried on with my spiel, and after five minutes Corrado leaned forward and said something very softly to Marcello, who shrugged his shoulders and without excusing himself, unfolded again from his chair and glided out of the room. Corrado proceeded to ask me two or three questions about the McArthurGlen concept, and then said, "Have you had lunch, Mr. Murphy?"

For the next two hours, over a simple but elegant Tuscan lunch, the two brothers and I found ourselves in a far-reaching and totally unscheduled conversation. The brothers described their growing interest in real estate, and how they had land holdings throughout Tuscany and beyond, including the plant in which they had their offices. But rising labor costs were forcing the Fratinis to consider transferring their manufacturing from Italy to North Africa, resulting in the loss of two hundred local jobs. It was, they said, a dilemma. As an important employer in Tuscany they wanted to offer something back. Our conversation turned to the possibility of forming a joint venture for Italy, and even the possibility of using their soon-to-be-shut-down factory site as a McArthurGlen site. Wouldn't it be convenient, Corrado suggested, if McArthurGlen opened an office in Florence?

For me, the entire conversation was somewhere between fanciful and lyrical. This was no Rossatti. This was the type of partner I had envisioned. The more we discussed a potential partnership, the more I liked it. I left a few hours later. With Corrado's help, I settled the Calvin Klein rent at 5 percent. The Fratinis pretended they had been outmaneuvered by me. I pretended it was the lowest rent ever agreed for Troyes. We all thought there was great potential in a partnership.

Eventually, we did convert the Serravalle zoning permit into one that would accommodate an outlet center, but it didn't take three to six months. It took two years. True to form, getting to the initial "Yes" had been the easy part. Our approval in Serravalle was heralded by many as lightning fast for Italy.

With an approval in hand, I hired a young, energetic man named Luca d'Ambrosis to open our office in Milan. Luca was experienced in dealing with the high-fashion brands and was well positioned to help adapt our concept to the Italian market. Once we announced that Serravalle was indeed proceeding, there was buzz in the fashion world and a buzz in the tiny village itself. One morning Luca called me in London to say we needed to have a proper ground-breaking.

Sure, I thought. Ground-breaking. A handful of local officials with shiny shovels turning over the soil with photographers clicking away. "No problem," I said, "go ahead. Organize a ground-breaking. Have fun."

"Ah," Luca replied, "but you must come down from London for this. There will be a blessing."

"A blessing?" I asked.

"Ah yes, always a blessing. This is Italy and all important projects start with a blessing and you should be here."

So I arranged to be there, to be present for "the blessing."

This was not to be any old blessing from the local parish priest, or even from the local monsignor. For a project that involved the creation of 250 to 300 new jobs in a small village like Serravalle, and a project that was bringing such glamorous high-fashion brands and a foreign investor to town, this blessing was from none other than the bishop. And on the great day the bishop arrived in full regalia, with his miter and crosier, holy water, and incense, supported by a host of priests and nuns, and a press corps of a few dozen. The bishop blessed the land, blessed the tractors, blessed the crowds, blessed the photographers, and even blessed the upcoming lunch. Included in those blessings was one for the American who had brought the jobs to little Serravalle. As a lifelong Catholic with a spotty record of observance I found myself hoping that all those blessings included absolutions, future confessionals, and next Sunday's church presence. I wondered if maybe what I had really needed in France and Germany was to have a bishop or maybe a cardinal on my side to secure the help I really needed.

Not everything was a blessing that day. Just before the ceremonies began, I was handed a note informing me that Mr. Rossatti had called. I had continued trying to avoid him but by that time he must have heard about the ground-breaking. Undoubtedly the news would have infuriated him. It was time for me to conclude that unfinished business.

By this point the Fratinis and I had long since agreed on terms for a joint venture in Italy. In the process I met Jacopo Mazzei, the Fratinis' in-house partner for all real-estate projects. It was in working closely with Jacopo that I began to learn about Italian history at a different level.

When Jacopo Mazzei enters the room over 700 years of Tuscan heritage accompanies him. Lean, with an athlete's build, classic Italian good looks, and an easy smile, Jacopo embodies the elegance of Florentine culture. His family has been at the epicenter of Tuscan history and culture since his forefather, Lapo Mazzei, was the first person to mention the word "chianti" in print, in a letter dated 1398. The family has long played an important role in the history of Florence, and has been producing *chianti classico* at their Fonterutoli estate since 1435. The family has also carried the title of Marquis since the founding of the republic in the mid-nineteenth century. The Mazzeis had been so renowned for their winemaking expertise for so many centuries that it was to them that Thomas Jefferson turned, on the advice of Benjamin Franklin, on how to import winemaking and high-quality vineyards into America. At Jefferson's request, Philippo Mazzei moved to Virginia in 1773, bringing with him olive trees and grapevines from Italy. He designed the vineyards which were planted at Monticello and the surrounding area. But with Jacopo's understated manner, it was years before I learned any of this, and none of it from him. Clearly, Jacopo's and the Fratinis' approach to working with me was radically different from Rossatti's.

After the ground-breaking ceremonies in Serravalle, Corrado walked over with Jacopo to shake my hand.

"Welcome to Italy, Byrne. Now you are really in business. If you encounter any problems here, you must call Jacopo or me. We are here to solve your problems."

I reached into my pocket and pulled out the message that Mr. Rossatti had called.

"Well, Jacopo," I said, "there is a little something that perhaps you can handle . . ."

I never heard from Mr. Rossatti again.

It was always surprising to stumble across seemingly mundane topics that the normally fun-loving Italians take so seriously.

One afternoon I was enjoying a quick lunch at an outdoor café adjacent to the Duomo in Milan with Luca d'Ambrosis and Giovanni Belloni, a well-known broker from Florence. It was classic Italian weather in late spring with warm sunshine and clear skies, and it seemed fitting that we linger a bit longer over an espresso, taking in the swirl of Milanese life around us. As always, there was constant chatter and joking with the two Italians, much of it at my expense as the visitor in town.

When the espressos arrived, I took a first sip as I watched the ritual of both Luca and Giovanni scooping small heaps of sugar into the demitasse cup, followed by relentless stirring of the tiny spoon, around and around, as they chatted incessantly in Italian, neither of them looking down at their cups, nor even at each other. I concluded, nearly unconsciously, that the espresso was somewhat bitter for me and so reached for the small pitcher of cream on the table. I was about to pour a bit when—

"NO, NO, NO, Byrne!" Luca exclaimed.

"Mmm-nnn!" Giovanni grumbled from the throat, caught with the demitasse cup at his lips. "Mmm-nnn!"

"No—Byrne. Don't do that!" Luca continued, as I held back the pitcher. "That's espresso. No. If you want cream, order a café Americano, not espresso."

They both maintained serious looks on their faces, Giovanni shaking his head yes in agreement as he swallowed his sip.

"Well, maybe a cappuccino instead?" I countered.

"No, no—not that," responded Giovanni with gravity. "Cappuccinos are only with breakfast. Not with lunch."

"And never with dinner," Luca added solemnly.

I found that there are more layers to peel back in Italy than even in France, more layers and each harder to penetrate. I acknowledge that I actually lived in France and have only worked and visited Italy (although for more than ten years now) but that is not the reason. The power and omnipresence of the central government in Paris, with all highways, and railroads, and directives leading to and from Paris, is a direct reflection of the Napoleonic model of planning and control. Paris and what it stands for is a conscious and unconscious reference point for the nation and the people at all times. Not so Rome and the Italians.

In Italy it is not just that there is deep disdain for the central government but a distrust as well. With a parliamentary system involving twenty-three political parties and yielding sixty-one governments since World War II, such a sentiment is not surprising. The government in power has to struggle just for baseline credibility. Such basic challenges then spills over into the fundamentals of government: If you don't respect the central government, goes part of the reasoning in Italy, then why pay taxes to it? Studies that I read estimated that 25 percent to 30 percent of the real GDP in Italy was a "cash economy," i.e., no taxes were paid because only cash is exchanged and the revenue is not reported. With a challenge of that magnitude, I have often thought Italy as a weak nation state but a strong collection of proud and preferably semiautonomous city-states.

It was only in the 1860s that Garibaldi and others managed to corral the various independent regions of the Italian peninsula into a single country. With such a short history of sovereignty, half of America's longevity, one senses that Italians remain more abjectly aware of their local and regional affiliation than their national one. They are more proudly Florentine, or Roman, or Venetian, for example, than they are Italian (until, of course, the World Cup arrives). Aspects of that regionalism is expressed in terms of parochialism and division, not only in north versus south, or workaholic Milan versus noble Rome or aristocratic Florence. It is also expressed through rivalry evolving into distrust, a distrust which seems palpable. In a business setting the distrust about who is really zooming whom can be dizzying. It is a distrust that can be an advantage for an American arriving with a new idea. In some ways Italians are more open to forming an alliance with an American than with each other. Americans are perceived as capable business people, but also often straightforward to the point of naïve. Americans can be good partners for Italians. But the flipside is also true: If you want to do business in Italy, you'd better have a partner there you can trust, one you can really, really trust. There is, after all, a reason why they don't trust each other.

In Italy there are more undercurrents swirling around than in any other European country in which I worked. I don't begin to understand them all. And the undercurrents are not just about business. There seems to be many unresolved matters between pressures of the far Left and the far Right. Combine that with the troubles in recent decades involving the Red Brigade, the Mafia, and a puzzling lack of jailtime spent by those responsible for very public criminal acts, and I remain perplexed. Most recently the country enjoyed the longest serving government in power since World War II, but it was headed by the country's richest man (Silvio Burlesconi), the same man who also owned and controlled most of the country's media and, on most days, clearly controlled the legislature. Italy is a complex and mysterious country to understand but a fabulous one to visit and enjoy. With the right partner, which I certainly had, it can also be a fabulous one in which to conduct business.

Nine months later Serravalle opened with seventy of Italy's and the world's most famous brands, ranging from Versace to Gucci, Zegna, Etro, Dolce & Gabbana, Alessi, and dozens more, all offering fabulous savings to fashion-conscious Italians. The outlet was designed in a classic village setting with a very Italian piazza in the center, replete with a bubbling fountain.

Serravalle was the culmination of all that we had learned in our eight years of developing across Europe. We had come a long way from the modest, inexpensive design of Cheshire Oaks and Troyes. We had also come a long way in our understanding how a shopper shopped, what brands a site required, how to ensure that all brand signage was visible from all angles of a shopper's stroll, and how the careful positioning of the restaurants, bars, and bathrooms in the right places maximized the flow of shoppers in front of shop doors.

Sensing that Serravalle might be a special center, we had invested heavily in its design and architecture. Unusually, we built a two-story structure throughout, although we needed only one story for shopping. Grand vaulted arches were anchored by Doric columns, which in turn created a series of arcades leading from one end of the center to the other, all of them flanking that grand piazza in the center. We added marble and granite in key spots, with outdoor cafés designed as though they were in Milan. It was our best center yet, and very possibly the best designer-outlet center in Europe or America.

And on a late September day it was overrun with shoppers from the outset, swamped in fact, once again almost out of control. The parking lot held three thousand cars, nearly triple the capacity that we provided in our first centers, and even then it was insufficient. As we had hoped, Italians take their fashion seriously, and the line of cars on Opening Day was backed up out of the lot, onto the road for nearly a mile down to the highway, and then back up onto the highway for another mile. The ribbon-cutting ceremony was cut short in the middle of Santo Versace's remarks when he acceded to the crowds chants of "Open! Open! Open!" and abruptly cut the ribbon himself to let in the hordes.

To celebrate the opening and to entertain our shoppers during the cool September evening hours we built two stages in the piazza. Three different bands entertained the crowds, and thousands of shoppers were eventually dancing and singing across the piazza. At ten o'clock we unleashed a twenty-minute barrage of fireworks, a display seen for miles and miles around the Piedmont region. The music, fireworks, and kaleidoscope of colors, mixed with the shops, the famous brands, and the good cheer and enthusiasm in the bars and restaurants—it was our grandest opening yet. I felt on top of the world. It was as much of a high as the Troyes opening had been, and even a greater high than The Warner opening with Frank Sinatra and Shirley MacLaine almost exactly eight years before.

Of the five thousand or so people who flocked to the Serravalle opening, perhaps 150 were members of our staff, or advisers, friends, and family—people from the law firms, the banks, construction companies, and architects from other countries, government officials from Italy, our partners from BAA, and many from Jones Lang Wootten.

An hour after midnight the local hotel lobby was filling up fast with people, fatigued by the day's events and yet still excited by its spectacular success. We had chartered several buses for the short transport from the center to the hotel, and as each arrived the energy and volume inside ratcheted up more and then more. A convoy of cars arrived. Slightly behind them was one tiny Fiat Uno that came roaring up the drive packed full of young professionals who had flown in from Berlin, Paris, and London, some old friends, some new from the day's events. A sharp curve, a large tree, and suddenly tragedy.

Senseless, instantaneous, heartbreaking tragedy.

The small Italian car slammed straight into one of the proud old oak trees lining the drive up to the hotel, leaving several people whiplashed and injured, and leaving one bright, promising young German woman dead.

She had only recently graduated from university and had joined the Jones Lang Wootten team as a researcher in their Berlin office. Her first client was McArthurGlen. She had been thrilled to be part of the team for such an exciting new concept. Her manager felt she had great promise and had sent her to the Serravalle opening on what was her first international business trip.

Neither the driver of the car nor the person who rented it, were from McArthurGlen. But everyone in the company was profoundly affected. From that point onward, first the atmosphere and then the culture around McArthurGlen changed. It was as though the young, aggressive, "anything is possible" company had been forced to grow up.

Over the years I had seen our young European employees flourish in the entrepreneurial freedom of McArthurGlen. I had seen some of them join us in their first real job, and over time become accomplished managers. Others were moving out of their home country to open new offices abroad and to oversee new centers. I had seen young people who couldn't believe what they accomplished at such early ages. New centers would open in Austria, or Scotland, or Wales, and new sites were being pursued in Germany, France, and in Italy and Holland, and we sent young managers out to new territory to expand the company's horizons. The results, and the fun, and the sense of optimism became self-perpetuating and we pressed on for more.

What had started as a solo effort in my Paris hotel room was now a dynamic pan-European enterprise. We had some of the most important pension funds and insurance companies as our partners in our completed projects. We were a real company with very real responsibilities, and perhaps the gung-ho attitude that drove the company early on was no longer appropriate.

And I wondered later if in some way our can-do culture had contributed to that tragedy at Serravalle. Had we created a culture of such gung-ho spirit and "never ever give up" approach that it had contributed to an aura of invincibility that made those in that Fiat Uno that fateful evening not want to stop? Had that spirit led them to pack more people into that small car than should have been there? Had they seen only continuous success with this hard-driving McArthurGlen clan, and assumed that anyone associated with the company would be winners and there would be no losers? No losers until the car careened out of control.

It was a tragedy that night, a heart-wrenching senseless tragedy. It was also a turning point in the maturing of McArthurGlen.

THIRTY-ONE

Moving On

The year 2000 was a momentous one for me. In January, our fourth daughter, Kyle Camden Murphy, was born in London. Kyle's middle name is taken from the beautiful Maine harbor where Pamela and I made landfall after the fateful voyage fifteen years before.

In September 2000, Serravalle opened.

And at year-end 2000, just over eight years after my first reconnaissance trip to Europe, I resigned from McArthurGlen.

It was time to move on. McArthurGlen was well established as the market leader across Europe. We had nearly one billion dollars in sales at the shopping center level, with eleven projects operating across Europe, selling five hundred brands in approximately 1,500 stores. By that point most of the well-known luxury brands were already or about to be in our centers, including Prada, Versace, Hugo Boss, Armani, Zegna Brioni, Polo Ralph Lauren, Escada, and many more. Our centers were attracting approximately 40 million shopping visits per year, and had created over 8,000 jobs across Europe. The centers had also won dozens and dozens of awards for tourism, architecture, historic restoration, community relations, and more. We had centers in England, Wales, Scotland, France, Italy, and Austria. We had not only created a new concept and a new company in Europe, but in fact created a new multibillion-dollar industry. At one point we had considered taking the company public. During a presentation from JPMorgan, their lead banker, John Zehner, told us their research indicated we were the most active pan-European retailers at the time.

Based on our market share as measured by square footage at year-end 2000, I estimate that the modern outlet industry in Europe was generating five billion dollars in total sales. Eight years before it was generating zero. We had created a new sales channel for brands in Europe, and one which could provide, if carefully executed, a win-win-win solution for the brands, the retailers, and the communities in which the projects were located. At the time I left, McArthurGlen faced only one significant competitor on a continuing basis—Roger Morgan's Fashion Retail. We were the market leader in the industry, and were larger than Fashion Retail by a wide margin. But to say that by such measurement that we had "won" the race with Morgan to a certain extent misses the point.

Roger and his team were, and are, excellent developers whose projects were of such high quality it forced us to create even better ones. I know the reverse is also true. The increase in quality benefited not just ourselves, but also the brands and the communities in which we operated. Morgan was a very tough competitor throughout and we, and he, were better off for it. As Roger said when we finally discussed the rivalry—fifteen years after it started—"Competition is good."

In the end McArthurGlen became the company we had set out to make it: the market leader, not just in size but also in trailblazing where the industry was going. Roger, too, succeeded in creating the company he set out to create: a focused, high-end player with one or two centers in each of the key European markets where he chose to operate. There are many, many more stories of the battles McArthurGlen and Fashion Retail engaged in, more than a reader wants to learn about. The battle sites ranged from all over the UK, to outside Madrid and Barcelona, to sites in Holland and Belgium, many locations within Germany, and, notably, the Disneyland Paris site.

As for the townships in which we operated, I know we made a significant positive impact on their local economies. In Troyes, we created 220 direct jobs by 2000 and by our count were attracting nearly three million visitors annually, two-thirds of whom would otherwise not have come there. Intercept surveys conducted in June 2002 by an independent firm for the Troyes Chamber of Commerce showed that of those three million, over 600,000 visited downtown Troyes, and spent approximately 20 million dollars (at current exchange rates) on meals, hotels, museums, and general shopping. That's 20 million dollars per year in the downtown economy that otherwise wouldn't have been spent there. Our concept of "commercial tourism" worked. Parisians and others came for our outlets, and then spent time and money in the surrounding environs. In my research I can find no documentation of a significant number of downtown stores closing as a result of McArthurGlen's is arrival. Over the years independent stores have closed, but it was primarily due to the growth of national retail chains, and not due to outlet stores. Just the opposite: shops in the center of town benefited from the measures we put into place. That's because we took the time and made the effort to put those measures in place. If we hadn't, the results might have been quite different. Today, the debate in Troyes is not whether outlet stores and outlet shoppers are good for the economy, but rather how can Troyes defend its position as Europe's number one outlet destination.

In England, there is a similar story. The long-term effect of our Cheshire Oaks project is perhaps best expressed by Stephen Ewbank, the chief executive of the borough of Ellesmere Port & Neston, the township in which the project is located. He has written that the public/private effort required to create Cheshire Oaks, created "a brilliant partnership, the building of the largest Designer Outlet Village in the UK, the regeneration of the Borough of Ellesmere Port & Neston, the creation of two thousand new jobs and the transformation of the image of Ellesmere Port and the land surrounding the village into a superb leisure and tourist destination." When the outlet concept is carefully executed, it can be a powerful force.

A similar story can be told for all the other towns in which we operated: Bridgend in Wales; Ashford, York, Swindon, and Mansfield in England; Livingston in Scotland; Serravalle in Italy; Parndorf in Austria. Even in Roubaix, France, now ten years later, there is a rebirth of the town's center, with a vibrancy not seen in many decades. Though the McArthur-Glen center is not performing up to the company's portfolio average, it is achieving the average of all outlet centers in France. McArthurGlen will never make a return on its investment there commensurate with its risk, but at least we will have been a key contributor to the town's ultimate regeneration.

Even more exciting than our projects was the company we created as exemplified by the people we attracted. At the height of our expansion drive we had approximately 180 people employed across seven different

European offices: London, Paris, Berlin, Dusseldorf, Vienna, Milan, and Amsterdam. At any given time I could walk into our London offices on Portman Square and hear hallway conversations involving three or four languages from nationals of four or five different countries. The average age always remained notably young, and the energy around the halls reflected it. We had an unstated policy of promoting from within if only because our entrepreneurial culture was founded on the principle that what we didn't know we would figure out, and do so fast. Those who consistently figured out the next puzzle were promoted. It led to a very enthusiastic atmosphere.

Our biggest management challenge was in harnessing all the energy that accompanied that enthusiasm. Many cultural biases are inherited into any pan-European operation. We wanted to eliminate the biases and create a company *esprit*, which transcended nationalities. Our approach included holding frequent events, off-site retreats, and exercises, which required much transnational interaction, usually based on a sense of fun. In Adrian Wright's words, we wanted to create a team based on the strengths of each country. In his view we wanted British police, French cooks, German engineers, Italian lovers, and Swiss timekeepers. What we didn't want were German policemen, Swiss cooks, French engineers, British lovers, and Italian timekeepers.

So how does one keep the various national oars rowing in the same direction and to the same cadence? Answer: through the combination of having simple objectives that all parties buy into, and then having the ability to listen, listen, listen, and to hear. The last part is the most important.

Americans have an advantage when operating overseas. Despite our reputation for being brusque and heavy-handed there is respect for the long-standing success of American business. There is often a willingness to grant the benefit of the doubt to American managers regarding the many new concepts and innovations emanating from the United States. But this benefit of the doubt is precariously balanced, as though on an old-style weighing scale with two plates on which a new substance is measured against known values. On one plate is a heaping of respect for America and what it stands for. On the other plate is resentment for what America has achieved and how it sometimes handles those achievements. When starting up an American-inspired venture abroad, if the listening and hearing skills of the American manager is not acute enough to take into real consideration the cultural context in which the venture is operating, the weight of resentment will quickly outweigh that of the respect. The benefit of the doubt has worn off. The scale has tilted out of equilibrium.

We were most successful at McArthurGlen when we derived clear objectives and worked hard in listening to each office on how best to achieve them. We put in place a profit-sharing scheme to reward success in meeting the objectives in one's home market but also to encourage and to reward cooperation across borders. Interestingly, the plan met with only partial success. The more effective tactic was the listening and the hearing. Hard-edged entrepreneurial tools only go so far in many European settings.

Not that all aspects of our operations flowed smoothly, either internally or externally. It wasn't until after a certain employee left McArthurGlen that we discovered a mother and sister had quietly been put on the company's payroll. Shame on us for not having better checks and balances. In another country we didn't realize that there had been cash kickbacks from some brands to someone working in our leasing program. When that person left one brand called the office and asked, "Who gets the special payments now?"

In a different twist it wasn't until several months after we lost a competition to be the chosen developer for a certain town that we learned a certain secretary to a certain politico wasn't playing a straight game. The politico's office was coordinating the selection process, and the secretary was the designated recipient for all incoming information. As such, she was relaying all of our information to the competition as it came in. It became clear that the secretary, and possibly her boss, were receiving healthy stipends for doing so.

But as exciting as all our achievements were, after Serravalle's opening it was time for me to move on, for several reasons. There was and remains a real limit to how many outlet centers can operate in Europe. The growth of McArthurGlen had peaked and the subsequent three to five years was not going to compare to what we had achieved in the prior three to five years. Joey had moved to London and, with the slowdown in the development activities, there wasn't a need for both of us. And, by late 2000, it had also become clear that there was a new and extremely powerful force which was infiltrating not only the retail industry but the economies of all developed nations—the Internet.

In late 2000 I had been spearheading an effort to bring McArthurGlen online by creating a joint venture with GUS, the largest catalog company in the United Kingdom. McArthurGlen brought the brands and retail know-how; GUS brought the logistics. Ultimately, I concluded that my brilliant idea of McArthurGlen selling online was not so brilliant at all and we scuttled the joint venture. In the meantime, I'd become fascinated with the virtual world, and wondered where and how did it intersect with the physical world? In other words, where did the Internet and real estate cross over? My conclusion was that they did so in a physical environment known as a "data center." I left McArthurGlen to start a new company, once again importing a concept from America to Europe. "Data centers" were originally known as "co-location centers" or "Internet hotels," and were born in Silicon Valley to help incubate hi-tech startups. By 2001, the concept had grown far beyond that. I thought that data centers had a bright future in Europe, and I felt I knew well how to introduce American concepts into the European landscape. It seemed like a natural time to leave one platform to start up another one.

THIRTY-TWO

Breaking Barriers

I chose Paris because I didn't know any better.

I chose Paris because I was in a rush to launch our new company and, like most Americans, I was naïve about the world beyond our borders. I thought France presented a number of attributes that would support a start-up company focused on carefully distributing excess stock from well-known brand names. France offered its wide array of famous brands and its superb highway network that could whisk shoppers out to bucolic locations to find those brands at reduced prices. What I hadn't understood is the extent to which the economy of France is dominated by the government, whether obviously or subtly. I hadn't realized that the French economy is structured for large and established companies such as Peugeot and Crédit Agricole. I hadn't understood that in France the emphasis is always on job preservation, and not job creation. I also hadn't understood the extent to which elected officials push or pull macro- and microeconomic levers to preserve that status quo, levers which elsewhere are left to market forces. In other words, I hadn't understood the context into which I had so hastily parachuted.

What I discovered was the obvious: Context matters. A lot.

After that disastrous evening hearing in Normandy, described in the opening chapter, when the protesters accosted François and me with the torches and the coffin, François and I met with certain officials to assess what had happened and why. We visited with the president of the powerful Chamber of Commerce, a businessman who owned a printing press. On leaving his office he handed a book to us.

"Read this," he advised, "this describes part of what you are up against. It is a force behind the scenes."

The book was entitled *An Ameria That Scares,* by Edward Behr, a *Newsweek* reporter. The message our host wanted to convey was not so much in the book's contents as in its title. It played on the stereotype of America as an all-powerful, insensitive, bulldozing nation. It exemplified the underlying fear that lingers in certain quarters, the same fear that was whipped up (for self-serving interests) to form the demonstration against François and me that night. To a greater or lesser degree this happened to us on many other nights in many other settings. Variations of this perception are why so many French articles about McArthurGlen used the prefixes "Mega," "Super," or "Giant" when referring to us. Given that I started out alone in that rented apartment with no one to call, it could be taken as a compliment. More, though, it reflected the fear of what America represented as an agent of change to certain audiences in Europe.

"Vital statistics" will describe part of any country's character, but only part. It is just as important to understand the culture of the people with whom you are working—their history and aspirations, their anxieties and prejudices, to create a *bon contact,* as it is to know their income, ages, and home ownership statistics.

What has amazed me over fifteen years of working in Europe is the extent to which so many ex-pat professionals working in foreign countries either don't understand that context matters or, worse, recognize that it does matter but refuse to make any effort to act accordingly. Such an approach can transform a state of naïveté into an expression of hubris. The former is unfortunate. The latter begs trouble.

One starting point in understanding the "European context" is realizing that there is no one "Europe," at least not in the way there is an "America." In America there is one media market in one language for messaging and movies from San Francisco to New York. There is essentially one America, a nation of 300 million people, with an underlying sense of shared heritage (nearly all Americans know of George Washington, Daniel Boone, and Abe Lincoln) and shared expectations ("I am working to make my mark in the world . . ."). But Europe shares no common heritage, no common language, and no unitary shared culture. The European Union now comprises twenty-seven countries with 494 million people and twenty-three official languages, all packed into a land mass only slightly larger than the continental USA.

The European context is also more diverse and subtler than numbers alone would suggest. It's not only that there is no "one Europe," but also that the nation state in Europe is not the strong overriding authority one might naturally assume. I found that instead of a collection of nation states, Europe is more a collection of economically competing *regions*, which frequently either transcend or ignore national boundaries. Cities or regions of different countries will work with each other against cities or regions of their own respective countries. The cities of Lille in France, and Brussels in Belgium, for example, are very willing to join forces to compete against Grenoble in France, which has teamed with Geneva in Switzerland, to win inward investment. Similarly, the region wrapping around the Mediterranean, encompassing parts of Italy, France, and Spain, may ignore national boundaries and work together regarding regional and trade and tourism.

The major drivers of this regionalization process are the familiar ones: globalization, the incredible speed and dexterity of international capital (both enhanced by the power of the Internet), and, significantly, the inefficiencies of Europe's multilayered structure. World events and world commerce are often moving far too fast for communities focused on their well-being to wait for helpful action from their nation's capital or from the European Union's headquarters in Brussels. (One of the great challenges for twenty-first century Europe is how to respond quickly and efficiently to shifting global forces when by necessity Europe is organized in an inefficient manner.) Usually, the national government is too slow and the Brussels' apparatus is too clumsy to help the regions to respond to these forces. The communities need and, therefore, often resort to more nimble alliances and organizations to respond to the pressures of globalization, be they local, regional, or supernational in nature. (Ironically the trend is currently being sanctioned and even promoted in Brussels and many European capitals.) This self-reliance reinforces a regional identity, which at first glance does not have a strong presence compared with a country's national identity but which in fact can be strong enough to trump it. When I secured the final approval to proceed in Troyes, I did so by highlighting that the real issue was of Paris dictating to the provinces what they could or couldn't do with their own economy. Because the motivations to do so for those in the prime minister's office were self-serving and political in nature, the power of regionalism won out when those motivations were unveiled for all to see. The implication for arriving foreigners is that there are more layers of the culture one may need to investigate before uncovering where the relevant decision-making authority actually lies.

Caution, however, is advised. As always in Europe, there may be more layers of nuance than one can readily see. At McArthurGlen, we were sometimes so eager to recognize regional affiliation and to promote the neo-phenomenon of borderless Europe that we ignored other aspects of context. During one presentation to a small Belgian town's mayor and his council members, I was extolling the power of our center to attract masses of Germans to that locale who otherwise would never have stopped in, each ready to leave behind significant sums of money in the local economy. After I had held forth for some fifteen minutes or more, the mayor slowly stood up and politely raised his hand to interrupt.

"Mr. Murphy," he started up in a somber tone, "we like your concept, and we'd like the Germans to come visit . . ." and then, in reference to the prior one hundred years' history of periodic waves of armed and uninvited Germans rushing across their borders, the mayor went on ". . . just not all at once. . . ."

Dozens of heads nodded in agreement, acknowledging not only the mayor's dry humor, but also the fact that history matters.

Taking context into consideration doesn't mean compromising principles. In fact it may mean being able to return to principles. Clearly, when the Disney people came storming into Europe to develop and operate their Disneyland Paris theme park "the Disney way," they didn't pay enough attention to context—of how to market to a variety of different cultures, how to offer an ambience more in keeping with European expectations, and how to interact with their own employees. When Philippe Bourguignon and Steve Burke arrived to remedy the situation they addressed all those issues and more. But in doing so they never diluted Disney's basic concept of family fun in a crisp, clean environment, of offering thrills and experiences unique to the Disney company. At McArthurGlen when we moved from country to country opening centers, we changed the design of the buildings, the tone of the marketing, and the approach to development every time. But the principle of offering famous brands at reduced prices, structured in a way that protected the traditional retailers, never changed.

It took some bruises and setbacks before it became apparent to me that by madly rushing to hurriedly establish McArthurGlen in France I was in fact losing time. By not stopping to listen and observe more, to understand either the historical, or political, or other aspects of the cultural context, I lost time overall by setting myself up to learn another lesson the hard way. I had to remember that not everyone thinks or acts, or even wants to think or act, like an American. When operating in a foreign culture, if you never make an effort to understand the context in which you are operating, then you deserve the unintended consequences which are headed your way. Most of them will be unpleasant.

While we were developing the outlet center at Swindon, there was a temporary go-cart operation set up in one of the empty buildings on site. The operator provided well-maintained, high-speed go-carts, which zipped around a Formula One–style track. There was always a steady trade of business there, especially in the evenings. From time to time people from McArthurGlen frequented the track. One evening, after an exhilarating series of races, Joey went to pay for his go-cart, and inquired if there was any merchandise he could buy as a memento for his son—racing jackets, key chains, helmets, or the like.

"No," said the proprietor, "I'm often asked that, but I don't carry any."

"Why not? It could be a whole new income stream for you," Joey countered. "Clearly, there's demand."

"I have a good business here. I'm happy," the owner said ever so casually as he fiddled with the credit-card machine. "Not everyone lives like an American," he added pleasantly.

I have often been asked by those who have heard the story of the early days of McArthurGlen in France: "Why didn't you give up? Why not at least move to another country and start over?"

The honest and perhaps uninspiring answer is because it never occurred to me, or to Pamela, to give up. By the time the waves of opposition had engulfed me I was too far into the effort, not only emotionally and professionally but also economically, to walk away. Pamela and I had a lot at stake. And I believed in what I was pursuing: I honestly felt that what I was bringing to Troyes and to France would benefit all parties concerned. I also strongly believed that I was not being treated fairly. I would have felt sick for ages with self-disappointment if I had walked away under those circumstances. Fairness, I think, is a very American sentiment. It can be a strong motivator. In a foreign culture it can also be a romantic but misleading notion. I knew then that if I waited for fairness to save me I would now still be sitting in an open field on the edge of Troyes, waiting for Godot.

I responded in France in a way that I think many Americans would have done: when faced with a problem, however daunting, I set out to solve it. If one approach didn't work, I'd try another. Initially I perceived the problem as primarily economic, and tried solving it along strictly commercial lines. When I realized it was essentially a political problem, I worked first on a local level, then on a regional level, and finally on a national scale until I found the combination required to break down the barriers that stood in my way. I never would have guessed that ultimately I would have to stand up to directives emanating from the prime minister himself, and then even beyond him to the Supreme Court of France. I just took it one step at a time and became more determined with each one.

In the end, people do what they think they really need to do. I needed to see it through in France.

Pamela and I loved our twelve years of living in Paris and London. We loved the diversity of the people and the cultures, the richness of the cities, and the lifestyle of being able to leave London and arrive in Florence or Madrid or Stockholm in two hours' time. We go back to visit as often as we can. And yet, as much as we loved it, after twelve years of living in Europe, Pamela and I decided to move back to America with our four children. We did so because, in general, America is optimistic and Europe is not.

That dichotomy is not surprising. America is very young and the history of our westward expansion, of rugged individualism and homesteading, is not far back in time or in the American collective memory. With millennia of history and culture to draw upon, Europe, has so much more to remember and review, and does so naturally. Just strolling through the cities of Europe is a reminder of the rise and fall of entire nations and civilizations which long predate America's founding days. America has a culture of looking forward, of projecting and almost living in the future. And it is in the looking forward, instead of to the past, that America expresses its optimism and finds its energy.

It is very much in the American belief system that one person alone can still make great scientific discoveries, create new products or companies, write books that can change the course of history, generate fabulous wealth, or leave behind one's own indelible mark for future generations to observe. Charles Lindbergh, Thomas Edison, Eleanor Roosevelt, Martin Luther King Jr., Bill Gates, John Glenn, and endless others are household names representing personal achievement and triumph often after overcoming incredible obstacles. What quickly struck Pamela and me upon our return to the States was that the American Dream is very much alive and well. It is a Dream that is just not present in Europe.

We wanted for our four girls what most American parents want: for them to grow up knowing in their bones that they could be whomever they wanted to be and do whatever they wanted to do. Corny? Perhaps. But it's not a sentiment held dear in Europe. Pamela and I felt that such optimism is embedded into Americans early on, when they're young and on the school fields, and surrounded by living examples of people who have worked hard and made their way up in the world.

For Joey and for me, having that optimism—backed up by our intense drive and our ability to live and breathe our vision for the future—was our competitive advantage. We overcame obstacles that others honestly believed were too great to overcome and didn't even bother trying. The irony was that when we did overcome them, those same obstacles usually became even harder for the next person to surmount. Once we secured a zoning permission to open Cheshire Oaks, there was not a chance the British authorities would allow another outlet center to open within several hours' drive. It was the same in France, Austria, Italy— nearly everywhere in Europe. We determined that the intense European focus on preserving what is already there versus also considering what else could be created, eventually became a protective shield once we were up and running. But to actually get up and go, to overcome all that was thrown at us, we needed to be aggressively optimistic about what was possible.

Some have dismissed our success by saying it was merely a case of our not knowing what we *didn't* know. I have heard the argument that we blindly fought against odds we didn't realize were stacked against us, and were just lucky. If that were true, then it is also true we made our own luck. This was so in part because we became more adroit at working in foreign environments. We didn't care that we were trying to achieve what others had deemed not possible. When Dominique Cocquet, a French friend, and the number-three executive at Disneyland Paris charged with all real-estate matters, arrived for the Grand Opening of Troyes, he was amazed at what we had achieved.

"Didn't you know," Dominique asked me, "that to open a center like this isn't meant to be possible in a political environment like this?"

When Pamela and I moved back to the States we discovered there is a flip side to that optimism. There is a price, in today's metropolitan America anyway, to the belief that "we can do it, whatever it is—we can meet the challenges, however many there are—in fact, we can do it all." One sees parents in a manic drive to "do it all," right now, right away, because what they know as a fact, as a basic thesis for their daily lives is that what we achieve now is directly linked to where we will be in the future, and especially so for our children.

A typical scene is finding myself at the wheel of our seven-seater Volvo XC-90, Starbucks Decaf Grande Latte (semiskinned, Splenda artificial sweetener) in my right hand, left hand on the wheel. There are three to five children in the car, from two or three different families. I might have a Bluetooth earpiece connecting brain to a BlackBerry phone, which itself is connected to the charger, which in turn is connected to the car battery, which keeps all this action running nearly on time, or at least not more than ten minutes or three long traffic lights behind schedule. The chatty and cheerful kids in back have just finished an afternoon game at school, after the last school bus has left. I am there to zip them to prearranged drop points. Some of the kids are on a tight time table because their out-of-school team (soccer, or ice hockey, or lacrosse, or karate) has one of its three-times-per-week practice. Others in the car don't have another team event but there is the music lesson, for which they practice for the forty-five minutes beforehand, which is why I must get them home on time. As I drive I may field a call from another parent, who is explaining that Lisa, his wife-the-working-mom, is traveling to a conference in Chicago, and he is with Bobby, the little brother, at his language tutoring session. Do I, the driver with the Bluetooth earpiece and half-empty Starbucks Decaf Grande Latte, mind dropping Margaret, their daughter in the back of my car, at the piano teacher's house during the rounds of drop-offs? Sorry I didn't call earlier, says the dad on the phone, I was in a conference at the office, and well . . . you know.

Weekends arrive with more of the same, where parents morph into taxi drivers with little or no spousal time available. This is affluent and nearly affluent America, both urban and suburban, in the twenty-first century— spinning to the next tightly scheduled appointment, sandwiched between the orthodontist and the dermatology appointments, just after the community service committee meeting, the day before the monthly Boy Scouts, or Little League, or volunteer Parent Council meeting. Sunday is blocked out all afternoon to help with a sixth-grade science project demonstrating the pull of gravity. The family schedule seems to teeter one forgotten appointment away from systems failure. Parents often seem breathless and ask each other as they wait in the back of the school theater after the latest performance: "Why are we living like this?"

It is the same question Pamela and I asked ourselves when we experienced the pace of life in our native country. For all the stresses of life in the Old World, we never spun ourselves around like that, and neither did our friends. Here in America, we often look at each other and reminisce about the long Sunday afternoon lunches, where a visiting family would arrive at noon, and at four-thirty or five the adults were still chatting around the table, coffee cups half-full, and the children were amusing themselves around the house. America knows how to live in the future. But Europeans deserve credit for living in the present. Striking the balance is the challenge.

Lifestyle issues notwithstanding, the emphasis in America on team participation and team building, on learning to adapt quickly to changing circumstances, to compete from an early age—these characteristics are vital in today's polyglot, multinational, never-static global marketplace. We may not like the pace or the potential side-effects, and both need to be managed. But for those who choose to participate in international affairs, America does provide a formidable staging ground. That it does so is, in fact, one of America's competitive advantages.

But with our focus on speed and innovation, and in achieving more in less time, a key weakness is in not taking the time to understand the context in which we're operating. Context matters. Culture matters. Ignoring them in any endeavor—commercial, legal, diplomatic, military—can be costly . . . very, very costly.

Context is also, by definition, dynamic. Policies change, economies change, politicians change, and the environment evolves as all this transpires. With the arrival of Nicolas Sarkozy as President, the overall tone in France today is much different than when I arrived in the waning days of the Mitterrand era. The general malaise hanging in the air then has been replaced now by an acceptance of a need for real change, a change which Sarkozy represents. In Germany, the ongoing debate over the need to modernize many social institutions recently helped elect the first woman, and the first person from eastern Germany (Angela Markel), to be Chancellor. When I was working to expand McArthurGlen across Europe in the late 1990s, America was flying high with the high-tech boom, our status described at the time by President Bill Clinton as "the envy of the world." Not so today. In fifteen years of working in Europe, and in light of the war in Iraq, I have never seen anti-Americanism there as strong as it is now. The steps I took starting up McArthurGlen in the early 1990s would not be the steps I would take today if I were to redo it. For anyone running a business in a foreign culture, and especially for an American working abroad, the evolving landscape needs to be constantly reassessed, business plans reevaluated.

To understand more about the importance of context, one of the most productive and enriching steps an American can take is to spend meaningful time living outside America. It will test one's assumptions—assumptions about work life, home life, and American life. It will help put into place the most important context of all: America's dominant role in the international community. Obviously, America isn't only facing a European community in our international affairs, a community that is overwhelmingly friendly to

America. We are also facing the rising aspirations of powerful new players on the world stage, players with whom we may have even less in common than with Europeans, players not interested in being so friendly to America. Understanding the context in which they are operating can only help to understand how we should most effectively interact with them.

If you go looking to create your own opportunities in an international setting, bring your American optimism with you, bring your drive, bring your "can-do" attitude, but leave your hubris behind. Stick to your principles but put them in context. Often, it is that context which holds the answers. Listen, then act. In foreign lands, context is paramount. Your concept may be your own idea, but it's someone else's country. It's their ball, their playing field, and their rules.

But once you understand their rules and put them into context, remember that it's your optimism.

Epilogue

One of the most heartening aspects about the company we created at McArthurGlen is the number of other startups that have been launched by talented people coming out of there. The spirit of McArthurGlen lives on in many other incarnations. All have been successful.

Adrian Wright, Managing Director for the United Kingdom, has led a buyout of the UK men's retailer, Suits You. Ironically, that was the first brand we ever signed up at McArthurGlen.

François Moss, my early-on cultural interpreter and property adviser, joined with James Hoddell, his good friend and co-Development Manager at McArthurGlen, to launch their own firm, Pantheon Retail. They are developing designer outlet centers in France and in Italy.

Luca d'Ambrosis, initially Retail Director, and later Managing Director for Italy, is a partner in a start-up firm in Milan, specializing in real-estate fund management for institutional investors.

Patience O'Connor has started her development advisory firm in the United States. She is spearheading the two-million-square-foot redevelopment effort of a town on the Jersey shore.

Peter Nash moved back to Washington, D.C., and has his own land-development company focusing on the mid-Atlantic states.

Joey Kaempfer is still heading up McArthurGlen, based in London. He has certainly made his comeback and then some. Since Serravalle opened in

2000, Joey has steered McArthurGlen to opening three more centers: one in The Netherlands, and two more in Italy, as well as multiple center expansions. There are now fourteen McArthurGlen centers in operation with more in the pipeline. Gary Bond is also still with McArthurGlen, in charge of development across Europe.

After eighteen years at Jones Lang Wootten, including many as a senior partner there, John Milligan left to form his own development firm, Milligan Retail, which specializes in repositioning shopping centers in the United Kingdom and in Europe. Joining him are several McArthurGlen veterans, including Liz Bradley, our Director for European Leasing, and Adrienne Jones, who at JLW advised McArthurGlen from the outset. Also joining him is Paul Hanagraaf, who successfully launched and expanded in Europe the renowned American architecture firm RTKL.

John Nicolosi was married in London to a fabulous British woman, Louise Anderson. They have subsequently moved to Rhode Island, where John continues to work at McArthurGlen, flying to Europe monthly. He also works nearly halftime as a volunteer for severely handicapped adults. I have never seen him happier.

Roger Morgan remains Chairman of Fashion Retail, based in London, and has expanded the portfolio to nine centers. We cross paths from time to time, usually at conferences organized by the Urban Land Institute. Bit by bit the tensions eased over time. Seven years after I left McArthurGlen we finally addressed the origins of the McArthurGlen–Fashion Retail rivalry for the first time since it started. We compared notes on what happened and why. Not surprisingly, our recollection of events differ a little, but not much. When Mark Mogull, a mutual friend, heard us say that for five or more years we hadn't even spoken to each other, he was amazed.

"Why not?" Mark exclaimed. "You guys have known each other for thirty years."

"It was easier that way," Roger replied.

Now, we speak. During the rivalry, we were at least wise enough not to demonize each other in the process, thereby enabling a rapprochement later.

For my family the move to Washington, D.C., was the right decision. Pamela and the girls are all happy with their lifestyles in the upbeat American culture. True, everyone's agenda is more jammed-packed than what it would have been in Europe. But the activities are stimulating, rigorous, and rewarding. At the same time, we all miss the UK and Europe and visit as often as we can. Fortunately, our daughters realize that there is, in fact, a wide world beyond our borders and they remain interested in what that world is doing.

Pamela has often been asked how did our marriage survive the stress of the early McArthurGlen years. The response is that actually it was the marriage which enabled the company, and not the company which threatened the marriage. Woe is the entrepreneur who does not have a solid family foundation upon which he or she can fall back. Without it, something will oftentimes have to give, whether it be the startup or the family.

Pamela has been (thank God) the architect of our smooth transition back home, mixing in with that dedicated work with external relations at our daughters' school and charities. With our transition to America now complete she is plotting the return to her career.

As for me, I left McArthurGlen to launch a new platform developing and operating data centers across Europe. In a swirl of events, I formed a joint venture with a friend (William Palmer) and with Deutsche Bank. Two months later, in a stroke of what could be marketed as pure genius, but which really qualifies as pure luck, William and I told David Brush at Deutsche, much to his displeasure, that we did not want to proceed. Market conditions, we concluded, were just too risky. Six weeks later the IT/telecom bubble burst. David called to say thank you. We had dodged a very large and very fast bullet. If we had proceeded as planned, we would have lost 100 percent of the equity invested within six weeks. I am occasionally asked, "Which was the best deal that I had ever done?" I always answer, "A few select ones which I didn't do . . ."

About this time, The Carlyle Group, one of the world's largest private equity firms contacted me. They suggested that rather than launch my own data-center platform, I come aboard as a turn-around CEO for a data-center company they had already launched. The company, named Digiplex, was in the midst of a pan-European rollout. In light of the IT/telecom bubble bursting, it seemed a good time for me to be riding Other People's Money, and so I agreed.

After my first day on the job, I had dinner with Dan Cummings, the

Carlyle partner to whom the poisoned Digiplex chalice had just been passed. Over sushi I told him that based on what I had learned that day, this wasn't a "troubled investment." It was a train wreck. Fourteen months later, the train crashed.

In the interim Dan Cummings and I, together with our CFO Jack Barker, dramatically restructured Digiplex and created enormous value, but it wasn't enough. The company folded, the banks took over, and the investors lost everything. In fact every other investor in European data centers in those early years suffered large losses, as there was far too little demand to soak up the massive capacity which had been created.

As soon as the company's assets went into insolvency, I knew it was time to act. I tried to buy the whole European portfolio from the banks, but in the end was only able to purchase the Digiplex operation in Oslo, Norway. Today, some six years later, Digiplex Norway is a highly successful data-center operation in its fourth phase of expansion. In turning around the company it became clear that reliable engineering talent was needed so I, the non-engineer, started an engineering services company (Aldwyns) in England. Ironically, my partners for Digiplex Norway are principals from The Carlyle Group, the investment house behind the original Digiplex. It can be a small world. Treat people with honesty and respect in one sphere and you are likely to see them in another.

A year before moving back to America, I wanted one last project, preferably one very special project, to round out my time in Europe. And I found it in the form of Palazzo Tornabuoni, a fifteenth-century Medici palazzo in the heart of Florence. It was the home of Alessandro Medici, who became bishop, cardinal, and then Pope Leo XI. In the process, as befits a Medici and a pope, Alessandro commissioned many incredibly beautiful frescoes and mosaics, which remain there to this day. For the redevelopment of the palazzo it is perhaps no surprise that my partners on the project are the Fratinis and Jacopo Mazzei of Florence, the same people who were my partners in Italy for McArthurGlen.

The restoration returns me to my roots of urban redevelopment, back to The Warner project fifteen years earlier. We have returned the ground floor to retail use, which now features Bulgari, Bottega Venetta, Polo Ralph Lauren, and other luxury brands.

We are also restoring the upper floors to their original use: apartments, enabling current residents to live where the Medics lived. But we are doing so in a new way. We are establishing Italy's first, and perhaps Europe's first, Private Residence Club, where members will own a one-eighth share of a restored apartment. The Club is directed toward the American and British markets, where there are many lovers of Florence who are keen to visit there often, but without the worry of owning a residence so far from their primary home.

Despite appearances to the contrary, there is a pattern to my various ventures over the years. I have worked on taking three different American business concepts to Europe: designer outlets, data centers, and Private Residence Clubs. Now that I am based back in America, I have formed with others a new venture (Matapeake Partners) to continue that process, and to raise overseas capital to invest in America. It is not a vocation easily explained in a sound bite.

It is, however, a fascinating one.